Care, Dare, Share:
Lead and Thrive with Heart, Mind, AI

Allegra Patrizi

To my children who inspire me to always do better for them, to be curious, and to seek new learnings,

To my beloved husband, the kindest and wisest person I know,

To my parents and my family, for having given me a strong basis to build from in life,

To all those who shaped my career. Sometimes you supported me, sometimes you challenged me, in all cases, you helped me become the leader that I am.

To my teams: you were wonderful, you coalesced into the most inspiring of movements, your energy was extraordinary, and all the credit goes to you for everything we have achieved together.

And last but not least, to my horses: with your kind power and boundless generosity, you taught me trust, heart, partnership.

Advance Praise for *Care, Dare, Share: Lead and Thrive with Heart, Mind, AI*

"A book that brings leadership to its fullest expression: combining strategic clarity, courage in decision-taking, and human depth. *Care, Dare, Share* provides a rigorous framework for action, grounded in real-world experience, to lead lasting transformations in the age of AI. An inspiring and immediately actionable guide for today's leaders."

> - Nicolas D'Ieteren, Chairman of the Board of Directors of D'Ieteren Group

"Allegra Patrizi masterfully shows that in the age of AI, our most powerful intelligence is our humanity. She provides a roadmap for leaders to escape the "Rationality Mirage" by blending empathy, courage, and collaboration."

> - Diane Govaerts, CEO of Ziegler Group and Manager of the Year, Belgium 2022

"Allegra Patrizi expresses a profound truth when she says that "data informs, humanity transforms". She defines a rich path to impact in the world that is emerging: more technology leveraged by (much more) humanity."

> - Pierre Gurdjian, Chairman of the Board of Directors of Solvay, Founder of Belgium's 40 under 40

"Care, Dare, Share - Allegra Patrizi leads you through her concept of leadership in times of AI by giving insights into her own personal journey. A worthwhile discovery!"

- Clara C. Streit, Non-Executive Chair of Supervisory Boards

"Why has the life expectancy of Fortune 500 companies shrunk to less than 18 years and the one of CEOs to less than 7 years? How can you reverse this trend and improve your chances of success? In the age of AI and big data, Allegra Patrizi, in her book *Care, Dare, Share*, delivers a compelling human centric answer."

- Enrico Cucchiani, Chairman of Open Fiber, former CEO of Intesa Sanpaolo, former Chairman of Allianz spa

"Collaborating with Allegra Patrizi in my role as chairman of the works council of Aegon, we have had many constructive conversations about the impact of organisational changes on people and vice versa, about the influence of people on the intended changes. I am happy and also a little proud to see that these conversations have co-contributed to this excellent book *Care, Dare, Share* by Allegra Patrizi."

- Han de Vos, former Chairman of the Works Council of Aegon The Netherlands

"Allegra combines deep executive experience with humanity, and it shines through every page of *Care, Dare, Share*. She shows that lasting transformation is never just about strategy or technology, but about leaders who connect, dare, and build trust at scale. This book is a practical compass for anyone serious about leading change with both courage and heart."

- Peter Slagt, Partner at Bain and Company

"This book is a powerful reminder that true leadership isn't about perfection or control. It's about courage, empathy and presence. In a world increasingly shaped by technology, it dares to ask: what does it mean to be a human being?

What I found most inspiring is its insistence that bold leadership begins with listening, not just to data or strategy, but to people. It explores how we can work alongside technology without losing sight of human sentiment, intuition, and emotional intelligence. Allegra Patrizi doesn't shy away from complexity. Instead, she offers a vision of leadership that is both future-facing and deeply grounded in humanity.

If you're navigating change, managing teams, or simply trying to lead with integrity in a digital age, this book will challenge and uplift you. It's not just a guide, it's a call to lead without ignoring the heart."

- Lilia Christophi, EMEA Data and AI Financial Services Partner at PWC

"What does it take to be a better leader in the era of AI? With her warm and authentic tone, Allegra shares actionable strategies and real-world case studies that genuinely inspire leaders to blend Empathic Intelligence and Human Intelligence with AI. A must read!"

- Isabelle Langlois-Loris, Partner at Egon Zehnder, Chairwoman of the Solvay Schools Alumni Association

"A three legged stool is better than a pedestal. *Care, Dare, Share* is that solid platform for transformation. Read, absorb and practice Allegra Patrizi's unique, robust methodology and you won't go wrong."

- Sue O'Brien, Founder and CEO of the Mentor Hub

"At Aegon The Netherlands, I saw *Care, Dare, Share* turn scepticism into real momentum. Combining the proven concept with AI, elevates leadership to a whole new level."

- Chantal Spoelstra, Deputy Company Secretary Aegon Asset Management, former Deputy Company Secretary Aegon Nederland N.V.

"Allegra Patrizi masterfully resolves the central tension of modern leadership blending human empathy with AI-powered strategy. Care, Dare, Share is a powerful guide for creating sustainable value."

- Basil Geoghegan, Partner at PJT Partners

"How do you harness AI's transformative power while keeping people at the heart of everything you do? *Care, Dare, Share* delivers exactly that blueprint, providing leaders with a modern framework to innovate boldly yet thoughtfully."

- Richard Huston, Founder and CEO of Vamos.dev

"Allegra Patrizi manages to tap into the Zeitgeist with ambition and foresight. Her book *Care, Dare, Share* is a manifesto not only for success in business but also life in general. Make her manual your operating system."

- Stephanie Ferrario, Founder and CEO of SHECAN Media

"In her book *Care, Dare, Share*, Allegra Patrizi captures the essence of true leadership: "Humanity". Drawing on her experience as a Director and CEO of major listed and non-listed companies, as well as her role as a mother of three, Patrizi uses examples of management failures and successes to explore leadership. With disarming simplicity, she uses difficult moments in her life to remind us that excessive reliance on data, rationality, and AI yields negative results when key factors such as emotional intelligence are underestimated. In short, her vision aligns with that of ancient Greek philosophers and of major religions in that it places people at the centre. It is a wonderful read that I recommend to everyone."

- Giacomo Di Marzo, European Parliament's Vice-President's Secretariat, former advisor to Antonio Tajani, Chair of the Committee on Constitutional Affairs and of the Conference of Committee Chairs in the European Parliament

"A profound and essential read. Allegra Patrizi brilliantly demonstrates that in the age of AI, our humanity is the ultimate competitive advantage. *Care, Dare, Share* is the playbook for unlocking it."

- Ronan Breen, Managing Director in Investment Banking

"In our world, you can't rely on spreadhseets or authority. You succeed through empathy, courage, and trust – or you fall. We watched Allegra Patrizi start riding at 40 and achieve what seemed impossible and improbable through sheer resilience and an intuitive grasp of these principles. Her book *Care, Dare, Share* brilliantly codifies the very philosophy she used to build an international equestrian partnership from the hoof up. It's proof that to achieve any bold vision, in life or in business, you must first lead with heart."

- John Hardwick and Adrien Cherpîon, International Riding Instructors and Coaches

Table of Contents

Foreword

The future of leadership is heart-led, AI-powered.

Right now, somewhere in a boardroom, a leader is drowning in data and dashboards. They are making a decision that will ripple through hundreds of lives, armed with more data than any generation before them. Their dashboards are glowing with AI-powered predictions that can optimize supply chains and analyse market trends in milliseconds.

Yet, there's a brutal truth hiding in plain sight: 70-80% of these data-rich transformations will fail.

Why? Because the data, for all its precision, is deaf. The algorithms, for all their power, are blind to what truly matters. This is the Rationality Mirage of modern leadership: a relentless pursuit of optimization that prioritizes data and rationality, creating brilliant yet deaf, data-rich algorithms and transformations that are destined to fail. This book is your guide to escaping it.

Transformations fail not because of poor execution, but because we have abdicated the distinctly human act of leadership - deep, empathic listening - to the cold logic of the machine.

The Transformation Delusion We Are All Facing

We are told that we face a difficult choice: ignore AI and be outpaced by competitors, or lean into AI and risk losing the soul of our organisation.

This is a false choice. The real danger isn't in choosing one over the other. The danger lies in the delusion that AI, a tool of logic, can solve the fundamentally human problems of trust, culture, and purpose. We ask our algorithms to answer questions they were never designed to ask.

If you want to see this delusion in action, consider the widely reported story of Zillow's home-buying business, which serves as a powerful cautionary tale. The following is an interpretation of public events, intended to illustrate a key leadership principle.

The company, a titan of data, launched a bold initiative called "Zillow Offers." Their dream was to use their powerful AI, the "Zestimate," to predict housing prices with such accuracy that they could buy homes directly, make minor repairs, and resell them for a quick profit. It was the ultimate data-driven dare.

For a time, it seemed to work. The algorithms, glowing on dashboards just as we discussed, were a marvel of operational streamlining. But the data, for all its precision, was deaf. The AI could price a house, but it couldn't *care* about a neighbourhood's soul or feel the emotional currents of fear and exuberance that truly drive a market.

Imagine the scene in Zillow's boardroom in mid-2021. The dashboards were glowing with AI-powered predictions that could analyse market trends in milliseconds. The "Zestimate" was a marvel, projecting confident profits on the thousands of homes it was buying. The data was king, and its logic seemed absolute.

Real tensions can arise in such a situation. On one side, the data models are glowing, projecting confident profits with near-certainty. The quantitative evidence seems absolute. On the other side is the qualitative, on-the-ground human intelligence, the whispers from agents and regional managers about a change in market 'feeling.' In a culture heavily reliant on data, it's easy to see how such human insights, while politely acknowledged, might not carry the same weight as the seemingly infallible logic on the screen. This outcome serves as a powerful illustration of a core leadership challenge in the AI era. The situation suggests that daring with data is not enough; it must be integrated with a deep care for the human wisdom that provides essential context. The financial losses, which were widely reported to be over half a billion dollars, highlight the immense cost of a potential disconnect between brilliant technology and on-the-ground human insight.

The future of leadership is not about balancing technology and humanity. It is about leveraging technology with a profoundly amplified humanity. To do this, we must move a powerful truth from the footnotes of leadership to the headline: Data informs. Humanity transforms.

The most powerful intelligence of all is our own humanity.

I have led teams through massive transformations – mergers, market shifts, cultural divides. From my 20-plus years in the C-suite, as Chief Risk Officer, Chief Technology Officer, Chief Executive Officer, one truth stands clear: transformations fail when leaders forget the people behind the numbers.

The most impactful leaders are those who blend intelligence with heart, boldness, and humility.

Most initiatives collapse not from bad technology or flawed strategies. They crumble because we ignore the human heart. We create change fatigue. We deliver short-lived improvements that collapse the moment momentum fades. Organisations revert to old behaviours because we never addressed the soul of the system.

What if I told you that the most powerful act in our frenetic digital age is to slow down and listen?

Here's what I've discovered through all the transformations I have been involved in: AI will revolutionize operations, yes. But the decisions that shape trust, culture, and purpose? Those still rest with us.

The future belongs to leaders who dare to stay human.

No algorithm can carry the weight of moral complexity, trust, culture, or purpose. No machine can read the unspoken tension in a room or know when to push forward versus when to pause and heal. The essence of leadership remains irreducibly human. That's your job, as a leader.

This is collaborative leadership - where AI amplifies human capability rather than replacing it. Where empathy isn't a "soft skill" but a strategic imperative. Where vulnerability becomes the foundation of unshakeable trust.

This is not a linear playbook - it's a journey of expanding leadership.

It begins with self-awareness, where empathy unlocks insight. It moves through courageous action, where bold decisions reshape outcomes. And it culminates in shared momentum, where trust becomes a cultural force.

This journey of expanding leadership is not a simple linear path; it is a self-reinforcing **flywheel**. Each phase builds momentum for the next, creating a virtuous cycle of human-centred, AI-powered leadership.

The **CARE, DARE, SHARE Leadership Flywheel** below is your master map for this journey.

It shows how the human insights and trust generated in **CARE** fuel the bold innovation of **DARE**. The successes and learnings from **DARE** are then amplified and scaled through **SHARE**, which in turn builds a more intelligent and connected culture, deepening the capacity for **CARE** in the next, more powerful cycle. As the flywheel spins, your impact naturally expands - from the Self, to your Team, to the entire System.

CARE, DARE, SHARE Leadership Flywheel

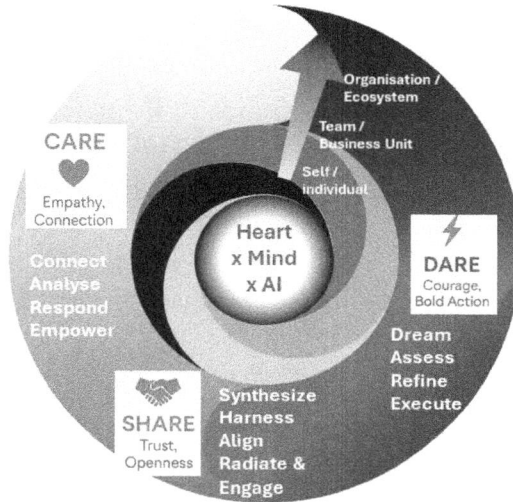

Fig. 1. The CARE, DARE, SHARE Leadership Flywheel: from self to organisation-wide iterations of the CARE, DARE, SHARE methodology create the foundation for successful, long-lasting transformations.

Your Three Leadership Intelligences

Leaders who thrive in this new world master timeless qualities - integrity, vision, resilience, and the ability to inspire - while adding distinct intelligences that are nowadays essential:

- **Empathic Intelligence (EI):** For connection, culture, and trust
- **Human Intelligence (HI):** For strategic insight and lived experience
- **Artificial Intelligence (AI):** For data-driven precision

These intelligences fuel three leadership pillars that define modern impact:

CARE

Empathy in action. Understanding stakeholder needs through emotional intelligence, enhanced by AI's analytical power. Whether you're addressing a large enterprise that must upgrade its performance to thrive, team burnout at a tech startup, understanding parent concerns as a school principal, rallying volunteers around a nonprofit mission, or supporting a family member through change.

DARE

Innovation with courage. Having the courage to focus on what will truly make a difference, to take bold, calculated risks, to disrupt and innovate - backed by human wisdom and AI's foresight. Not reckless gambling, but strategic bravery informed by both data and intuition. Whether you're developing a new billion-dollar business line, pivoting your small business model, redesigning curriculum for better learning outcomes, launching a community health initiative, or making a life-changing career decisions.

SHARE

Trust at scale. Combining vulnerability, inclusion, and collaboration to unite teams and amplify impact. Creating cultures where people feel safe to fail forward, bold enough to dream big, and constructively supported to learn and succeed. Whether you're building culture in a remote team, creating psychological safety in a classroom, fostering collaboration among diverse community stakeholders, or strengthening relationships in your personal life.

What You'll Discover

This book is your practical guide to making CARE, DARE, SHARE your own. Across fourteen chapters, you'll master:

- **The CARE Framework** (Connect, Analyse, Respond, Empower) to activate empathy

- **The DARE Framework** (Dream, Assess, Refine, Execute) to drive innovation

- **The SHARE Framework** (Synthesize, Harness, Align, Radiate, Engage) to foster collaboration

Your Leadership Legacy

Leaders and organisations today face an intricate web of challenges - digital transformation, cultural integration, and ethical decision-making - alongside unprecedented opportunities for innovation and growth. Care, Dare, Share equips you to navigate these with confidence, ensuring your decisions are data-driven yet empathic, bold yet grounded, and collaborative yet strategic.

Every chapter includes real-world case studies, actionable tools, and reflection questions designed to help you immediately apply what you learn. These are based on my own 25+ years of C-level experience, as an executive, as a board member, and as a senior advisor, but also on in-depth documentation and senior interviews with people who were closely involved in the case studies presented. To share the lessons from my leadership journey as openly as possible while respecting confidentiality, some of the case studies have been anonymized. The data, and outcomes described are real, but the names of the institutions and their products, as well as some dialogues, and detailed events, have been adapted.

Transformation isn't something you implement - it's something you embody. And all these case studies should help you do just that, embody Care, Dare, Share.

The most effective leaders of tomorrow will be those who blend technological fluency with emotional depth. Those who understand that AI's role isn't to replace humans, but to amplify their judgment and capabilities.

AI doesn't automate leadership; it demands we deploy humanity at scale. This book is the operating manual for the Generative Leader - the one who uses empathy (Care), courage (Dare), and connection (Share) to make that future a success.

Who This Book Is For

Leadership isn't confined to corner offices or corporate hierarchies. If you influence others - whether you're running a Fortune 500 company, launching a startup from your garage, teaching in a classroom, leading a nonprofit, coaching a team, or even navigating your own personal transformation - you are a leader. And this book is for you. Because Care, Dare, Share is a philosophy: to lead with utmost humanity, boldness, and humility. This philosophy will transform how you approach influence and impact in our interconnected, AI-augmented world, regardless of your title or setting.

CARE shows up when a startup founder takes time to truly understand why their best developer is considering leaving, using both emotional intelligence and data analytics to address retention.

DARE manifests when a high school principal courageously redesigns the entire grading system to better serve student learning, backed by educational research and community input.

SHARE comes alive when a nonprofit leader creates space for volunteers to share their own stories and ideas, building a movement rather than just managing tasks.

These aren't corporate concepts - they're human ones. The frameworks in this book scale from intimate one-on-one conversations to global organisational transformations because they're rooted in timeless principles of human connection, courageous action, and collaborative trust.

Every meaningful transformation starts with leaders who model the change they seek. Leaders who treat empathy as strength, courage as clarity, and vulnerability as the foundation of trust. These leaders don't just implement change - they embody it. And in doing so, they inspire similar behaviours throughout their large organisations or the few people around them.

That's where transformations become unstoppably powerful and long-lasting: they energise, they are embraced by the people, not imposed onto them.

Data informs. Humanity transforms.

Your leadership journey has the potential to create a future where technology serves humanity's highest aspirations.

The path forward requires leaders who understand that in our quest to build smarter organisations, we must never lose sight of what makes us fundamentally human.

This book is a new leadership compass for the AI era - anchored in emotional intelligence, guided by strategic boldness, and scaled through collective intelligence.

Are you ready to lead with both heart and intelligence?

Let's begin to Care deeply, Dare boldly, Share generously.

Explore The Leader's Compendium: From Insight to Action: a practical toolkit of diagnostics, prompts, and frameworks designed to help you apply the CARE, DARE, and SHARE principles in real time. Think of it as your leadership field guide.

You can find it on www.AllegraPatrizi.com or www.Care-Dare-Share.com

Chapter 1: The Day I Took The Job

Leadership reveals who you are - especially when you've spent years hiding behind competence.

June 15, 2021 – The Hague.

It was 8:02 in the morning, the office was quiet. The announcement of my appointment as CEO of Aegon The Netherlands had recently been published, and I was standing alone by the tall windows of the 2nd floor. Below me, the city moved with its usual rhythm - trams, bikes, busy lives. Inside, I felt anything but rhythmic.

I wasn't nervous. It was something deeper - uneasy. Like I had stepped into a role everyone expected me to fill, but inside, I knew I was crossing a threshold into something entirely unknown. Until that point, I had led mostly technical teams - analytical, focused, fact-driven. This was different. This was about people, legacy, emotion, and transformation.

In this new reality, the data pointed toward clear opportunities: the need for a unified strategic direction, a response to commercial pressures, and a drive for greater operational efficiency. It was the perfect diagnosis for a leader falling victim to the Rationality Mirage, offering a clean, quantifiable, and dangerously incomplete picture.

As those first few days went by, walking the halls revealed a deeper truth the data could not see: a profound disconnection. A human system quietly breaking under the weight of metrics that measured everything except what mattered. The fragmentation wasn't a separate problem; it was the direct result of leading by spreadsheet.

This wasn't just an operational challenge. It was a human one.

And if we wanted to be successful at transforming this business, we had to tackle the human aspect with tact and intelligence.

It dawned on me. I was afraid. Not of dealing with the challenges painted by the data. I was afraid of missing what really mattered.

And I remember telling myself:

Care. Dare. Share.

I didn't know it yet, but those three words would become my leadership compass. It was the compass I needed to navigate away from the purely rational and escape the trap that reduces leadership to a spreadsheet.

A compass, to find emotional clarity when the path ahead was blurred, to make bold moves when inertia threatened to stall us, and to connect people who had stopped trusting in each other.

Since that moment, I have used that compass every single day. In board meetings. In town halls. In moments of crisis. In moments of hope.

And now, in this book, I want to give it to you.

Pause and reflect: Where, in your experience, have you seen data tell one half of the story while human experience tells you the other half?

The Challenge: Beyond the Balance Sheet

The irony wasn't lost on me. As a woman and a foreigner leading in the Netherlands - with less-than-brilliant Dutch language skills - I was about to discover that my tucked-beneath humanity might become my greatest leadership strength.

Somewhere deep inside, I had always known another kind of leadership. One built not just on logic, but on listening. Not just strategy, but soul.

My experience as a single mother of three, my Italian heritage, my years living in different countries - these had given me something precious: deep empathy for people and cultures. An ability to listen across perspectives, to sense unspoken tensions, to celebrate differences, to understand the struggles of normal people going by their normal life.

But in the technical environments I'd grown up in professionally, these human instincts had been quietly parked. There had never been space - or permission - to lead with heart.

The old playbook said: vulnerability is weakness. Cold rationality is your compass. Results come from analysis, not emotion.

The new reality demanded to embrace empathy.

This wasn't just a change in role - it was a transformation in how I showed up as a leader. I had to dare to exercise the parts of myself that I had kept professionally dormant. I had to trust that leading with both mind and heart wasn't just possible - it was essential.

Your turn: what is your leadership style? Do you tend to use your brain or heart as a first resource?

The Transformation: We Started by Listening

Instead of creating another strategy deck, with the executive committee, we did something radical: We connected.

We made a commitment to visit clients – for me, it was two per week, whenever possible. But this wasn't just about me getting closer to customers. We ensured that the entire executive committee would also regularly meet with clients. If we were going to lead the transformation, we needed direct contact with the people we served, not filtered reports about their needs and concerns. And role modelling starts from the top! So, as an executive committee, we needed to be the change we want to see.

We also began listening across the organisation with systematic intentionality. We went around the company, creating space for colleagues to tell us what they saw, what they felt, and what they viewed as the priorities going forward. We held countless town halls. But these weren't the traditional one-way presentations that employees had grown accustomed to. Instead, we created genuine dialogue - authentic two-way conversations with an approachable human leader. And for those who wished to say things in Dutch, despite English being the official language, we did welcome it. Sometimes I needed a bit of help with the Dutch language, but that too reinforced the feeling of approachability and co-creation.

Some of the stories were filled with hope and dreams, some other with pain and frustration. We listened to them all, with no judgement.

Soon, something beautiful happened: formal barriers dissolved. People saw us not as distant executives, but as fellow humans navigating the same complex world.

But we didn't just listen with empathy - we listened with discipline. For every story, we asked: What does this mean for the business? What patterns are emerging? Where does data confirm or challenge what we're hearing? For every insight we gathered, we analysed it rigorously to test for impact and meaning. We listened with purpose, combining human empathy with analytical rigor to understand not just what people were saying, but what it meant for our organisation's future.

Try this: In your next team meeting, spend the first ten minutes asking: "What's one thing about our customers that keeps you up at night?" or "What's the one single biggest pain point our colleagues have to endure in our processes?"

The Breakthrough: Three Pillars Emerge

Six months into the role, we had something that was co-created with our people AND rigorously tested for potential and feasibility, not something imposed from above: a new strategy based on clear and straightforward pillars, that was both the result of listening and analysing.

Besides that, we developed simple behavioural guidelines that we had all decided to adopt together - not complex corporate jargon that no one can remember even if their life depended on it, but simple words that everyone could understand and connect with.

Language that was ours - shared, not handed down. We called it "potato language", because it had the comforting warmth, the sublime simplicity, and the magic effectiveness of a jacket potato.

We returned to the organisation with these insights through a second round of in-person town halls, and this time the energy was completely different: we had shown we could listen, and now we dared to tell them where we would go, what we would do, how we would behave, based on all we had understood.

Through those in-person town halls, we addressed directly every employee of the company, at every location. People didn't just hear about change - they saw themselves reflected in it. They recognized their voices in the strategy and the agreed behaviours we were presenting.

The energy and alignment this created were extraordinary. From the executive committee members to the reception clerk, everyone could relate and repeat, in their own words, the meaning of what we had agreed collectively. Some, of course, were more articulate than others, but all represented the meaning pretty faithfully.

And that is when the magic of alignment happens. Thousands of people moving with shared clarity, energy, and rhythm - like a team working in perfect sync.

The results followed swiftly and dramatically:

Commercial momentum built across all business lines as everyone realized their impact on client perception and on the support they could bring to the front-line teams to deliver effective solutions to clients.

Cost control improved as people understood and embraced efficiency, pockets of savings started popping up, and waste was reduced.

Operational excellence took root as silos began to break down, as people felt accountable to "keep the rats out of the kitchen" (that was one of the agreed behaviours that went around the whole organisation, and although clearly a bit iconoclastic, it became the viral mantra in every team to incite people to catch the problems, solve them and share the learnings with the rest of the organisation). People had shifted from hiding problems or passing them on to the next person to being proud of solving them and letting it be known.

Our long-standing balance sheet volatility began to reduce significantly as we addressed fundamental structural issues and as we evolved from a slightly reactive approach to a more proactive approach to financial markets.

But more than the metrics, the mood had changed. Teams were energized, aligned, and cooperative. Customers were responding positively. People believed again - in the work, in the mission, in each other. Performance started to shift upward across every dimension that mattered. And so, quarter after quarter, we would hold some more townhalls to celebrate the success. And that started our flywheel: more energy, more success, more confidence, more energy, more success, more confidence.....

That's when I realized: we had cared, we had dared, and we had shared.

The philosophy wasn't named yet, but it had come to life in the most practical way possible.

We **Cared** - by listening deeply, connecting across the organisation, and treating empathy as a strategic skill. We had demonstrated that understanding people wasn't separate from driving results; it was the foundation for sustainable, relevant transformation. Because at the end of the day, the only really successful transformations are the ones that are built on solving real problems for real people: clients, employees, or investors.

We **Dared** - by changing how we led, not just what we did, and trusting that courage, humility, and kind authority could drive performance. We had taken bold steps in inviting others to co-create our future. We dared to make choices, which is often so difficult in large organisations because every department has its hobby horses. We dared to simplify and to focus on what would make a real difference to the real problems we needed to solve. And we also dared to stick to our decisions, once they had been taken, accepting that it may not be the popular decision, but it was certainly one that had been pondered, taking into account the various perspectives.

We **Shared** - by dissolving barriers, embracing transparency, and building something together. We had moved from a culture of hierarchy and information hoarding to one of collaboration and accountability. We as leaders accepted to own the responsibility when things were not going well with certain actions or projects, and to share the success with everyone involved. The exact opposite of what often happens in many organisations....

The transformation was profound and lasting. We doubled the value of the company while significantly improving our people scores and client satisfaction.

Two years later, the company was sold, for a range of reasons, including its renewed trajectory and strong performance. And to this day, when I meet former colleagues, union and workers' council members, regulators, they still speak of that moment in time. The energy. The possibility. The exhilarating feeling of real, human, collective transformation.

Pause and reflect: Where in your experience did you face a transformation where you needed to Care, Dare, Share? How did you deal with it at the time?

Taking It Further After Aegon

After Aegon, I have had a number of roles, as an Executive, as a Board Member, and as Senior Advisor. In December 2024, I decided to take a break from executive roles to help several organisations with my unique combination of C-level experience and AI expertise, to finalise the gathering and structuring of all the data I had amassed during the last 4-5 years for this book, as well to refine and test all the Care, Dare, Share methodologies in as many environments as possible to complement my previous executive experiences.

Among the companies I have played an important role in, were a mobility services player, a local consumer lending company, a bank based in a European country, a logistics company with global presence, and a top, multi-regional, accounting services firm.

In all these cases, I have actively used the CARE, DARE, SHARE approach.

Large regional accounting firm

For example, the large accounting services firm I helped was facing a "productivity paradox": highly skilled professionals were overwhelmed by repetitive, low-value tasks that hindered both client impact and job satisfaction. So, applying the CARE, DARE, SHARE approach, we started by listening deeply to a selection of 2000+ employees and many clients, identifying the need to free experts from digital drudgery and deliver faster, more strategic insights to clients. This care for internal well-being and external value creation became the human-centric driver behind its bold AI transformation. A very substantial investment was committed in generative AI, a significant DARE, becoming one of the first large accounting firms in their region to build a proprietary tool, which we shall call "MyPal". Rather than relying on public models, the firm dared to prioritize trust, building AI within a secure, private environment. They also committed to upskilling every employee on ethical and effective AI usage, transforming their entire workforce into AI-powered professionals. With a strong governance framework about AI usage, they dared to lead with ethics, not just speed.

MyPal got progressively rolled out across the entire regional workforce, enabling the SHARE part: cross-team collaboration and real-time intelligence sharing. Insights on AI usage were tracked and re-shared, creating a culture of collective learning and continuous improvement.

The unexpected positive effect was that this development has also enabled the firm to be credible in advising clients on their own AI transformations, sharing not just technology, but lived experience and ethical frameworks.

Results include 100% workforce AI enablement, the launch of new advisory services, and recognition as a regional leader in responsible AI deployment.

Bank operating in Europe

At the bank based in a European country, a very innovative app, which, for the purpose of this book, was developed, we will call it "Zaya". Zaya aimed at helping customers perform a vast amount of simple banking tasks, which in normal times would clog call-centres and often take an inordinate time to perform, resulting in frustration both for customers and call-centre colleagues. Zaya got recognitions in its country as one of the best AI applications. Zaya was also one of the first conversational banking platforms in its country, and enabled a whole new level of intuitive and helpful banking experiences for customers.

New products were introduced, such as innovative accounts and unique credit cards propositions. All of this resonated deeply with customers because they spoke to human feelings.

After about 9 months of Care, Dare, Share transformation, the results were strong and very encouraging:

- High single-digit improvement in income
- Improvement in risk, significant
- More than 50% increase in profits
- Above sector average engagement scores with employees
- Double-digit increase in cross-selling

Logistics player with global presence

The large logistics player I was involved with, found itself at the convergence of urgent pressures and strategic opportunity. As global logistics demand surged, fuelled by e-commerce and rising customer expectations, the company faced increasing operational strain, legacy systems fragmentation, and growing scrutiny over its environmental footprint.

The pandemic had further exposed vulnerabilities in visibility, planning, and agility. Recognizing that incremental change wouldn't suffice, they decided to launch an ambitious transformation. The goal: to build a logistics network that was not only smarter and faster, but greener and more human-centric, capable of serving a rapidly changing world with care, courage, and shared purpose.

So we started by tackling workforce anxiety by launching large-scale upskilling programs and committed to drastically reducing emissions, with different targets over 10, 20, and 30 years. We dared to invest significantly in robotics, AI, and fleet electrification. Finally, we scaled impact across the ecosystem, offering carbon-neutral services to clients and forming partnerships to accelerate collective progress.

The results here, as well, like in the other cases, were strong: double-digit productivity gains, AI-driven efficiency, and industry-wide influence in sustainable logistics.

We will explore all these cases in further depth in this book.

This work, combined with my experience from Aegon NL, convinced me of the power of CARE, DARE, SHARE: how CARE for people, DARE to invest boldly, and SHARE knowledge systemically can transform even the most traditional sectors.

From Practice to Philosophy

These weren't isolated successes or lucky breaks. They revealed a deeper truth: CARE, DARE, SHARE isn't just a management style or a set of tactics. It's a human-centred transformation model that is particularly suited for the age of AI.

If you think of it, the paradox is that as things got increasingly digital across businesses, the level of "transactionality" has gone up, not down, and the level of engagement with people as humans has gone down, not up. Whereas, one could have hoped that as tedious, transactional tasks were being automated, people in help-centres would have been freed up to be more, not less, focused on customers as humans. Zaya or MyPal, for example, freed up humans to deliver empathy where it matters.

CARE, DARE, SHARE aims at resolutely putting the human back at the centre of the business model. It recognizes that humans long to be understood, cared for, recognised in their needs, including emotional needs, and that AI and data insights amplify human wisdom rather than replace it.

This is the future: Heart, Mind, AI – together, combined through the CARE, DARE, SHARE framework. We started explaining the core of this framework in the foreword, but to be sure we are all on the same page, whether we have read or not the foreword:

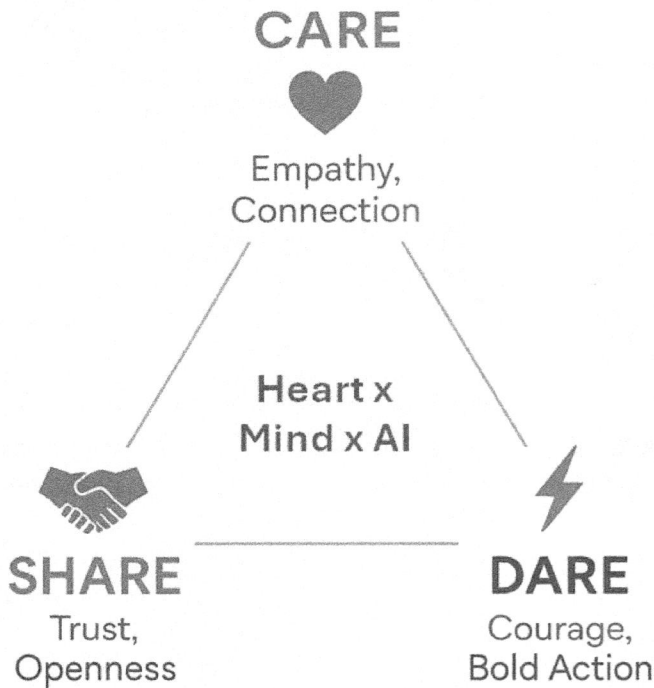

CARE

Empathy,
Connection

Heart x
Mind x AI

SHARE
Trust,
Openness

DARE
Courage,
Bold Action

Fig. 2. The Care, Dare, Share model: a compass for bold, emotionally intelligent leadership in the age of AI

CARE is empathy in action - rooted in emotional intelligence and enhanced by AI's analytical precision. It's the deep understanding of stakeholder needs through emotional intelligence, whether addressing team pain points, anticipating customer needs, or dealing with regulatory concerns about operational processes.

DARE is innovation, focus, and simplification with courage - powered by human wisdom, creativity, and experience, sharpened by AI's foresight to take bold, strategic, well-calculated risks. It's about having the courage to challenge conventional wisdom while being grounded in both human insight and data-driven analysis.

SHARE is trust at scale - enabled through vulnerability, inclusion, celebration, introspection, and collective ownership. It's about creating environments where transparency and authentic human connection drive sustainable transformation and constant, honest learning.

Where Do You Stand On The CARE, DARE, SHARE Compass and Why This Matters?

If you don't care enough to truly understand your people, AI will optimize for metrics that don't matter.

If you don't dare to lead with both mind and heart, you'll build efficient systems that slowly hollow out your humanity.

If you don't share the journey transparently, you'll create change that happens to people, not with them.

Leadership is a journey - but not a straight line. It loops, accelerates, and sometimes stalls.

That's why this book offers two practical tools: the **Leadership Flywheel** and the **CARE, DARE, SHARE Compass**.

The **Leadership Flywheel**, which you saw in the Foreword, is your master map. It visualizes the dynamic system for generating leadership momentum, starting with empathy (CARE), moving through strategic courage (DARE), and culminating in collective impact (SHARE). It shows how your influence grows with each cycle from self to organisation-wide.

The **Compass**, on the other hand, helps you navigate your journey on that map in real time. It lets you assess where you are strongest (e.g., CARE) and where you may need to grow (e.g., DARE or SHARE), so you can consciously apply energy where it's needed most to keep the flywheel spinning faster and more effectively.

Some leaders get stuck in one direction - caring but never daring, or daring without sharing. The Compass brings clarity and intentionality, helping you lead not just from instinct, but with conscious alignment and purpose across all the axes.

Think of the **Leadership Flywheel** as your map for creating momentum. And the **Compass** as your trusted guide for the journey.

We kept the Compass deliberately simple and practical, so that you can come back to it often, as you progress through the book, to assess how you are developing on CARE, DARE, SHARE.

Your scores across CARE, DARE, and SHARE will help you recognize your strengths, imbalances, and areas of greatest potential growth.

Use it not as a judgment - but as a guide. A snapshot of your leadership imprint, ready to evolve.

Step 1: Answer each of these simple questions with a score of 1 to 5 (1 = Rarely/Never, 2 = Sometimes, 3 = Often, 4 = Usually, 5 = Always).

CARE

- Connect: Building Emotional Bonds
    - Do I listen deeply to understand the emotions and concerns of my team or stakeholders, and do I create psychological safety? (1-5)
    - Do I ask open-ended questions to uncover what truly matters to others? (1-5)
- Analyse: Leveraging AI for Empathic Insights
    - Do I combine human intuition with data and AI tools to identify emotional patterns in feedback, moving beyond what is happening to understand why? (1-5)
    - Do I actively create an "Actionable-Truth-Zone" by seeking and rewarding uncomfortable truths that are critical for improvement? (1-5)
- Respond: Acting with Tailored Empathy
    - Do I move beyond one-size-fits-all solutions by tailoring my actions and communications to the specific emotional and practical context of my stakeholders? (1-5)

- Do I act on feedback in ways that show I've heard my team or customers? (1-5)
- Empower: Creating Conditions for Growth
  - Do I act as an orchestrator rather than a hero, focusing on building the emotional intelligence and capabilities of others so the team can thrive without me? (1-5)
  - Do I give my team opportunities to act autonomously, take ownership, and make decisions with confidence? (1-5)

DARE

- Dream: Vision with Strategic Imagination
  - Do I ground our team's vision in the real human needs we uncovered during the CARE phase, ensuring our boldest ideas solve meaningful problems? (1-5)
  - Do I use strategic imagination to envision future possibilities unconstrained by current limitations, using AI to explore and model what could be? (1-5)
- Assess: Balancing Data and Intuition
  - Do I rigorously evaluate bold ideas using a clear framework, combining data-driven insights with my intuition to evaluate opportunities? (1-5)
  - Do I seek diverse perspectives as well as data-driven analysis and AI-powered insights to validate (or challenge) my strategic intuition before deciding and committing significant resources? (1-5)
- Refine: Crafting Resonant Solutions
  - Do I use real-world feedback and lived experience to evolve our solutions from being functionally correct to emotionally resonant? (1-5)
  - Do I apply a systematic process (e.g. AI or feedback loops) to ensure that what we learn from pilots is codified and designed for successful scaling? (1-5)
- Execute: Leading with Confidence

- Do I lead implementation by communicating the human impact first ("why this matters to you") rather than focusing solely on the technology or project plan? (1-5)
- Do I measure the success of our execution across three dimensions: immediate performance, long-term learning, and strategic readiness for the future, leveraging AI predictive abilities and adjusting plans during implementation? (1-5)

SHARE

- Synthesize: Connecting Collective Knowledge
  - Do I actively break down "knowledge islands" and silos by creating systems and rituals that connect scattered insights from across the organization into a cohesive whole? (1-5)
  - Do I act as an architect of collective intelligence, using AI to spot patterns and my human wisdom to help the entire team generate insights that no single person could alone? (1-5)
- Harness: Coordinating Collective Action
  - Do I design and orchestrate collaboration by first identifying the connective tissue between teams and initiatives? (1-5)
  - Do I use AI not just as a communication tool, but as an intelligence amplifier that helps coordinate shared learning and synchronized action across organizational silos? (1-5)
- Align: Uniting Stakeholders with Emotional Intelligence
  - Do I proactively map and address the emotional landscape and differing perspectives of all stakeholders to build a foundation of trust? (1-5)
  - Do I align team efforts around shared goals using data and emotional insights, and ensure that all stakeholders understand their role in collective success and feel like co-creators? (1-5)

- Radiate and Engage: Amplifying and Sustaining Collaboration
    - Do I "radiate" progress by sharing successes, failures, and learnings with authentic transparency to build trust and inspire action? (1-5)
    - Do I build sustainable "engagement" by creating systems for recognition, continuous learning, and shared purpose that outlast any single project? (1-5)

Step 2: Sum your results for each of Care, Dare, Share.

Each sub-framework (e.g., Connect, Analyse) has 2 questions. Sum the scores for the 2 questions (possible range: 2–10).

Each framework (CARE, DARE, SHARE) has 4 sub-frameworks. Sum the scores of the 4 sub-frameworks (possible range: 8–40).

Step 3: Plot your footprint on the Compass

The compass is a radar chart with three axes (CARE, DARE, SHARE), each scored from 8 to 40. Plot your scores on each of the CARE, DARE, SHARE axes, and then connect the points as a triangle. The larger the triangle, the better.

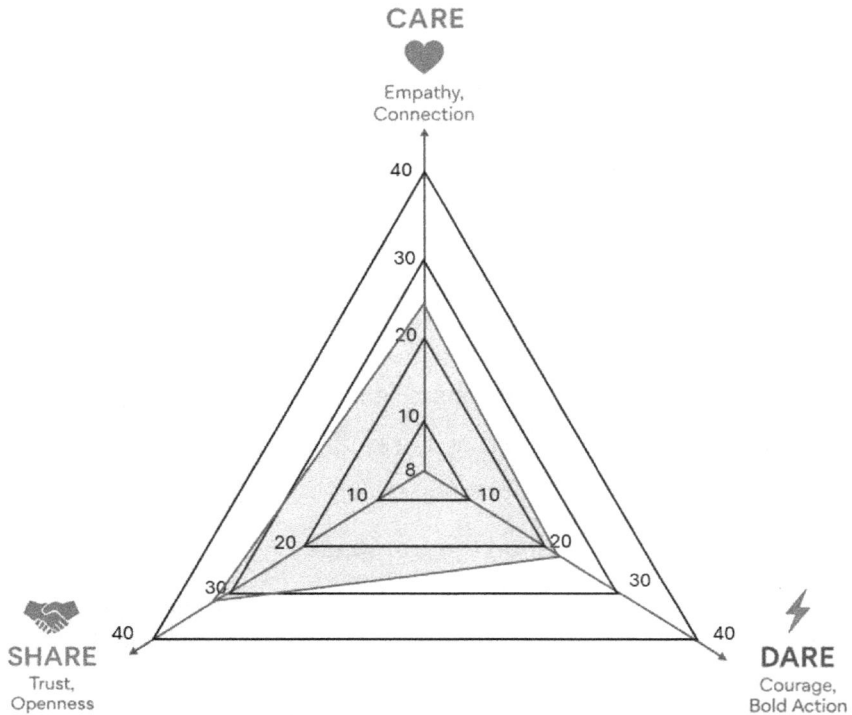

CARE

Empathy, Connection

40

30

20

10

8

10 10

20 20

30 30

40 40

SHARE
Trust, Openness

DARE
Courage, Bold Action

Fig. 3. The CARE, DARE, SHARE Compass, your continuous self-assessment tool to expand your leadership

Step 4: Interpret the Compass

Balanced profile: Similar high-ish (above 24) scores on each of the axes (e.g., 28, 30, 32) suggest a well-rounded leader who integrates empathy, courage, and collaboration. Focus on refining all areas.

CARE-Dominant (e.g., 36, 24, 26): Strong in empathy but may need to strengthen bold decision-making (DARE) or collaboration (SHARE). Revisit Chapters 6–9 (DARE) or 10–13 (SHARE).

DARE-Dominant (e.g., 24, 36, 28): Excels at innovation but may need to deepen emotional connection (CARE) or alignment (SHARE). Focus on Chapters 2–5 (CARE) or 10–13 (SHARE).

SHARE-Dominant (e.g., 26, 24, 36): Strong in collaboration but may need to enhance empathy (CARE) or execution (DARE). Revisit Chapters 2–5 (CARE) or 6–9 (DARE).

Low Scores (<24 on any axis): Indicates areas for growth. Start with the corresponding chapters (e.g., low CARE → Chapters 2–5) and focus on one sub-framework where you got low scores (e.g., Connect).

High Scores (>36 on all axes): Suggests advanced leadership. Focus on mentoring others or scaling CARE, DARE, SHARE (Chapter 14).

As you progress through the CARE, DARE, SHARE journey, regularly assess yourself on these questions to track your progress in expanding your footprint on the Compass.

Your Next Step

Your Chapter Challenge: What is one way you've been leading with only your mind, when your heart has critical data to contribute?

The future isn't just about building smarter organisations. It's about building more human ones, enhanced by artificial intelligence in service of our highest aspirations.

Your transformation begins with a choice: Will you lead with the wholeness of who you are?

Let's explore how you can make CARE, DARE, SHARE your own.

In the next chapter, Chapter 2, we'll explore the first pillar: CARE - How empathy becomes your AI-enhanced superpower for understanding what others truly need.

Chapter 1 Takeaways & Reflection

Lead with both brain and heart - because data alone doesn't transform.

◇ **Key Takeaways**

- **CARE - Empathy in Action:** Listening before leading unlocks trust and insight and surfaces what the data missed. Showing up with vulnerability makes leadership more approachable and human.

- **DARE - Courage to Simplify and Focus:** Dare to pause the strategy deck and co-create direction through live, open conversations. Choose clarity over perfection, create shared language ("potato language") and bold behavioural shifts ("keep the rats out of the kitchen").

- **SHARE - Trust at Scale:** Make transformation participatory, not performative. People see their ideas in the final strategy - and own it. By celebrating progress and learning from failures openly, reinforces the flywheel of confidence → performance → momentum.

- **When alignment happens, it feels like music.** Transformation clicks when every team member... acts on the same priorities - rhythm, harmony, shared purpose.

- **AI accelerates - but empathy directs.** Tools, (e.g. Zaya, MyPal, robots-, can supercharge performance, but only if built on deep human insight.

◇ **Reflection Prompts**

- *What is your footprint on the CARE, DARE, SHARE Compass and where do you want to expand?*
- *Where do you need to stop talking and start listening?*
- *What uncomfortable decision or simplification are you avoiding right now - and why?*
- *What signals of disconnection might you be overlooking?*
- *What piece of "potato language" could unite the team?*
- *What bold, human-first action are you willing to take this week to re-energize alignment?*

Chapter 2: Connect - Building Emotional Bonds (CARE: C)

You don't lead by directing. You lead by connecting.

Walking the halls during my first weeks as CEO at Aegon NL, the data on my spreadsheets told one story, but the faces of our employees told another. I saw brilliant people working in silos, a sense of fragmentation that no metric could capture. I remember a conversation with a mid-level manager who told me, "You know, every business line at the moment has its own vision, we don't have a truly connected vision across Aegon NL."

It was then that I knew that before we could build any new strategy, we had to rebuild our connections. You don't lead by directing. You lead by connecting.

This is your leadership shift: From directing to connecting. From knowing to understanding. From commanding to caring.

Your Connection Blueprint: The CARE Framework

To solve this profound sense of disconnection, the first step of our leadership compass became essential: **CARE**. We had to build a structured practice for tuning into the emotions, values, and perspectives of their stakeholders, starting with the first principle: **Connect**, which is all about building emotional bonds through deep listening.

This is where the CARE framework comes in:

- **C – Connect:** Build emotional bonds through empathic presence and deep listening

- **A – Analyse:** Extract insights by marrying human intuition with data (for instance, after a series of candid conversations reveal a general feeling of 'burnout,' you could use sentiment analysis tools on internal communications platforms like

Slack to quantify how frequently words like 'overwhelmed,' 'exhausted,' or 'stretched' appear. This factualises the empathic insight, allowing you to see which teams are most affected and to track changes over time).

- **R – Respond:** Act in ways that align well with what you've heard and learned

- **E – Empower:** Create conditions where others can connect, lead, and grow

This shift from directing to connecting isn't unique to a Dutch insurer. In fact, it was the catalyst for one of the most remarkable corporate turnarounds in recent history at Microsoft.

When Satya Nadella took over, he didn't just see a business problem; he saw a soul problem. The company's infamous "stack ranking" system had created a toxic, "know-it-all" culture where collaboration went to die. In an early leadership meeting, he confronted this head-on.

"For years," he might have said to a room of brilliant but siloed executives, "our culture has rewarded being the smartest person in the room. What happens when the world requires us to be the best learners in the room?"

The resistance was palpable. One executive later admitted his first thought was that this "empathy stuff" was perceived as "soft fluff". Sensing this, Nadella shifted from corporate strategy to human connection. He shared his personal story of how raising his son with special needs had reshaped him, teaching him to move from a place of certainty to one of deep empathy and curiosity.

By modelling this vulnerability, he gave his leaders permission to do the same. He wasn't just directing a change; he was embodying it. This was CARE in action, creating the psychological safety that would allow a "learn-it-all" mindset to flourish. This wasn't a performance; it was authentic vulnerability in service of connection.

The ripple effects were immediate and profound. Teams that had been competing against each other began collaborating. Departments that had hoarded information started sharing insights. Employees who had been disengaged began contributing ideas. The shift wasn't just structural - it was emotional. People felt seen, heard, and valued in ways they hadn't experienced before.

The result? A trillion-dollar market cap and a culture where innovation flourished because connection created trust.

As the Microsoft story shows, connection isn't just the first step. It's the anchor. Without emotional connection, your analysis remains academic, your responses feel impersonal, your recommended actions feel imposed, and empowerment risks becoming manipulation in disguise.

Connection is not manipulation. It's not superficial rapport. It is the work of building a genuine, often intuitive, understanding of what really matters to your people, your customers, and your broader stakeholder network. It's about learning to lead with both insight and heart.

But here's what makes connection in the age of AI both more challenging and more essential: as our work becomes increasingly digital, our human need for genuine connection intensifies. Paradoxically, the more automated our processes become, the vaster the data set we can tap into to come to insights, the more people crave authentic human interaction. The leaders who understand this paradox - who can leverage AI's analytical power while deepening human connection - will define the future of leadership.

The Science of Connection: Why Emotional Intelligence Matters

Emotional intelligence isn't "soft" - it's your hardest competitive advantage:

When people feel seen and understood, their brains release oxytocin (the "trust hormone"), boosting collaboration and reducing stress.

Feel ignored or misunderstood? The amygdala triggers fight-or-flight, impairing focus, creativity, and connection.

This biological reality has profound implications for leadership. When you create genuine connection, you're not just being nice - you're literally changing brain chemistry in ways that enhance performance, creativity, and collaboration.

Studies show that emotionally intelligent organisations can boost productivity by up to 30%. And companies that train for emotional intelligence experience 20% higher productivity and 30% better retention. Google's Project Aristotle, which studied hundreds of teams to understand what made them effective, found that psychological safety - largely a function of emotional connection - was the single most important factor in team performance.

This discovery by Google is built on the foundational research of Harvard Business School professor Amy Edmondson, who first defined the concept of 'psychological safety.' Edmondson found that the highest-performing teams were not those with the smartest individuals, but those where members felt safe enough to be vulnerable, to admit errors, and to take interpersonal risks. Connection, as we practice it in the CARE framework, is the most direct way a leader can cultivate this safety.

Success in leadership is determined more by how well leaders manage emotions - both their own and others' - than by technical skill alone. Why? Because even in what appear to be rational, logic-driven discussions, our decisions are never devoid of emotion. Emotions subtly colour our reasoning, cloud our judgment, and influence what we accept or reject. We feel at peace with a decision only when both our rational and emotional selves are in alignment. When they're not - no matter how sound the logic - we hesitate. We make excuses. We stall.

Think about the last time you had to make a difficult decision. Maybe it was about restructuring your team, changing a product direction, or entering a new market. You probably gathered data, ran analyses, and built compelling business cases. If something didn't feel right - if your gut was telling you something different - you likely found yourself second-guessing, seeking more information, or delaying the decision. That's the emotional brain at work, and it's more powerful than we often acknowledge.

Whether we like it or not, emotion is always part of the equation. And as leaders, we must acknowledge it, understand it, and work with it - our stakeholders' and our own.

Emotional intelligence acts as your organisational radar system - sensing resistance before rebellion, burnout before turnover, opportunities before competitors. It consists of four foundational capabilities:

1. **Self-Awareness**: Recognizing your emotional patterns, triggers, and blind spots. Without this, authentic connection with others is impossible. Understand not just what you feel, but why you feel it, and how those feelings influence your decisions and interactions. Leaders who are victims of the Rationality Mirage, and say, for example things such as, "I'm completely rational" are, in reality, not as rational as they would want and unconsciously wield authority in disguise - people comply but resent it. These are leaders who have not developed the humility of understanding their own emotional biases in decision-making. People feel that, and at some point, will revolt.

2. **Self-Management**: Regulating your own emotions - especially under pressure. Leaders who stay grounded in turbulence create psychological safety for others. This isn't about suppressing emotions, but about channelling them constructively. Emotions are amongst the strongest triggers for action one can imagine. By channelling them constructively, leaders and organisations can harness the energy emotions create towards very significant positive transformation and achievement.

3. **Social Awareness**: Reading emotional context - what people feel even when they can't articulate it. This includes understanding the unspoken dynamics in meetings, the energy shifts in your organisation, and the emotional undertones in customer feedback. I personally find this one the hardest, but also the most powerful. It is a subtle mix of picking up cues, detecting body language, and intersecting these with spoken and unspoken rules to come to an assessment of what is happening behind the words being spoken. This requires cultural knowledge, intuition, and deep attunement

4. **Relationship Management**: Using emotional insight to build trust, defuse conflict, and foster cooperation and inspiration. This is where emotional intelligence becomes leadership intelligence - using your understanding of emotions to create positive outcomes for everyone involved. The stronger the trust the leader establishes, the greater the buy-in to the proposed course of action will be.

The Art of Deep Listening: Techniques for Authentic Connection

Real connection begins with a fundamental shift: Instead of planning your reply while others speak, cultivate **empathic presence** - being fully immersed in their experience. Asking yourself, "What is this person feeling? What are the fears, the hopes, the aspirations?" "Where do they feel safe, where do they feel unsafe?"

This shift from transactional listening to empathetic presence is more than just a behavioural change; it's a neurological one. Neuroscientists speak of 'mirror neurons,' brain cells that fire both when we perform an action and when we see someone else perform it. When we listen with true empathy, we are literally activating the neural pathways that allow us to 'feel with' the other person. This isn't a 'soft skill'; it is a biological mechanism for building trust at the deepest level.

This shift requires the humility to believe that others have insights worth hearing, combined with the professional will to act on what you learn. It's about approaching every interaction with genuine curiosity rather than predetermined conclusions.

Here's how to deepen your listening:

1. **Listen for Emotions, Not Just Facts**: If someone says, "This system is confusing," "The timing for this is not right" the subtext may be fear of underperformance or failure, or job insecurity. Emotional content often carries more weight than factual input. Train yourself to hear the feeling behind the words. Are they frustrated? Anxious? Overwhelmed? Excited but uncertain? The emotion often points to the real issue that needs addressing.

2. **Create Space for Silence**: In a world that values speed, silence can feel uncomfortable. But when you ask a question, wait. Profound insight often follows a moment of quiet reflection. Some of your most important discoveries will come not from what people say immediately, but from what they share after they've had time to think.

3. **Listen With Your Whole Body**: Physical presence matters. Body language never lies. Put away distractions. Turn towards the person. Maintain soft eye contact. These cues tell people they matter. But go beyond the basics - notice your and their posture, your and their breathing, your and their energy. Are you leaning in with interest or holding back with judgment? Your body language communicates as much as your words. For example, if you find the two of you leaning towards each other, in mirror positions, that shows a high level of engagement and communion of minds. Conversely, different or divergent positions show non-alignment. Any shift in position reflects getting closer or further apart. We have all mastered this art as children or even as adults during emotionally charged situations (love, grief, attack...), but we let our language understanding capabilities overtake body language signals in most interactions. But words are very easy

to manipulate; body language is very hard. So do use your body language sonar when you want to build trust and rapport.

4. **Listen for Patterns**: Over time, you'll begin to notice patterns in what people share. Are multiple team members expressing similar concerns? Are customers describing the same emotional journey? Are stakeholders using the same language to describe different problems? These patterns often reveal systemic issues that individual conversations might miss.

5. **Ask Open-Ended Questions.** Good questions open doors. They unlock not just information, but emotions and insights. Closed questions gather data. Open questions build trust. The quality of your questions determines the quality of your connection. Instead of asking, "Are you happy with the new process?" try "What's your experience been like with the new process?" The first question invites a yes or no answer; the second invites a story. Ask for perspective, emotion, and insight. Invite people to share not just what they think, but what they feel and what they need by asking, for example: "What's working well for you right now?", "What's keeping you up at night?", "If you could change one thing about how we work together, what would it be?", "What support do you need to be successful?", "What am I missing?", "What would success look like from your perspective?", "What's the biggest challenge you're facing that others might not see?", "What opportunities are we not taking advantage of?", "Where can we improve?"

6. **Follow-up With Interest**: Great questions deserve great follow-up. When someone shares something meaningful, resist the urge to immediately move to the next topic or offer solutions. Instead, go deeper: "Tell me more about that.", "What does that feel like?", "What would need to change for that to improve?", "How long have you been thinking about this?", "What would you do if you were in my position?". These follow-up questions signal that you're truly listening, not just waiting for your turn to speak. They often reveal the most valuable insights. And as the famous theory of the 5 whys

teaches us, by drilling down through a series of dressed-up "why" questions, you can get to the core issue, not just the surface symptoms, and identify actionable solutions.

Practice this Week: In your next three conversations, ask one follow-up question for every initial response. Notice how the quality of information changes.

Making Time to Connect

In practical terms, authentic connection requires time - particularly one-on-one or at most one-to-few time. Don't rush it. A 45-minute conversation can yield more transformation than five rushed meetings. Better to do fewer, deeper interactions - and share the work across your senior team - than to cram connection into an overloaded agenda. Depending on the size of the organisation, once you will have had conversations with 20-30 clients (increase that if you have fundamentally different clients, e.g. businesses in one area and retail in another, lower that if you are a startup), 30-50 internal conversations (triple that if you are a colossal multinational, half that if you are a small business) in different functions and different seniority levels, 3-5 conversations per relevant key stakeholder type (e.g. unions, regulators, large investors, etc.), you and your executive team will have plenty to go by. After that, you can increase the effectiveness leverage by having larger meetings in the form of one-to-many (town hall, open questions sessions, breakfast with the leader, etc.), as the likelihood of finding new themes decreases significantly.

This requires intentional calendar management. Block time for connection the same way you block time for strategic planning. Treat these conversations as mission-critical, not as nice-to-haves that can be cancelled when urgent matters arise.

Consider creating different types of connection time:

- **Weekly one-on-ones**: For regular check-ins with direct reports

- **Monthly skip-levels**: For connecting with people deeper in your organisation

- **Quarterly stakeholder rounds**: For maintaining relationships with key partners, customers, and external stakeholders

- **Annual connection audits**: For a systematic review of all your key relationships

The key is consistency. People need to know they can count on your attention and presence. Sporadic connection efforts often create more frustration than no effort at all.

Cultural Sensitivity: The Global Connection Challenge

In a global workplace, emotional intelligence must be culturally intelligent.

Emotions are universal, but how we express them varies dramatically across cultures, generations, and contexts.

In some cultures, direct feedback builds trust. In others, it damages it. In some, showing vulnerability fosters respect. In others, it undermines authority. In some contexts, silence indicates agreement; in others, it signals disagreement. The key is to approach each interaction with curiosity, not assumption.

When I led the teams at Aegon, at the European bank, or at the logistics company headquartered in Northern Europe, I had to learn to adapt my Italian expressiveness to the local norms. The intention behind my care stayed the same - but how I expressed it had to shift. Connection doesn't mean losing who you are - it means adjusting how you show up. And interestingly, together with the teams, we found a balance which allowed us to have open, genuine conversations, but with the kindness and well-meaning that is expressed so differently from one country to the other.

This cultural sensitivity extends beyond nationality. Different generations have different communication preferences. Different functions within your organisation may have different norms. Different personality types respond to different approaches. The art is in reading these differences and adapting your style while maintaining your authenticity. And whenever you get it (a bit) wrong, and that will happen more often than you think, be vulnerable, stop and apologize, or at least acknowledge that you realise it may not have come across right and explain where you are coming from. People will appreciate this deeply, as it will allow them to consciously give an interpretation to your behaviour that is different from what they may have instinctively assumed had they just followed the usual pattern of behaviour and interpretation that prevails in their community.

Some practical "speed-adapt" strategies:

- **Observe first:** Notice how different groups communicate before jumping in

- **Ask about preferences:** "What's the best way to give you feedback?"

- **Adapt your medium:** Some connect better in writing, others in person

- **Respect timing:** Some cultures value punctuality, others prioritize relationship-building

- **Understand hierarchy**: Some contexts require formal respect for authority; others thrive on egalitarian interaction

Mining the Digital Goldmine: Listening at Scale

In the digital age, your people and customers are already sharing how they feel - through reviews, surveys, internal chats, and social platforms. You don't need to guess; you just need to listen intentionally.

In the age of AI, you can easily throw vast amounts of unstructured data into a model to extract the key messages. Obviously, the more you structure the question you expect answers to the better the outcome will be.

Here are some advanced digital listening techniques you can leverage:

- **Look beyond ratings:** A 3-star review saying "Product worked, but no one answered questions" reveals more than glowing 5-stars

- **Social listening:** Set alerts for emotional language - "frustrated," "excited," "confused," "delighted"

- **Go beyond satisfaction scores:** Ask about hopes, worries, dreams. Use questions like "Describe your ideal experience with us" or "What would make you excited to recommend us to others?"

- **Internal communication analysis:** Are people asking the same questions repeatedly? Is tone changing over time?

- **Digital body language:** Who's withdrawn in video calls? Working unusual hours? Stopped participating in chats?

- **Response Time Patterns:** Notice how quickly people respond to different types of messages. Delayed responses might indicate discomfort or disagreement. Immediate responses might signal strong engagement or concern.

- **Participation Patterns:** Track who participates, who asks questions, and who volunteers for projects. Changes in participation often reflect changes in emotional engagement.

The Trust Equation

In summary, all this boils down to building trust. And as C.H. Green, D. Maister, and R. Galford outlined in their "The Trusted Advisor", trust can be summarized by the following equation, where, as you can see, the various components get determined by the emotional intelligence capabilities and the successful implementation of the techniques that we have just described:

Trust= (Credibility+Reliability+Intimacy) / Self-Orientation

Your emotional intelligence directly impacts each element:

- **Credibility**: It refers to the knowledge and expertise a person has. It encompasses how believable and competent someone appears based on their words and actions. For example, if someone is knowledgeable about a subject, they are seen as credible. For a leader, this is rarely a challenge as their voice is perceived as authoritative.

- **Reliability**: This measures how dependable a person is. It involves whether they follow through on their commitments and deliver on promises. A reliable person consistently meets expectations and deadlines, which builds trust over time. This is heavily influenced by self-awareness. A person with low self-awareness will come across as (emotionally) unpredictable because he or she believes she is using a certain compass to make decisions, while in reality, emotions play a great role and affect the accuracy of that compass significantly. As with a real compass, the gap between the displayed north and the true north varies significantly from one place to another on the globe, and a sailor must take that into account, lest the boat be significantly off course after just a few hundred miles.

- **Intimacy**: It relates to the emotional safety felt when sharing personal information with someone. It reflects how secure individuals feel in confiding their thoughts and feelings. High intimacy fosters deeper connections and trust. The possibility of intimacy is directly influenced by the ability of the leader to self-manage and by the focus that the leader puts in truly hearing the person he or she is talking to.

- **Self-Orientation**: This is the degree to which a person is focused on themselves versus others. A lower self-orientation indicates that a person is more concerned about the needs and interests of others, which enhances trustworthiness. Conversely, a high self-orientation can diminish trust. This is directly linked to how open a leader appears to be to the suggestions and ideas of other people, as opposed to using discussions only to validate his or her preconceived hypothesis. This is obviously directly influenced by the ability of the leaders to be completely focused on the perspectives of the person they are interacting with through open-ended and follow-up questions, appropriate cultural interpretation, and time allocation.

Reflect: Where is your trust equation strongest? Where does it need work?

The Ripple Effect: From Connection to Transformation

When people feel emotionally connected, they trust. When they trust, they speak up, take risks, feel supported and energized, innovate, and collaborate. Connection becomes your flywheel - each genuine interaction builds momentum for the next.

This isn't just feel-good leadership - it's your strategic multiplier. Emotionally intelligent cultures outperform the rest in growth, retention, and resilience. They adapt faster to change, recover more quickly from setbacks, and sustain performance over time.

Consider the compound effect: when one leader creates genuine connection, it models behaviour for others. When that behaviour spreads, it creates a culture where connection becomes the norm rather than the exception. When connection becomes cultural, it attracts people who value authentic relationships and repels those who don't.

Most importantly, connection creates psychological safety - the foundation for any meaningful transformation. When people feel safe to be vulnerable, to admit mistakes, to share ideas, to challenge assumptions, transformation becomes not just possible but inevitable.

Think about the organisations you've seen that successfully navigated major changes. Almost invariably, they had leaders who had built strong emotional connections throughout the organisation. These connections created the trust necessary for people to embrace uncertainty, the communication channels necessary for rapid adaptation, and the resilience necessary for sustained change.

When Connection Transforms Business: Case Studies

Case Study: Southwest Airlines - The Employee-First Revolution

Southwest's success wasn't built on airfare - it was built on emotional intelligence at scale. The leadership understood something crucial: if employees feel valued, they will pass that value on to customers.

But Southwest's approach went deeper than just treating employees well. They created a culture where connection was systematized, not left to chance. Every leader, from the CEO to front-line supervisors, was expected to spend time connecting with their people.

Leaders didn't inspect - they connected. They asked questions, removed obstacles, and followed through. When baggage handlers needed better tools, they got them. When flight attendants offered suggestions, they were heard - and changes followed.

The company created what they called "Culture Committees" at each location - groups of employees responsible for maintaining connection and celebrating achievements. They instituted regular "Message to the Field" communications from leadership, but these weren't just announcements - they were conversations that invited response and dialogue.

Southwest also pioneered the practice of "servant leadership" in aviation. Leaders at every level saw their role not as directing work, but as removing obstacles that prevented great work. This required constant connection to understand what those obstacles were.

The result? Consistent customer satisfaction, low turnover, and resilience in tough markets. Southwest maintained profitability for 47 consecutive years - a record unmatched in the industry - largely because its connected culture created customer loyalty that transcended price competition.

Case Study: Starbucks - The Experience Economy

Howard Schultz knew Starbucks was selling more than coffee - it was selling an emotional experience. Connection wasn't a buzzword; it was a business model.

Schultz understood that every interaction was an opportunity to create an emotional connection. He institutionalized this understanding through comprehensive training programs that went far beyond operational procedures.

Starbucks trained employees in the LATTE method to handle conflict with empathy:

- Listen to the customer's concern

- Acknowledge their feelings

- Take action to address the issue

- Thank them for bringing it to your attention

- Explain what you've done to prevent it from happening again

But the real genius was in how Starbucks designed for connection. They designed stores to foster community - comfortable seating, ambient lighting, spaces for both solitude and gathering. They encouraged baristas to learn customer names and remember preferences. They created seasonal drinks and experiences that gave people reasons to connect with the brand emotionally.

Schultz also modelled vulnerability and connection as a leader. He shared his own story - growing up in public housing, his father's struggles with work injuries, and his own journey from salesperson to CEO. This authenticity created a culture where personal stories mattered, where employees felt comfortable bringing their whole selves to work.

Connection wasn't just good hospitality - it was strategic. It made Starbucks synonymous with warmth and belonging, creating customer loyalty that allowed the company to charge premium prices and expand globally.

Case Study: Microsoft - A Culture Code Rewritten

Under Nadella, Microsoft went from silos and competition to collaboration and connection. But this transformation required systematic culture change, not just inspirational leadership.

Gone were the stack rankings that pitted employees against each other. In came coaching conversations, dialogue, and vulnerability. Nadella himself modelled this - sharing his personal learning journey, rather than broadcasting top-down edicts.

The company instituted "One Week" hackathons where employees across divisions collaborated on projects they were passionate about. These weren't just innovation exercises - they were connection exercises, breaking down the silos that had prevented collaboration.

Microsoft also transformed its performance management system from annual reviews to ongoing "Connects" - regular conversations between managers and employees focused on growth, development, and support rather than evaluation and ranking.

The company created "Inclusion Journey" programs that helped employees understand different perspectives and experiences. They established Employee Resource Groups that fostered connection across traditional organisational boundaries.

Perhaps most importantly, Microsoft leadership began sharing their own learning journeys openly. They talked about mistakes, about changing perspectives, about moments of doubt. This vulnerability created psychological safety throughout the organisation.

The transformation was stunning: soaring engagement, revived innovation, and a growth from $300 bn to $2.8 trillion market cap. But the real success was cultural - Microsoft became a place where people wanted to work, where customers wanted to partner, where innovation flourished because connection created trust.

Connection in Action: Your 3-Phase Plan

Here is your practical plan to establish a connection.

Phase 1: The One-on-One Listening Movement

Schedule dedicated connection sessions with your direct reports and the audience you want to connect to (clients, colleagues, stakeholders, etc.). Not status meetings - human understanding sessions.

Your playbook:

- Open with: "How are you - really?"
- Explore: "What's energizing or draining you?"
- Check feelings: "How do you feel about team dynamics?"
- Collaborate: "How can I support you better?"

Map your connections across all stakeholder groups. Of course, depending on which group you are exploring, the big themes to probe should be adapted:

- **Teams**: Do you know what drives each person? What are their career aspirations? What motivates them beyond compensation? What challenges are they facing outside of work that might affect their performance?
- **Customers**: What's their emotional journey with your products or services? Where do they feel frustrated, delighted, confused, or supported? What stories do they tell about their experience with your organisation? If you are in retail businesses, the key is to understand whether your customers

feel treated as a person, i.e., are you giving them the recognition for who they are and what they go through in life (e.g. are you being the no-frills, effective, to the point provider with the busy self-directed professional, while leaving more space for interaction and human connection with the lonely yearning for company)? Equally, if you are in B2B, are your services/products helping them grow their own business, do you make them look good with their own clients, do you reflect in the way you serve them a good understanding of their ambitions, their constraints, their circumstances?

- **Peers**: What tensions or opportunities remain unspoken in your cross-functional relationships? Where are the silos? Where is governance used as an excuse for creating obstacles and derailing initiatives? Where could a better connection unlock better collaboration? What support do they need that you could provide?
- **Leadership**: Do you connect to their pressures and priorities - not just their metrics and directives? What keeps them up at night? What would success look like from their perspective? Are the roles cut for what people excel at?
- **External Stakeholders**: How do partners, suppliers, regulators, or community members perceive working with your organisation? What could you do to strengthen these relationships?

Phase 2: Digital Connection Strategy

- Set up emotional language alerts for your industry
- Redesign surveys to ask about hopes and worries
- Schedule virtual coffee chats with no agenda
- Send personal video messages instead of emails

Phase 3: The Ripple Effect

Document what you've learned. Share insights with your team. Model vulnerability by admitting what surprised you. Create space for others to practice these connection skills.

Measure your progress: Track participation rates, response quality, and voluntary feedback. But most importantly, notice how you feel in conversations and how others respond to you.

Assess yourself with the CARE, DARE, SHARE Compass (chapter 1): Is your Care dimension expanding?

Your Connection Journey: The Foundation of CARE

Here's your leadership choice: Continue operating with transactional efficiency, or embrace connection as your strategic multiplier.

The most effective leaders create cultures where connection becomes the norm, not the exception. Where empathy isn't a "soft skill" but a strategic imperative. Where vulnerability becomes the foundation of unshakeable trust. This is the first and most critical step in bursting the Rationality Mirage, which thrives on disconnection and transactional relationships.

But in a culture governed by the Rationality Mirage, advocating for 'connection' can feel like a career-limiting move. The key is to translate it into the language of the boardroom. Connection isn't just about feeling good; it's a primary strategy for risk mitigation. High-trust, high-connection teams identify and solve problems faster, before they escalate into crises.

Think of it this way: what is the cost of disconnection? It's the cost of employee turnover, of disengagement, of an idea that is never shared. The single greatest expense on any company's P&L is the cost of untapped human potential. When you frame it that way, building connection isn't a soft initiative; it's a core financial strategy.

Your Chapter Challenge: This week, have one conversation where you ask, "What am I missing?" and then truly listen to the answer. Notice how both the quality of information and the quality of relationship change.

Connection is the foundation that makes everything else possible. The insights you gather through genuine connection will inform every other leadership act to come.

Connection is also an ongoing practice, not a one-time achievement. The relationships you build require continuous nurturing. The emotional intelligence you develop needs constant refinement. The cultural sensitivity you cultivate must evolve with changing contexts.

It all starts with this: the intention to see the human being behind every role, to listen not just with intelligence but with empathy, and to lead with both head and heart. This isn't about becoming a different person - it's about becoming more fully yourself while remaining genuinely curious about others.

The connections you forge today are the roots of your future impact. Every authentic conversation, every moment of empathic presence, every act of genuine care creates the foundation for the transformation you want to see.

And the intuition you develop through this practice - the ability to sense what people need before they can articulate it, to recognize patterns in emotional responses, to identify the human problems behind business challenges - becomes your most trusted compass. This intuition, grounded in genuine connection, will guide every other aspect of your leadership journey.

Transformation begins with connection. Everything else builds from there.

In the next chapter, Chapter 3, we'll explore how to turn your emotional insights into analytical clarity - blending empathy with evidence to understand what your stakeholders need, and why. We'll learn how to combine the human intelligence you've gathered through connection with artificial intelligence and data analysis to create insights that are both emotionally resonant and strategically sound.

Chapter 2 Takeaways & Reflection

Lead with both brain and heart - because data alone doesn't transform.

⬦ **Key Takeaways**

- **Connection precedes clarity:** Deep listening surfaces what data alone can't: fear, hope, misalignment, and unspoken tensions that determine success or failure.
- **Emotional intelligence changes outcomes:** Practicing self-awareness, attunement, and presence shifts brain chemistry - reducing threat responses and enabling trust, collaboration, and performance.
- **Listening is a leadership discipline:** Intentional, open-ended, follow-up questioning reveals what metrics can't. Leaders who make space for silence, emotion, and nuance unlock deeper insight.
- **Digital doesn't mean distant:** AI can amplify listening at scale - but the act of noticing who's silent, withdrawn, or emotionally checked out still falls to the human leader.
- **Connection is pattern recognition:** Noticing recurring emotions, themes, and non-verbal signals helps you move from isolated anecdotes to actionable insight.

⬦ **Reflection Prompts**

- *Where have you mistaken communication for connection?*
- *What emotional signals might you be missing - in self or others?*
- *What's one conversation you need to slow down and really listen to this week?*
- *How are you building trust across cultural, generational, or functional lines?*
- *What practice - personal or team-wide - could make connection more consistent and systemic?*

Chapter 3: Analyse - Leveraging AI For Empathic Insights (CARE: A)

Data becomes powerful when it evolves into understanding that can shape choices.

After weeks of town halls and client visits at Aegon, my office was filled with feedback. We had hundreds of powerful stories and emotional truths. But anecdotes alone don't make a strategy. I was faced with a new challenge: how do we transform this flood of human experience into clear, actionable intelligence? How do we find the patterns in the pain? Data becomes powerful only when it evolves into understanding that can shape choices.

This is where the second principle of CARE became our guide: Analyse. We had to combine our human intuition with analytical power to see what the data was truly telling us.

You connect through deep listening. You absorb your stakeholders' stories and feel their emotions. Then, you can transform those insights into actionable intelligence by combining your human intuition with AI's analytical power.

This is the future: AI amplifying human understanding when wielded with emotional wisdom. The goal isn't to replace emotional intelligence with artificial intelligence - it's to enhance it.

AI can process vast amounts of data and identify patterns that human analysis might miss, but it takes human wisdom to understand what those patterns mean and human empathy to know how to respond.

The Power of Empathic Analytics

Traditional analytics answers "what" and "when." Sales decreased 15%. Complaints increased in April. Turnover peaked in Q3.

Empathic analytics answers "why" and "how people feel about it."

It's the difference, for example, between knowing customer satisfaction dropped 15% and understanding that customers feel treated like commodities during onboarding. It's the difference between seeing engagement decline and understanding that people feel uncertain about their career growth.

It's the same difference between observing your friend crying and actually understanding what drove them to that point - and how to help.

This is where AI becomes your emotional intelligence amplifier. Modern AI tools can process vast amounts of unstructured data - surveys, reviews, communications, support tickets - and identify emotional patterns that would take human analysts months to discover. For example, a platform like Qualtrics or Brandwatch can scan thousands of customer reviews and not just classify them as 'positive' or 'negative,' but also use topic modelling to pinpoint that the word 'frustrating' is most frequently associated with your 'onboarding process,' giving you a precise, factual target for improvement.

The crucial distinction: AI doesn't replace emotional intelligence; it extends it. Your human intuition guides what to look for. Your empathy interprets what the data means. Your wisdom decides what actions to take.

Empathy, when fuelled by analysis, transforms into tailored care.

This practice of using AI to amplify human understanding is the future of leadership.

Netflix demonstrated this perfectly when it revolutionized how streaming platforms understand their audiences[1]. Traditional

---

[1] Netflix's journey toward emotional AI began early. They launched their first recommendation system in 2000, but the real breakthrough came in 2007 when streaming gave them access to real-time viewing data for the first time. This marked the beginning of their evolution from simple preference matching to sophisticated emotional engagement analysis that now drives over 80% of viewing hours.

analytics told them what people watched and when they stopped watching. But Netflix's breakthrough came when they trained their AI systems to detect not just viewing behaviour, but emotional engagement patterns.

In their quest to reduce the billions lost annually to subscriber churn, Netflix developed what industry analysts call "emotional engagement scoring" - AI that analyses how viewers interact with content at an emotional level. The system tracks subtle signals: pause patterns during emotional scenes, rewind behaviour at key moments, browsing patterns after watching certain content, and even the time gaps between episodes that indicate emotional investment.

What made this approach revolutionary wasn't just the detection - it was what the AI had been trained to notice: not just whether people watched, but how they felt while watching. The system could distinguish between passive consumption and genuine emotional connection. It revealed that viewers who felt emotionally disconnected from content were 12 times more likely to churn, even if their viewing hours remained steady.

This is where data became empathy in action.

Instead of generic content recommendations based solely on genre preferences, Netflix created what they call "emotional journey mapping." They began personalizing not just what people watched, but when and how content was presented based on emotional readiness. A viewer showing signs of stress might receive comfort content recommendations. Someone displaying curiosity patterns might get complex narratives that reward deeper engagement.

The results were transformational: Netflix's AI-driven personalization now drives over 80% of viewing hours and has reduced churn by up to 12% in key markets. More importantly, engagement quality - the depth of emotional connection viewers feel with content - has become their strongest predictor of long-term subscriber loyalty.

The key insight: Netflix discovered they weren't just competing for screen time - they were competing for emotional connection. By understanding not just what people watched but how content made them feel, they transformed from a content delivery platform into an emotional experience curator.

Your Leadership Challenge: Creating The Actionable-Truth-Zone

Before diving into AI-powered empathy tools, confront an uncomfortable truth: Most organisations are drowning in comfortable lies.

Data gets filtered. Reports get massaged. Metrics get chosen to support predetermined conclusions rather than reveal uncomfortable realities. Yes-men get promoted. Truth-tellers get labelled as "negative".

But transformation requires brutal facts - creating environments where reality is faced directly, not through rose-tinted spreadsheets.

When you're honest about gaps, you can be strategic about growth. When you acknowledge where you're failing, you can focus resources on where you're succeeding. It is about solving the organisation's issues, not about making the leader feel good. When you're precise about problems, you can be precise about solutions.

Think about your last leadership meeting: Did you start with "What's going well?" or "What are we not seeing?" That single question reveals whether you're building a culture of truth or a temple of yes.

The most successful leaders I've worked with understand that false confidence leads to wasted investment, while shared truth builds trust. So, to avoid that, they create what I call a "Actionable-Truth-Zone" - a commitment to data-driven honesty that permeates every conversation.

Very few leaders dare to do so. Many prefer to think they do, but unconsciously push away any bearer of non-sugar-coated messages - usually because of low self-awareness and a tad of insecurity.

The courage to build an 'Actionable-Truth-Zone' is a practice in what philosophers call 'intellectual humility' - the recognition that our own beliefs and data may be incomplete or wrong. It reflects the principles of 'radical transparency' championed by leaders like Ray Dalio at Bridgewater Associates, who argue that the biggest tragedies in organisations come from people holding dangerously different views of reality without surfacing them. AI can be a powerful tool for revealing these hidden realities, but only within a culture that has the humility to look for them.

Ask yourself: Which leader are you? Which leader do you want to be? Are you truly accepting the bearer of bad news? Or criticism?

This cultural shift is particularly crucial when implementing AI-powered analytics. AI systems are only as good as the questions we ask them and the actions we take based on their insights. In a painting analogy, you should see AI as most powerful when a skilled and experienced human draws the shapes and the frames and AI colours the areas, and never ever, ever, the contrary.

If your organisational culture rewards optimistic interpretations over accurate ones, your AI tools will become expensive confirmation bias machines rather than instruments of genuine insight.

Building Your Actionable-Truth-Zone

1. Establish Psychological Safety for Truth-Telling

The first step is creating an environment where people feel safe to share difficult realities. This means rewarding honesty over optimism, accuracy over agreeableness, and insight over confirmation. People need to know that bringing bad news won't result in blame or punishment - it will result in gratitude and action. It means creating a culture where direct feedback is understood not as criticism, but as a profound investment in a person's growth. I often reminded my teams that **"tough love is also love"**: that caring enough to have the difficult, honest conversations is the ultimate mark of respect for their potential.

In practice, this looks like:

- **Start meetings with "What are we not seeing?"** rather than "What's going well?" This simple shift in framing signals that you value insight over reassurance.
- **Celebrate team members who surface problems early** rather than those who hide them until they become crises. Create recognition programs that reward early warning signals.
- **Ask "Where might we be wrong?"** about every major assumption. Make this a standard part of your planning and review processes.
- **Treat bad news as valuable intelligence,** not personal failure. When someone brings you concerning data, thank them before you address the issue.
- **Model vulnerability** by sharing your own mistakes and uncertainties. Leaders who admit their own blind spots create permission for others to do the same.

2. Host Monthly "Brutal Truth" Sessions

Schedule monthly sessions where the explicit goal is to examine uncomfortable realities. But frame these constructively, not destructively. You're not gathering to criticize or assign blame; you're gathering to understand and improve.

This phase requires courage. It means admitting where strategies aren't working, where initiatives are failing, where the organisation is struggling. It means as a leader to say publicly, "I failed, I regret, and this is my solution....". Not only this makes you a more genuine leader....and to be honest, you are not really admitting anything people had not really seen, as anyhow, everyone had seen your mistake, even if you hoped they actually had not. But when you do address these issues, everyone understands why the changes are necessary. People support what they help create; they support what they understand.

To prepare for these, you may want to create regular "gap reports":

- **Customer experience gaps:** Where are customers having difficulty, and what emotions are driving their frustration?
- **Employee engagement gaps:** Where are team members struggling, and what support do they need?
- **Process efficiency gaps:** Where are systems breaking down, and what's the human cost of these failures? Where are we wasting resources?
- **Strategic execution gaps:** Where are we falling short of our goals, and what capabilities do we need to develop?

To prepare these reports, a few tools can prove very valuable, such as:

- Sentiment Analysis: Sentiment analysis tools can process thousands of customer reviews, employee surveys, or social media mentions to identify emotional trends. The way to make them particularly insightful is to go beyond just tracking overall sentiment scores, and dig deeper around:
  - Specific emotions people express about different aspects of their experience (e.g. frustration with your product but delighted with your service? Employees are excited about new projects but anxious about job security?
  - Differences across demographic groups (e.g. younger vs older employees)
  - Gaps between what people say publicly and what they express privately
  - Emotions change over time and in response to specific events (e.g. before, during, and after major changes)

  For example, an advanced application of this is using a tool like Gong.io or CallMiner, which applies voice analysis to customer support calls. The AI can flag conversations where a customer's tone indicates high stress or frustration, even if their words are polite. This provides a factual, quantifiable measure of emotional friction that might otherwise be missed by human agents who are focused only on the words being spoken.

- Engagement Surveys: You can use traditional engagement surveys (e.g. on a scale of 1-10. "How satisfied are you with your job?" "How likely are you to recommend this company to a friend?" "How well does your manager support your development?") but beef them up with AI-powered survey tools can analyse open-ended responses to identify themes, concerns, and opportunities that numeric ratings miss. You should aim to detect when people are saying one thing but feeling another, or to identify the specific words and phrases that signal deeper issues or emerging opportunities, and track emotional responses to specific events.
- Customer Feedback Platforms: Your customers are constantly telling you how they feel - through reviews, support tickets, social media posts, direct feedback, and behavioural patterns. But this feedback is often scattered across multiple platforms and buried in unstructured text that's difficult to analyse at scale. AI tools can synthesize this feedback to identify patterns that human analysis might miss.

On a regular basis, for example, quarterly, you should focus on one of these reports and go into depth, asking yourself:

- What patterns in our data contradict our usual beliefs? Look for metrics that don't align with your narrative about how things are going.
- Where are we seeing emotional signals that we're not addressing? Identify the feelings behind the facts - frustration, confusion, excitement, fear.
- What feedback are we avoiding because it's difficult to hear? Acknowledge the human tendency to filter out information that challenges our beliefs.

- Where might our success be masking underlying problems? Sometimes good results in one area can hide deteriorating conditions in another.
- What would our harshest critics say about our current state? This helps you anticipate challenges before they become public.
- What are the sacred cows and the blind spots we refuse to challenge? This helps you anticipate thinking rigidities and aspects where competitors can blind side you.

3. Balance Truth With Hope

Present the full picture - problems AND progress. Pair every challenge with proposed solutions or next steps. You're not creating doom and gloom; you're creating clarity for focused action.

4. Develop Predictive Empathy Outcomes

Once you've mastered basic empathic analytics, you can begin to use AI for predictive empathy - anticipating emotional needs before they become problems. For example:

- **Burnout Prediction:** By analysing patterns in communication and collaboration, meeting schedules, and response times, AI can identify employees at risk of burnout weeks before traditional symptoms appear. This is precisely what platforms like Microsoft Viva Insights or Workday Peakon Employee Voice are designed to do. They can, for instance, generate a factual report showing that after-hours messaging from a specific team has increased by 40% over the last quarter. This is a quantifiable leading indicator of burnout that corroborates the qualitative 'feeling' of stress you picked up in one-on-one meetings, allowing for proactive, data-informed intervention. This type of insight allows for proactive intervention rather than reactive support.

- **Customer Churn Prediction:** AI can identify customers who are likely to leave based on emotional signals in their communications and usage (e.g. increasing frustration in support interactions, declining engagement, reduced feature adoption, changes in payment behaviour). This allows for empathic retention strategies rather than generic offers.
- **Team Dynamics Prediction:** AI can identify when team dynamics are shifting in concerning directions (e.g. increase in formal communication vs informal, changes in meeting participation), allowing leaders to intervene before conflicts escalate or collaboration breaks down.

5. Measure Success: Beyond Traditional Metrics

Traditional metrics like productivity and profitability are still important, but they don't capture the full impact of emotional intelligence. Metrics you may want to use:

- **For Employees:** Sentiment score trends over time, emotional volatility (stability of sentiment), engagement quality (depth of participation), psychological safety indicators, stress, and wellbeing markers
- **For Customers:** Emotional journey mapping, satisfaction depth (beyond ratings), advocacy strength (enthusiasm level), problem resolution satisfaction, relationship resilience

The Ethics of Emotional AI

As you implement AI-powered empathy tools, be transparent about emotional data collection and usage. Never let AI make decisions about emotional well-being without human judgment. AI should inform, not replace, human wisdom. Ensure emotional AI enhances safety rather than undermining it. People should feel supported, not monitored. Lastly and most importantly, AI systems can perpetuate or amplify human biases. You should therefore regularly audit your emotional AI for cultural biases in sentiment analysis, gender or age bias in emotion recognition, socioeconomic bias in engagement patterns, and language bias in text analysis.

People should understand:

- What communications are analysed?

- How is emotional data used?

- Who has access to insights?

- What controls do they have?

- How are biases kept in check?

Real-World Transformation: Spotify's Emotional Revolution

Spotify's breakthrough came when they realized users weren't just looking for songs they liked - they were looking for music that matched their emotional state or helped them transition to a desired emotional state.

Someone listening to upbeat music at 6 AM Monday was in a different emotional place than someone listening to the same music at 11 PM Friday.

The insight that changed everything: Their true competition wasn't other music services - it was anything that helped people manage their emotional lives. They were competing with meditation apps, therapy sessions, and phone calls with friends.

Music was just the medium. Emotional support was the product.

This led to mood-based playlists and emotionally intelligent recommendations. Instead of asking "What genre do you like?" Spotify began asking, "How do you want to feel?"

Results: Engagement rates increased 40% when they shifted from genre-based to emotion-based recommendations. Users spent more time on the platform, created more playlists, and showed higher loyalty.

Key lessons:

- Emotional context is as important as behavioural data
- People use products to manage their emotional lives
- AI enhances emotional intelligence when guided by human insight
- Emotional relevance creates stronger engagement than functional utility alone

Case Study: Airbnb's Empathy Revolution

In 2016, Airbnb faced an existential crisis. Discrimination was rampant - guests with African American names were 16% less likely to be accepted. The platform, promising to help people "belong anywhere" was systematically excluding people based on perceived identity.

Traditional analysis would have focused on compliance and penalties.

Instead, CEO Brian Chesky's team used AI to understand the human emotions driving discriminatory behaviour. They wanted to know not just what was happening, but why - and how everyone felt about it.

The AI analysed millions of interactions and revealed a shocking truth: The discrimination wasn't primarily driven by conscious bias, but by fear and uncertainty about unknown guests.

The emotional patterns were clear:

- Fear of property damage when hosts felt uncertain about guest trustworthiness
- Social anxiety among new hosts overwhelmed by hosting strangers
- Control needs when hosts felt they had little predictability
- Community pressure in certain areas

- Economic insecurity among income-dependent hosts

Airbnb's response was revolutionary. Instead of just implementing anti-discrimination policies, they redesigned the entire platform to address the emotional needs of both hosts and guests.

- Instant Book: Reduced host anxiety with automatic acceptance criteria

- Enhanced Profiles: Gave hosts context without demographic assumptions

- Host Protection: Comprehensive insurance addressing specific fears

- Community Building: Forums reducing isolation that led to discrimination

- Bias Interruption: Redesigned booking to emphasize shared interests over identity

The transformation was remarkable:

- By 2022, the discrimination differential between those who were perceived as white and those who were perceived black had shrunk to less than 3%, i.e., more than 80% from the initial 16% in 2016

- Host satisfaction increased as anxiety decreased

- Guest satisfaction improved in double digits

- Platform usage grew significantly as well

Most significantly, the platform that had been systematically excluding people became a model for inclusive hospitality.

Key insight: The most effective solutions address feelings, not just behaviours. This is a direct antidote to the Rationality Mirage, which is programmed to ignore the very feelings that drive human action. Understanding emotional drivers allowed systemic solutions rather than temporary fixes.

Case Study: Unilever's Wellbeing Analytics

Unilever, the global consumer goods giant, faced a challenge that many large organisations struggle with: how to understand employee wellbeing across 190 countries, 149,000 employees, and dozens of different cultures and languages. Traditional annual surveys were providing data, but not insight. People were reporting satisfactory scores on engagement metrics, but the company was still seeing high turnover, burnout, and disengagement in key markets.

The disconnect between reported satisfaction and actual behaviour suggested that something was being lost in translation - literally and figuratively. Employees in different cultures expressed dissatisfaction differently, and the annual survey format wasn't capturing the real-time emotional reality of work life.

In 2021, Unilever's leadership team, working with their global HR organisation and external technology partners, decided to implement what they called "Wellbeing Analytics" - an AI-powered system that could detect emotional patterns in employee communications, behaviours, and feedback in real-time.

Working with Microsoft's Workplace Analytics and custom sentiment analysis tools developed with academic partners, Unilever began monitoring emotional wellbeing indicators across its global workforce. They looked at various sources of insights, like:

- Communication Patterns (Email response times and tone, meeting participation and speaking time, instant messages sentiment and frequency, cross-team collaboration patterns, after-hours communication frequency)
- Behavioural Indicators (calendar scheduling patterns, meeting loads, use of wellness resources, learning and development engagement, physical office presence, and workspace usage)
- Feedback Analysis (open-ended surveys, exit interviews, manager feedback session notes, peer review comments)

The AI wasn't tracking productivity metrics or performance indicators - it was tracking emotional wellbeing signals that predicted both individual satisfaction and team effectiveness. The system was designed to identify patterns that suggested stress, isolation, overwork, or disengagement before they became serious problems.

Within six months, the AI had identified several patterns that human analysis had missed, partly because they were subtle and partly because they varied significantly across different cultural contexts:

- The "Always On" Culture: In certain regions, particularly in Asia and parts of Europe, employees were sending emails and messages at all hours, not because they were highly engaged or dedicated, but because they felt insecure about their job security. The AI detected that after-hours communication was often accompanied by language patterns suggesting anxiety rather than enthusiasm.
- The Meeting Trap: High-performing teams in North America and Northern Europe were scheduling so many "collaboration" meetings that individual contributors had no time for deep work. This led to weekend working, delayed projects, and eventual burnout. The AI identified this pattern by analysing calendar data alongside sentiment in team communications.
- The Feedback Vacuum: Employees who received frequent, specific positive feedback were more resilient during difficult periods and showed higher engagement scores. Those who received only annual reviews or generic feedback were more likely to disengage and eventually leave. The AI tracked the relationship between feedback frequency and emotional well-being across different management styles.
- The Inclusion Gap: People from underrepresented backgrounds were participating less in optional activities and showing lower engagement in team communications. The AI revealed that this wasn't because they weren't interested, but because they felt uncertain about cultural fit and belonging. The pattern was particularly pronounced among recent hires from different cultural backgrounds.

- The Innovation Paradox: Teams that were under pressure to innovate were actually showing decreased creativity and increased stress. The AI identified that innovation flourished in environments with psychological safety and moderate challenge but declined under high pressure and tight deadlines.

Instead of implementing generic wellness programs or broad policy changes, Unilever created targeted interventions based on the specific emotional insights the AI had revealed:

- Right to Disconnect: Established technology-enforced boundaries around after-hours communications, with different policies for different regions based on cultural context and local labour laws. The system automatically delayed non-urgent emails and provided alternatives for true emergencies.
- Meeting-Free Zones: Created protected time for deep work and implemented "meeting budgets" for teams. Managers received AI-powered insights about their team's meeting load and suggestions for more efficient collaboration.
- Feedback Coaching: Trained managers to provide more frequent, specific, and constructive feedback. The AI system provided managers with insights about their team's emotional well-being and suggested timing for feedback conversations.
- Inclusion Ambassadors: Created peer support networks for underrepresented employees, with AI-powered matching based on interests, career stage, and cultural background. The system also provided managers with insights about inclusion dynamics on their teams.
- Innovation Incubators: Redesigned innovation processes to include psychological safety measures and stress management. Teams working on high-pressure projects received additional support and resources.
- Cultural Adaptation: Customized wellbeing programs for different cultural contexts, recognizing that emotional

expression and support needs vary significantly across regions and cultures.

The transformation was both measurable and meaningful:

- Job satisfaction increased by 15% after only one year, a tremendous achievement in such a hard-to-move metric
- Productivity measures improved by 15% as stress and burnout decreased
- Employee NPS grew to 38
- Voluntary turnover decreased by double digits, with particularly strong improvements in key markets
- Innovation output (new ideas submitted) increased by 45%
- Employee Net Promoter Score improved by 50 points:
- Employees reported feeling "seen" and "understood" by their organisation in ways they hadn't before
- Manager confidence in supporting their teams increased dramatically
- Cross-cultural collaboration improved as cultural differences in communication were better understood
- The company's reputation as an employer of choice improved significantly

But the most significant result was cultural. Unilever had created a system that enhanced human connection rather than replacing it. The AI provided managers with insights that helped them be more empathic and effective leaders. It gave employees confidence that their well-being was valued and monitored. It created a feedback loop between emotional intelligence and business performance that reinforced positive behaviours.

This case proved rich in insights:

- AI can detect emotional patterns that humans miss in large-scale data, particularly across different cultural contexts and languages.

- Well-being is predictive of performance, not just a nice-to-have. Organisations that invest in emotional intelligence see measurable business returns.
- Personalized interventions based on emotional insights are more effective than generic programs. One-size-fits-all wellness programs often fail because they don't address specific emotional needs.
- Technology can enhance human connection rather than replace it when implemented thoughtfully and with clear ethical guidelines.
- Cultural context is crucial for emotional intelligence in global organisations. What indicates stress or satisfaction varies significantly across cultures.
- Emotional intelligence requires ongoing attention, not just annual surveys. Real-time monitoring and response create more supportive environments than periodic check-ins.

Your AI-powered Empathy Toolkit

Ready to implement AI-powered empathy? Here's your practical action plan:

Phase 1: Foundation (Days 1-30)

Week 1-2: Emotional Data Audit

- Catalogue existing sources of emotional data
- Identify gaps in current emotional intelligence
- Define success metrics for emotional AI

Week 3-4: Tool Selection Choose based on your specific needs (these are just some examples, the list can be very different depending on your sector and size of operations):

1. For Employee Insights:
    - Qualtrics: Advanced text analytics with sentiment analysis

- o Microsoft Workplace Analytics: Communication patterns

- o Slack Analytics: Team health and engagement

2. For Customer Insights:

- o Salesforce Einstein: Predictive analytics and sentiment

- o Zendesk: Support ticket sentiment and escalation prediction

- o Brandwatch: Social media sentiment monitoring

Phase 2: Implementation (Days 31-60)

Week 5-6: Pilot Testing

- Run AI analysis on existing data

- Compare AI insights with human observations

- Refine configurations based on results

Week 7-8: Action Planning

- Create response protocols for emotional insights

- Develop intervention strategies

- Train managers on using emotional intelligence data

Phase 3: Scaling (Days 61-90)

Week 9-10: Full Rollout

- Expand tools organisation-wide

- Implement real-time monitoring

- Create emotional intelligence dashboards

Week 11-12: Optimization

- Refine AI models based on outcomes
- Plan advanced capabilities

Your Transformation Moment

Here's your leadership choice: Continue operating with traditional analytics that tell you what happened, or embrace empathic analytics that reveal why it happened and how people feel about it.

The most effective solutions address feelings, not just behaviours.

For the leader facing scepticism, this is the most critical insight to prove. The temptation of the Rationality Mirage is to believe that the data tell the whole story. It never does. Consider the spectacular failure of Zillow Offers. Their algorithm, a masterpiece of rational data analysis, could predict housing prices with stunning accuracy. But it couldn't account for the irrational, emotional volatility of a market driven by human fear and greed. They were technically brilliant and emotionally blind, and it cost them half a billion dollars. This is the tangible, bottom-line cost of ignoring emotion.

The organisations that master empathic analytics don't just perform better - they become more human in an increasingly digital world.

They create cultures where people feel seen, understood, and valued. They build relationships based on genuine understanding rather than transactional efficiency. They develop emotional resilience to navigate uncertainty with grace.

When you understand how people feel, you can help them feel better. When you help people feel better, they perform better. When they perform better, everyone wins.

Your Next Step: From Insight to Impact

The insights you've gathered through empathic analytics are only valuable if you act on them. You've learned to listen with your heart and analyse with your mind.

Now it's time to act with both.

Your Chapter Challenge: This week, implement one "brutal truth" session with your team. Ask: "What are we not seeing?" Then listen - really listen - to what emerges. Use that insight as your first step toward AI-enhanced empathy.

The path from analysis to transformation requires courage. But with AI as your emotional intelligence amplifier, you have the tools to create change that's both profound and sustainable.

Your journey continues: You've connected. You've analysed. Now, in Chapter 4, you're ready to respond with precision and empathy - creating solutions that honour both the data and the human hearts behind it.

Chapter 3 Takeaways & Reflection

Empathy isn't just felt - it's decoded, clarified, and acted on.

◇ **Key Takeaways**

- **Insight needs courage:** AI can show you the truth - but only if you're willing to look. Facing uncomfortable patterns is the first step toward real change.
- **Empathic analytics go beyond the 'what':** Traditional data tell you what happened. Empathic data reveals how people feel and why it matters.
- **AI amplifies emotional intelligence:** It doesn't replace your gut - it sharpens it. The most powerful insights come when human empathy interprets what algorithms detect.
- **No illusion, only action:** Creating a truth-telling culture - where feedback is safe, bad news is welcome, and insights fuel decisions - is a leadership superpower.
- **Patterns predict pain - and possibility:** When you track emotion over time and context, you don't just see burnout coming - you prevent it. You don't just react to churn - you reconnect.

◇ **Reflection Prompts**

- *Where are you filtering out uncomfortable truths - about team, self, or strategy?*
- *Where in your organisation are you seeing symptoms but missing the emotional causes?*
- *Are you building a culture of clarity, or a culture of comfort?*
- *What AI insights have you ignored, diluted, or delayed acting on - and why?*
- *How can you better combine emotional intelligence and AI to inform the next big decision?*
- *What's the cost of continuing to make decisions based on incomplete emotional intelligence?*

Chapter 4: Respond - Acting With Tailored Empathy (CARE: R)

It's not the tools you have faith in - tools are just tools - they work, or they don't. It's the people you have faith in or not.

With our new analysis in hand, my executive committee and I had devised a first strawman of a strategy, and we started testing it with a few trusted people across Aegon NL. It was met with polite nods but not a lot of energy. We had listened and analysed, but our response felt hollow. It was a stunning failure that taught me the most important lesson: insight without tailored, empathic action is just another form of disrespect. This is where most leadership dies.

We had fallen into the classic corporate trap: you've connected deeply with your stakeholders. You've analysed what you've heard with both heart and AI. You have insights that could transform your organisation. And yet - despite the insights, the heartfelt stories, the clear signals - nothing changes.

Here's the brutal truth: based on Deloitte, 88% of employees believe their organisation cares about their wellbeing, yet only 56% feel their immediate manager demonstrates that care through specific actions. That 32-point gap? That's where most leadership dies. Insight without action is a fundamental disrespect of the gift people have given you by accepting to open up.

That failure forced us to develop the third principle of CARE: Respond. We had to learn how to translate our insights into actions that were precise, personal, and powerful. This isn't about launching another wellness program or sending another "we hear you" email. The Respond phase of the CARE framework is where leadership stops being performance and becomes transformation. It is the moment you actively defy the Rationality Mirage's dismissal of empathy and prove that you have not just heard, but understood. Where empathy evolves from feeling to strategy. Where strategy crystallizes into impact. This led us to co-create our 'potato language' - simple, shared words that everyone could connect with, turning a top-down mandate into a collective mission.

And for the leader operating in a sceptical environment, this is where you gain momentum. You don't need a company-wide revolution. You need one, undeniable success story. This is the 'stealth strategy' for cultural change: find a single, measurable business problem - like the mortgage intermediary issue I tell about in this chapter - and solve it by applying the CARE framework.

Case Study: Adobe - The Check-In Revolution

This realization - that the *way* you respond is as important as the response itself - is a lesson learned by the most innovative companies. Take Adobe, for example, when they scrapped their annual performance reviews after internal data revealed it was demoralizing employees and delaying feedback. In its place, it introduced "Check-Ins" - informal, flexible conversations between managers and team members on growth, not judgment.

This wasn't a rebrand of the same tool. It was a shift based on emotional insight: employees wanted timely recognition, clarity, and development - not bureaucratic rankings. The change increased retention, improved manager relationships, and helped build Adobe's reputation as a human-centric employer.

But the story was deeper than meets the eye: Adobe's transformation didn't happen overnight. Their analysis revealed that 78% of employees found annual reviews "not helpful" and 65% said they would be more motivated by frequent, informal feedback. The real insight came from exit interviews, where departing employees consistently mentioned feeling "invisible" between review cycles.

The implementation wasn't smooth. Managers initially struggled with the unstructured approach and felt it would favour a friendship-based performance system instead of a meritocracy. Adobe responded by providing conversation frameworks, not scripts - giving structure without rigidity. They also created peer mentoring groups where managers could share what worked.

Results after two years:

- 30% improvement in employee engagement scores

- 50% reduction in voluntary turnover

- 78% of employees reported feeling more supported in their development

- Manager effectiveness scores increased by 25%

The lesson? Sometimes the most empathic response is removing a process, not adding one. But removal must be coupled with something better, not just elimination.

The One-Size-Fits-All Trap

Think about the last time someone gave you generic advice for a deeply personal problem. How did it feel? Hollow. Dismissive. Like they weren't really listening.

Now imagine experiencing this repeatedly at work - where leaders *say* they understand but respond with solutions that miss the mark entirely.

A global tech company spent $2.3 million on a wellness program after surveys showed rising stress. The program barely moved engagement scores. Why? The real issue wasn't work-life balance - it was unclear promotion criteria, creating career anxiety.

Generic responses don't just fail. They actively erode trust. They signal that despite all your listening and analysis, you still don't get it, or you don't really care.

Question for you: Where have you seen generic responses damage trust in your organisation? What happened to the culture afterward?

The Anatomy of an Empathic Response

Empathic responses at scale follow a practical structure that balances data, judgment, and humanity. Think of this as your empathy architecture - a systematic approach to turning insight into impact.

1. Signal Recognition: Reading Beyond Words

Thanks to your efforts in the Connect (Chapter 2) and Analysis (Chapter 3) phases, you have identified the real emotional signals (behavioural, verbal, patterns, etc.) and underlying issues.

For example, a financial services firm discovered, after running the approaches highlighted in Connect and Analyse, that "frustrated" appeared 340% more in feedback after quarterly reviews. The real insight? People weren't frustrated with their ratings - they were frustrated with the lack of development guidance.

2. Context Mapping: The Hidden Multipliers

Now we need to devise the right solutions. For that, context allows to nuance the interpretation of the situation and to devise better solutions. Ask yourself: What else is happening around these signals?

- **Organisational Context**: Growth phase or restructuring? Market pressure or expansion?

- **Team Context**: Newly formed or disrupted? High-performing or struggling?

- **Cultural Context**: How do different backgrounds influence emotional expression?

- **Individual Context**: Career stage, life situation, tenure?

For example, a pharmaceutical company's Asian offices consistently showed lower "speaking up" scores. The Western solution? Assertiveness training. The actual solution after deeper context analysis? Redesigned meeting structures that honoured cultural communication preferences while achieving business goals.

3. Tailored Intervention: Precision Over Volume

From there, we can design a response that fits the emotional and practical context. Is it a recognition moment, a coaching session, a redesign of the process? Is it a tech fix or a human touchpoint?

Tailored interventions follow four principles:

Principle 1: Match Medium to Message

- High-stakes emotions → Face-to-face conversation
- Process confusion → Documentation and systems, individual support for high-value processes
- Recognition needs → Public acknowledgment
- Development concerns → Ongoing coaching

Principle 2: Scale Appropriately

- Individual issues → Individual solutions
- Team patterns → Team-level interventions
- Organisational themes → Structural changes

Principle 3: Consider Implementation Capacity

- What can realistically be sustained?
- Who has the skills and authority to execute?
- What other initiatives might this conflict with?
- How will you measure success?

Principle 4: Adopt Co-Creation

- Whenever possible, involve those affected in crafting the solution. Ask what would help. Don't assume you already know.
- Co-create, not just with employees but even with clients or other stakeholders. For example, in a B2B world, all it takes is

a few senior conversations and design sprints with selected clients. In a retail environment, think of experience labs, pilot programs, and other forms of testing directly with customers.

- Consider creating solution committees, involving cross-functional teams and people experiencing the problem, not just those managing it.
- Build ongoing feedback loops into your solutions. Don't just implement and walk away.

For example, a retail chain facing frontline turnover applied these 4 principles. And instead of doing the conventional, and expensive, action of raising wages. They co-created solutions with actual store employees. The result? A buddy system for new hires (i.e. one to one buddy to new hire allocation), flexible scheduling around life events, and rapid-response systems for customer complaints. These cost less than traditional approaches but had higher impact because they addressed what employees actually needed.

In another example, at a large financial services firm, mortgage intermediaries were increasingly dissatisfied. Many in the leadership team assumed the fix required a costly, multi-year IT overhaul. But by applying the Connect and Analyse phases of the CARE framework, we uncovered the real issue: relationship breakdown.

Intermediaries were constantly routed to new support agents, forced to re-explain complex client cases every time. Meanwhile, agents had no ownership incentive to see cases through, as they knew that the next call from that intermediary would not fall on them. This was further aggravated by an indeed clunky IT system. The frustration was mutual.

Instead of revamping the technology, we reassigned each major intermediary to a consistent mini-team of three support experts. This created personal relationships, better accountability, and full-hour coverage without changing shift patterns or headcount.

The impact was dramatic: satisfaction scores skyrocketed, and the firm jumped into the top three providers in the market. Even IT satisfaction improved - though the system hadn't changed at all. What changed was the human connection that helped people work *with* the (clunky) system, not around it.

Try this: Identify one challenge your team is facing. Instead of designing a solution, schedule 30 minutes to ask them what would help. What do you discover?

The ACTED Framework: From Insight to Impact

Tom Peters, the famous author of "In Search of Excellence" once said: "Leaders don't create followers. They create more leaders." His concept of "bias for action" meant avoiding paralysis by analysis. But in today's world, action alone isn't enough. We need a bias for precise action.

The challenge isn't just moving quickly - it's moving quickly in the right direction, with the right intensity, for the right people. This requires a framework that balances speed with specificity.

Here's a tailored adaptation for this new era - what I call the ACTED Framework for emotionally intelligent response:

A – Acknowledge the Emotional Reality

- Name the discomfort or unmet need. Say "I see you" in deeds, not just words.
- Good acknowledgment sounds like: "I hear that you're feeling overwhelmed by conflicting priorities from different stakeholders."
- Poor acknowledgment sounds like: "We value your feedback and are always looking to improve."

C – Co-Design Solutions

- Invite their voice. Give real authority, not just input.
- Include multiple perspectives. Set clear constraints. Create psychological safety for disagreement.

T – Tailor the Response

- Avoid one-size-fits-all fixes. Consider culture, generation, role, and personality. Set expectations for evolution. Create fast feedback loops and iterate to improve the response.
- The most powerful empathic responses aren't grand gestures - they're consistent, small actions that demonstrate ongoing care and attention.
- It is advisable to start small and scale smart, for example, by beginning with pilot programs before full rollout. This way, you can learn from early adopters and build successful momentum over time.
- Also, sometimes, straightforward empathic responses aren't sufficient. Complex situations require more sophisticated approaches that balance multiple stakeholder needs and navigate organisational constraints, for example, when different populations have conflicting needs, or at times of crisis where sensitivities may need to be sacrificed for speed and resolve. This is where the leader's judgment comes into the picture, but also where it is essential to explain to people the contextual considerations that led to the choice of a solution instead of another.

E – Enable Through Systems

- Make empathic responses sustainable, not dependent on heroic effort.
- Make it easy to participate.
- Embed responses into processes. Use technology to scale personal touches. Train people to continue the work.

D – Demonstrate Impact Visibly

- Show that feedback led to change. Close the loop. Build trust through transparency, both about successes and setbacks. Communicate continuously.
- Share specific stories of how responses helped real people. Track metrics, both quantitative and qualitative. Celebrate successes.

The Ripple Effect: When Empathy Compounds

When you respond with tailored empathy, the CARE Turbine spins ever more strongly:

1. People Feel Seen

This creates psychological safety, emotional connection, and increased engagement.

A manufacturing company's "manager walking rounds" program - 30 minutes daily talking with frontline workers - led to a 15% productivity increase and 40% reduction in incidents.

2. Systems Evolve

Empathic responses reveal structural improvements and innovation opportunities.

A healthcare system's response to nurse documentation frustration uncovered that nurses spent 40% of their time on paperwork. The resulting automation investment freed nurses for patient care, improving satisfaction by 25% and retention by 30%.

3. Trust Becomes Scalable

People who experience empathy extend it to others. Culture spreads person by person, moment by moment.

The most powerful aspect of empathic response is its multiplicative nature. One empathic action doesn't just solve one problem - it creates a template for how problems should be approached. This can, in turn, travel through the organisation down the organisational hierarchy, or across countries and departments, and become a powerful movement of transformation.

Case Studies: Where Empathy Tailored Responses Drove Real Impact

Let's examine how organisations have successfully implemented tailored empathy at scale. These aren't just success stories, they're blueprints and examples for translating insight into action.

Case Study: Vodafone - Policy That Listened

Vodafone's global parental leave policy was born from listening - not lobbying. Internal sentiment analysis and interviews revealed that both men and women felt pressured to return to work quickly, fearing career penalties.

The company responded with a bold, globally consistent paid parental leave policy - 16 weeks for all new parents, regardless of gender. They also provided flexible return-to-work options, like reduced hours for six months.

The implementation faced resistance from some regional leaders who worried about coverage and costs. Vodafone addressed this by:

- Sharing Success Stories: Highlighting teams that successfully managed parental leave coverage

- Providing Resources: Temporary staffing budgets and cross-training programs

- Measuring Impact: Tracking not just leave utilization but also team performance and employee satisfaction

The results? Employee engagement soared, particularly among millennials. Recruitment competitiveness increased. And retention after parental leave jumped by 20%. Even better, after three years:

- 98% of eligible employees utilized the policy

- 85% returned to work after leave (up from 65%)

- 40% increase in male employees taking parental leave

- 15% improvement in overall employee Net Promoter Score

- Recognition as "Best Place to Work for Families" in multiple markets

This wasn't charity. It was insight-based empathy, scaled through policy. The key was recognizing that parental leave wasn't just about time off - it was about career continuity, fairness, and cultural support. And from there, empathic policy design turned this aspect into a competitive advantage for Vodafone.

Case Study: Patagonia - Environmental Activism as Employee Empathy

Patagonia's decision to donate its $10 million tax windfall to environmental causes wasn't just corporate social responsibility - it was a direct response to employee values and concerns.

Internal surveys revealed that 89% of Patagonia employees cited environmental impact as a primary reason for working there. But focus groups uncovered deeper concerns:

- Employees worried the company was "selling out" as it grew

- Many felt guilty about working for a company that still contributed to consumption

- There was anxiety about whether leadership truly shared their values

The tax donation was accompanied by transparent communication, employee involvement, regular updates on environmental impact and activism, policies supporting employees' own environmental activism.

Results:

- Over 90% employee approval of the decision

- Very significant increase in job applications citing company values

- 4% employee turnover rate, about 25% improvement in employee retention
- Enhanced brand reputation and customer loyalty

Building Your Response Muscle: A 30-Day Plan

To build your empathic response and bring the ACTED framework to reality, this is your suggested practical approach:

Week 1: Signal Recognition

Choose one area where you have clear insight about clients, employees, or stakeholders' needs. Practice identifying behavioural, verbal, silent, and pattern signals. Use the Connect (Chapter 2) and Analyse (Chapter 3) methodologies of the CARE framework.

Week 2: Context Mapping

For your chosen area, map the organisational, team, cultural, and individual contexts influencing the situation.

Week 3: Response Design

Use the ACTED framework to design a tailored response.

Week 4: Implementation and Iteration

Launch your response. Measure initial impact. Gather feedback. Adjust.

Pause here: What's one insight you have right now that needs an empathic response? What would ACTED look like for that situation?

Put your learnings into practice - case examples where you lead

Case 1. Employees Feel Disengaged

Let's say your AI analysis shows high disengagement among early-career staff. Don't launch a company-wide training. Try this instead:

Insight: Early-career employees report feeling unseen and uncertain about growth.

Context Analysis:

- *Recent organisational changes have reduced informal mentoring opportunities*

- *Managers are overwhelmed and don't have time for development conversations*

- *Early-career employees are working remotely and feel isolated*

- *Traditional mentorship programs have had low participation rates*

How do you react? What solutions do you envisage? How will you measure success?

What they did:

Co-Design Process: Invite a focus group of early-career employees to share what would help them feel supported. Include mid-level employees who could serve as mentors.

Response Design: Launch a peer mentorship program with mid-level employees, with opt-in coaching circles and storytelling from senior leaders.

Detailed Implementation:

- *Matching Process: Use a combination of AI-suggested matches based on skills/interests and employee preferences*

- *Structure: Monthly one-on-one meetings, quarterly group sessions, and annual storytelling events*

- *Resources: Provide conversation guides, development tools, and recognition for mentors*

- *Support: Train mentors in coaching skills and create peer support networks*

System Enablement:

- *Embed mentorship into performance reviews and career progression*
- *Create a technology platform for matching and tracking*
- *Integrate with existing learning and development programs*
- *Recognize mentorship contributions in promotion criteria*

Measurement Plan: Track changes in engagement, retention, and internal mobility after 6 months.

Success Metrics:

- *80% participation rate among eligible employees*
- *25% improvement in engagement scores for participants*
- *15% increase in internal promotions for early-career staff*
- *90% satisfaction rate with mentorship relationships*

Case 2. Customers Express Confusion About Onboarding

Insight: New customers are struggling to understand how to use the product effectively, leading to early churn.

Context: The Product has become more complex, the support team is overwhelmed, and existing materials are outdated.

How do you react? What solutions do you envisage? How will you measure success?

What they did:

Co-Design: Include recent customers and the customer success team in solution design.

Response Options:

- *Humanized Onboarding Sequences: Videos featuring real employees explaining key features*

- *Live Support: Scheduled onboarding calls with success team members*

- *Simple Checklists: Step-by-step guides for common use-cases*

- *Peer Community: Connect new customers with experienced users*

- *Progress Tracking: Show customers their advancement through onboarding*

- *Opportunity Identification: Notice if there are specific additional needs that often surface in the first few weeks of onboarding, and explore ways to provide those as well*

Implementation: A/B test different approaches, measure completion rates and customer satisfaction, and optimize based on results.

Case 3. Frontline Employees Feel Voiceless

Insight: Frontline employees have valuable insights about customer needs and operational improvements, but feel their input isn't valued.

Context: Organisational hierarchy creates barriers to communication, and previous suggestion programs have failed.

How do you react? What solutions do you envisage? How will you measure success?

What they did:

Co-Design: Include frontline employees in designing new feedback mechanisms.

Response Options:

- *Rapid Feedback App: Mobile-friendly tool that routes insights directly to leadership*

- *Regular Skip-Level Meetings: Senior leaders meet directly with frontline staff*

- *Idea Implementation Tracking: Visible system showing which suggestions are being acted upon*

- *Recognition Programs: Celebrate employees whose suggestions drive improvements*

- *Decision Transparency: Explain why certain suggestions can't be implemented*

Implementation: Start with a pilot group, ensure quick response to initial feedback, and gradually expand based on lessons learned.

Your Response Revolution Starts Now

Here's what's at stake: In a world where AI can analyse everything, the organisations that win will be those that respond with precision, care, and humanity.

Your stakeholders aren't looking for perfection. They're looking for real change, and a sense that you really care about them, that they matter. That is where precision and humanity create the trust and inspiration that can move mountains.

For the empathy sceptics, you can position investments in empathy as direct investments in performance and innovation.

The gap between listening and responding is where trust lives or dies. Where cultures thrive or stagnate. Where ROI reaches great levels or remains stubbornly low. Where leaders become legends or footnotes.

When you demonstrate that responding with empathy and human-centric solutions directly reduces customer churn by X% or improves team productivity by Y%, you are no longer asking for permission to 'care.' You are presenting a proven strategy for profit growth. You have successfully translated heart into ROI, making it impossible for the Rationality Mirage to lure everyone.

Your Chapter Challenge: Tomorrow, find one person whose concern you've heard but haven't acted on. Have a conversation. Ask what would help. Design a response together.

Because real transformation doesn't start with grand gestures. It starts with showing one person that their experience matters enough to change something.

In Chapter 5, we'll explore how to scale this empathy by empowering others to respond with the same precision and care - creating cultures where empathic action flows through every level of your organisation.

Chapter 4 Takeaways & Reflection

Empathy without action is erosion. Tailored response is leadership.

◇ **Key Takeaways**

- **Tailored empathy builds trust**: Generic responses feel dismissive - even harmful. Precision and personalization show people they're truly seen and valued.
- **Insight ≠ impact - unless acted on**: The gap between listening and responding is where transformation succeeds or fails.
- **Context creates precision**: Emotionally intelligent leaders weigh cultural, team / individual contexts to choose how to act.
- **What AI does well**: Pattern recognition across large datasets, analysis without bias, processing feedback at scale, surfacing uncomfortable truths
- **What humans do better**: Context interpretation, emotional intelligence, relationship building, knowing when to break rules
- **The ACTED framework enables intelligent response**: Acknowledge → Co-design → Tailor → Enable → Demonstrate - five steps to translate insight into scalable impact.
- **Simplicity beats scale when it fits**: You don't always need massive transformation. Sometimes the best change is small, targeted, human.
- **Systems should scale care, not replace it**: Technology is to be used to respond with empathy, not automate empathy away.

◇ **Reflection Prompts**

- *What's one insight your team has shared that you haven't responded to yet? What might ACTED look like in that case?*
- *Where might you be offering one-size-fits-all fixes instead of tailored interventions?*
- *How can co-creation improve both impact and relationships?*
- *Are your current systems enabling empathy - or requiring heroic effort to demonstrate care?*
- *What's one small, specific action you could take this week to show someone: "I heard you - and it mattered"?*

Chapter 5: Empower - Fostering Trust And Growth (CARE: E)

Empowerment isn't giving the power away – it's sparking the power within.

You've mastered the first three steps of CARE. You Connect with genuine presence. You Analyse with empathic precision. You Respond with tailored care that meets people where they are. Now comes the ultimate leadership test: can you Empower others to lead with the same emotional intelligence - without you?

This is where most leaders stumble. They become the bottleneck to their own success, the emotional hub that everything flows through. But true empowerment isn't about creating dependency - it's about building distributed emotional intelligence that thrives in your absence.

Here's the paradox that changes everything: the more power you give away, the more powerful you become.

Yet most leaders resist this truth. They've climbed ladders by being indispensable, by having all the answers. Empower demands a radical shift - from being the star player to becoming the coach who creates champions.

What's at stake if you don't make this shift? Your organisation will never scale beyond your personal capacity. Your best people will leave for roles where they can grow. Your culture will collapse the moment you're not there to hold it together.

What does success look like? An organisation that maintains emotional intelligence when you're on a long vacation. Leaders who don't need you to be emotionally intelligent because they've internalized the skills themselves.

The Shift from Hero to Orchestrator

When I became CEO, I fell into the classic trap. I was the empathy expert, the emotional translator, the one who "got it." People lined up outside my office seeking emotional clarity. I felt important, but I was creating a time bomb.

One week epitomized my mistake: seventeen one-on-one meetings with people needing help with emotional challenges. I was proud of my accessibility, but in reality, I was teaching learned helplessness.

The wake-up call came during a brutal quarter. All of a sudden, in our mortgage business, intermediaries started expressing deep dissatisfaction, the backlog was growing fast, and employee engagement took a negative turn. Instead of diving into data myself, I asked our business-line leader: "What emotional signals are you seeing that our dashboards aren't capturing?"

Silence. Then he said "Let me take it away, good question!"

Our culture was to know perfectly every key indicator but not to read a room. We had spreadsheet literacy but no emotional literacy.

That's when I realized: empowerment isn't just giving people authority - it's giving them the emotional tools to use that authority wisely.

My realization that I had become an emotional bottleneck touches on one of the deepest truths of human motivation, described by psychologists Edward Deci and Richard Ryan in their 'Self-Determination Theory.' They found that humans have three core psychological needs: **autonomy** (the need to feel in control of one's own life), **competence** (the need to feel effective), and **relatedness** (the need to feel connected to others). The 'hero' leader, by solving every problem, inadvertently starves their team of autonomy and competence. The 'orchestrator' leader, by contrast, creates the conditions for all three needs to be met. Empower isn't just a management technique; it is the fulfillment of fundamental human drives.

Pause and Reflect: Where in your organisation are you the emotional bottleneck? What would happen if you weren't there for a month - would emotional intelligence survive?

The hero leader conducts every instrument. The orchestrator ensures every musician can read the music, feel the rhythm, and contribute their unique voice to the collective symphony.

Heroes create dependencies. Orchestrators create capabilities.

This isn't about working yourself out of a job - it's about multiplying your impact exponentially. When you Empower emotional intelligence throughout your organisation, you create something that outlasts your tenure and thrives regardless of who's in charge.

Empowerment Model

Traditional organisations concentrate emotional intelligence at the top, creating bottlenecks that worsen as companies grow. A CEO can personally connect with maybe 100 people, but modern organisations employ thousands across continents and time zones.

The Empowerment Model is a six-pillar approach to embedding emotional intelligence into the operating system of your organisation - so that care isn't just delivered, it's distributed.

The Empowerment Model changes everything. Instead of funnelling complexity upward, it distributes capability throughout the organisation. It's like moving from a fragile centralized power grid to a resilient network of solar panels.

The ultimate test of empowerment is this: can your organisation maintain its emotional intelligence when you're not there? True empowerment creates leaders who don't need you, the CEO, to be emotionally intelligent - they've internalized the skills and systems to do it themselves.

When you Empower others to lead with emotional intelligence, you create a legacy that outlasts your tenure and a culture that thrives regardless of who's in charge.

Building the Empowerment Model requires intentional system design. It's not enough to hope that emotional intelligence will emerge naturally - you need to create the structures, processes, and culture that support it - an Empowerment Model that becomes fully part of your business model, i.e. part of the organisational DNA.

This isn't a quick implementation - it's a systematic transformation that requires careful planning, patient execution, and continuous refinement. But the organisations that commit to this transformation create sustainable competitive advantages that are difficult for competitors to replicate.

The Six Pillars of the Empowerment Model

Pillar 1: Assess Your Current State

Before you can build an Empowerment Model, you need to understand where you're starting from. This assessment should be comprehensive and honest - it's better to discover problems now than to build solutions on a shaky foundation.

- Emotional Intelligence Audit: Survey managers and employees to identify emotional blind spots. This isn't just about self-assessment - it's about 360-degree feedback that reveals gaps between perception and reality. How well do managers think they understand their team's emotional needs? How well do employees think their managers understand their emotional needs? Where are the gaps?
- Feedback Flow Analysis: Map how information and emotional signals currently move through your organisation. Where do emotional concerns get stuck? Where do important insights fail to reach decision-makers? Where do people feel heard, and where do they feel ignored?
- Trust Measurement: Establish baseline metrics for psychological safety and manager effectiveness. This includes both quantitative measures (engagement scores, retention rates, promotion rates) and qualitative measures (focus groups, interviews, observation).

- Empowerment Inventory: Identify where decision-making authority currently resides and where it should reside. What decisions are being made at inappropriate levels? Where are people asking for permission when they should be empowered to act?

Pillar 2: Build Emotional Literacy

Your managers can read a P&L, but struggle to read the emotional signals in a room. They miss the quiet frustration, the burnout masked as overachievement, the hope flickering under cynicism. They've been trained to track what's measurable - but not what matters underneath.

Emotional literacy is the foundation of empowerment. Without it, authority becomes a risk - not a resource. This isn't about turning leaders into therapists; it's about helping them read the emotional pulse of their teams with the same fluency they apply to metrics.

How to build it:

- Weekly Emotional Check-ins: Pair operational metrics with emotional pulses: "What's our key blocker right now - and how is the team feeling?"

- Empathy Mapping: Have teams trace the emotional journey of customers, colleagues, or stakeholders through a key process. Reveal the friction beneath the flowchart.

- Emotional Debriefs: After major moments - wins, losses, launches - pause to ask: *How did people really feel? What did we miss emotionally?*

- Practical Manager Training: Teach supervisors to spot emotional cues, name them, and respond skilfully. Not one-off workshops - ongoing, coached, real-world practice.

- Psychological Safety Labs: Create role-play scenarios to rehearse difficult conversations in a low-stakes setting.

- Emotional Mentorship: Pair less experienced managers with emotionally mature leaders for regular reflection, guidance, and pattern recognition.

Try this: At your next team meeting, open with: "What emotional currents are you sensing this week?" Then just listen.

Pillar 3: Implement Listening Systems - Feedback Loops That Flow Both Ways

Traditional feedback flows downward. Empowered cultures require feedback loops that move up, across, and through the organisation - like a nervous system. Your body stays balanced because the brain adjusts to real-time signals from the ground. Without those loops, you'd trip with every step.

Most organisations are good at broadcasting messages, but poor at sensing emotional feedback. They launch strategies with detailed rollout plans - but no system to detect how those strategies are landing, or what emotional responses they trigger.

That's where AI becomes a game-changer. Traditional empowerment is reactive - we intervene after burnout, disengagement, or resignation. AI makes empowerment proactive: identifying subtle patterns, risks, and opportunities before they surface.

How to build a smarter emotional nervous system:

- Regular Check-In Rhythms: Replace infrequent, exhaustive engagement surveys with brief weekly emotional pulses. Two or three questions, real-time insight.

- Anonymous Feedback Loops: Go beyond suggestion boxes. Design mechanisms for psychological safety *and* honest dialogue - so truth rises without fear.

- Listening Networks: Build cross-functional groups responsible for interpreting emotional signals across the organisation. Think of them as emotional "air traffic controllers."

- AI-Powered Sentiment Analysis: Use smart tools to spot emerging emotional trends from digital communication - before they become culture issues.

- Cross-Functional Listening Forums: Gather insights from across silos. These emotional ambassadors meet regularly to detect organisation-wide signals hidden from any one manager's view.

- Predictive Empathy Analytics: Let AI highlight early warning signs - like shifts in tone, collaboration patterns, or response times - that flag disengagement before performance drops.

AI alone won't solve the problem. But when combined with human leadership, it helps you listen at scale - and act with speed.

Try this: After your next major announcement, ask three people at very different levels: "How did that feel to receive?" Don't defend. Just listen.

Pillar 4: Incorporating Emotional Logic into Decision-Making

Listening only matters if it changes what you do. Empowered organisations don't just hear emotional signals - they integrate them into decisions.

Every business decision has an emotional impact. The Empowerment Model trains leaders to anticipate that impact - not just react to it. This isn't about sentimentality; it's about foresight. Integrating emotional logic into your choices makes them more human, more strategic, and more sustainable.

Tools to incorporate emotional logic into decision-making:

- Emotional Impact Assessments: Ask: "How might this decision make different people feel? What unintended reactions could arise?"

- Stakeholder Emotion Mapping: Go beyond "who's affected" to "how will they feel?" Anticipate resistance, relief, fear, and hope.

- Empathy-Informed Rollouts: Design change initiatives that account for emotional transitions - not just operational ones.

- Emotional Stress Tests: Before big moves, simulate worst-case emotional fallout. Are you ready to support what you shake?

- Rapid Response Teams: Stand up trusted groups to quickly handle unexpected emotional friction during change.

- Recognition Systems: Reward emotionally intelligent decisions - not just outcomes. What you recognize shapes what you scale.

- Empowerment Escalation Channels: Make it easy for employees to ask for more responsibility - and to get the coaching that comes with it.

Try this: Before a major rollout, ask three stakeholders: "What worries you most about this change?" Don't solve - just note the themes. Then adjust accordingly.

Pillar 5: Embedding the Empowerment Model Into Processes and Systems

To hardwire the Empowerment Model into the DNA of your Business Model, you need to embed it into the deep-rooted processes and systems of your company. Approaches you can resort to:

- Leadership Depth: Sustainable empowerment requires building leadership depth throughout the organisation. This means developing emotional intelligence capabilities at every level, not just at the top.
- Peer-to-Peer Development: Create systems where employees develop each other's emotional intelligence. This might include peer mentoring programs, cross-functional project

teams, or employee resource groups focused on emotional intelligence.

- Distributed Leadership Opportunities: Provide opportunities for people at all levels to practice leadership in safe, supportive environments. This might include leading project teams, mentoring new employees, or representing the organisation at external events.
- Succession Planning: Ensure that emotional intelligence is a key component of succession planning. This means identifying and developing emotionally intelligent leaders throughout the organisation, not just at the senior level.
- Cultural Reinforcement: Create cultural norms and practices that reinforce emotional intelligence even when formal leaders aren't present. This might include peer recognition systems, storytelling traditions, or cultural rituals that celebrate emotional intelligence.
- Cultural Norms: Establish cultural norms that support emotional intelligence. This includes everything from how meetings are run to how conflicts are resolved to how success is celebrated.
- Continuous Learning: Create systems for continuous learning and improvement in emotional intelligence. This might include regular training programs, peer learning opportunities, or AI-powered feedback systems.

Pillar 6: Measure and Iterate

Empowerment is an ongoing process, not a one-time implementation. You need systems for measuring progress and continuously improving your approach.

Traditional metrics miss the emotional reality of empowerment. Financial metrics lag behind emotional metrics - by the time you see the impact on revenue or profitability, the emotional shifts have been happening for months. To manage empowerment effectively, you need metrics that capture the emotional reality of your organisation.

- Emotional Intelligence Metrics: Track progress on emotional literacy and empathic behaviour. This might include 360-degree feedback scores, emotional intelligence assessments, or behavioural observation metrics.
- Empowerment Indicators: Measure autonomy, trust, and decision-making authority at all levels. This includes both formal measures (span of control, decision-making authority) and informal measures (employee perception of empowerment).
- Continuous Improvement: Regular assessment and refinement of empowerment systems. This should include feedback from employees, managers, and other stakeholders about what's working and what needs improvement.
- Impact Measurement: Track the business impact of empowerment efforts. This includes traditional metrics (engagement, retention, performance) and newer metrics (innovation, agility, resilience).

The CARE Turbine

When empowerment is done right, it creates a compound effect. Each person who learns to lead with emotional intelligence becomes a force multiplier, teaching others through example and creating ripple effects throughout the organisation.

This compound effect is what separates successful empowerment efforts from failed ones. When empowerment is superficial - just giving people more authority without building their capabilities, for example saying to someone "I trust you can do this and that" without actually having a real sense they have the skills and capabilities to do it is not empowerment, it is actually the equivalent of "sink or swim". It is neither caring, nurturing nor growth enablement - and it often fails. But when empowerment is comprehensive - building emotional intelligence, creating supportive systems, linking to progressive growth in skills commensurate with the growth in challenge, and establishing cultural norms - it creates a growth momentum that becomes self-sustaining.

The CARE Turbine

- **Leader Models Emotional Intelligence** → People see the template of how to behave

- **People Feel Seen and Understood** → Psychological safety increases

- **People Feel Trusted** → They take ownership

- **Ownership Drives Performance** → Results improve

- **Success Builds Confidence** → Clever risk-taking increases

- **Confidence Foster Innovation** → The cycle accelerate

With a strong Empowerment Model, the CARE Turbine will keep happily spinning.

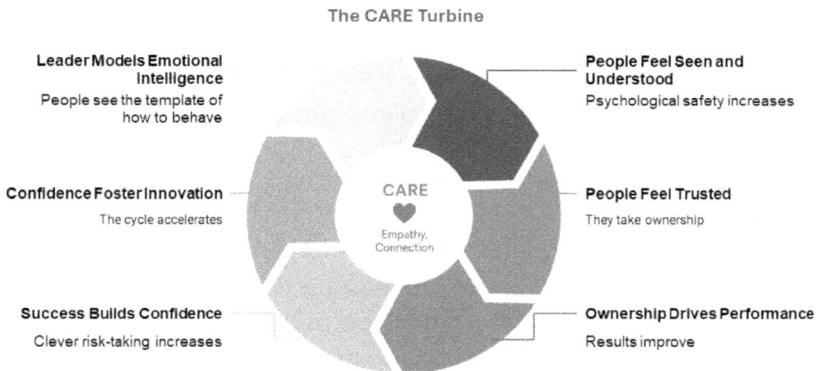

The CARE Turbine

Leader Models Emotional Intelligence
People see the template of how to behave

People Feel Seen and Understood
Psychological safety increases

Confidence Foster Innovation
The cycle accelerates

CARE
♥
Empathy,
Connection

People Feel Trusted
They take ownership

Success Builds Confidence
Clever risk-taking increases

Ownership Drives Performance
Results improve

Fig. 4. The CARE Turbine, the fundamental engine of the CARE phase.

Your Empowerment Moment: Think of someone in your organisation ready for more responsibility. What capabilities do they need to succeed? What emotional support will they require? How will you measure their growth? How do you get their CARE Turbine to spin?

When people feel safe, they don't just innovate - they become guardians of the culture. This creates an organisational immunity to the Rationality Mirage, as empowered individuals are the best defence against dehumanizing systems.

This CARE Turbine is the foundational engine of our leadership model. Once you get this turbine spinning, you generate the trust, confidence, and psychological safety needed to power the next, bolder phases of your journey: to DARE and SHARE.

Real-World Transformations: The Proof Points

The most compelling evidence for distributed emotional intelligence comes from organisations that have successfully implemented these principles at scale. These aren't just feel-good stories - they're business transformations that demonstrate the bottom-line impact of empowering emotional intelligence throughout an organisation.

Case Study: Microsoft - From Toxic to Thriving Through Distributed Empathy

When Satya Nadella took over Microsoft in 2014, the company was known for its cutthroat culture and stack-ranking system that pitted employees against each other. The transformation wasn't just about changing policies - it was about distributing emotional intelligence throughout the organisation.

The old Microsoft culture was built on individual brilliance and competitive dynamics. Employees were ranked against each other, creating an environment where helping a colleague could hurt your own performance review. Innovation was stifled because people were afraid to share ideas that might be stolen or criticized. The company was successful but emotionally unsustainable.

The Empowerment Model:

- Growth Mindset Training: Every manager learned to recognize fixed mindset language and respond with growth-oriented alternatives. This wasn't just a training program - it was a fundamental shift in how managers thought about human potential. Instead of seeing mistakes as failures, they learned to see them as learning opportunities. Instead of viewing skills as fixed, they learned to view them as developable.

- Inclusive Leadership Workshops: Middle managers were trained to spot and address microaggressions, unconscious bias, and emotional exclusion. This training went beyond awareness to skill-building - how to interrupt bias in meetings, how to create psychologically safe spaces, and how to ensure all voices are heard and valued.
- Employee Resource Groups: Grassroots communities that gave voice to diverse emotional experiences and needs. These groups became early warning systems for emotional issues and innovative solutions for workplace challenges. They provided emotional support for employees while also providing valuable feedback to leadership about the emotional climate of the organisation.
- Empathy-Driven Performance Reviews: The company moved from stack ranking to growth-focused performance discussions. Instead of comparing employees to each other, managers were trained to help each person identify their unique strengths and growth opportunities. Performance conversations became coaching conversations.

The Results: Employee satisfaction scores jumped from 63% to 91%. Revenue grew from $86 billion to over $200 billion. But perhaps most importantly, the culture shift created a virtuous cycle where empowered employees created better products, which created happier customers, which created more engaged employees.

The transformation wasn't just about changing behaviour - it was about changing the emotional operating system of the organisation. Microsoft went from a culture of fear and competition to a culture of growth and collaboration. This shift enabled innovation that wouldn't have been possible under the old system.

Case Study: Shopify - AI-Powered Career Empowerment

Shopify recognized that traditional career development was emotionally tone-deaf. Employees were frustrated by generic development paths that didn't account for their individual motivations, fears, and aspirations. The company's rapid growth meant that traditional one-size-fits-all approaches to career development were creating bottlenecks and dissatisfaction.

The old model assumed that everyone wanted to follow similar career trajectories - individual contributor to manager to senior manager to director. But Shopify discovered that many of its best employees had different aspirations. Some wanted to become deeper technical experts. Others wanted to move into customer-facing roles. Still others wanted to develop business skills. The traditional career lattice wasn't serving anyone well.

The AI-Enabled Solution:

- Career Aspiration Analytics: AI algorithms analysed employee communications, project choices, and performance patterns to identify genuine career interests beyond stated goals. The system could detect when someone was saying they wanted to be a manager but actually thrived most in individual contributor roles. It could identify people who were interested in new areas but afraid to express that interest.
- Skill Gap Empathy: Instead of just identifying missing skills, the system considered the emotional barriers to learning - fear of failure, impostor syndrome, work-life balance concerns. The AI could recommend learning paths that accounted for individual learning styles and emotional needs. For someone with impostor syndrome, it might recommend starting with small, achievable learning goals. For someone with work-life balance concerns, it might suggest flexible learning options.
- Personalized Growth Journeys: Development plans that accounted for individual learning styles, stress triggers, and motivation patterns. These weren't just lists of courses to take - they were comprehensive development experiences that included mentorship, stretch assignments, and emotional support systems.

- Emotional Learning Support: The system provided coaching and resources for the emotional aspects of career development. It could connect people with mentors who had overcome similar challenges. It could provide resources for dealing with impostor syndrome, fear of failure, or work-life balance concerns.

The Results: Internal mobility increased by high double digits. Employee retention improved by double digits. Most importantly, employees reported feeling "seen and understood" in their career growth, not just managed. The system helped people discover career paths they hadn't considered and provided the emotional support they needed to pursue those paths.

Case Study: Patagonia - Empowering Through Purpose and Autonomy

Patagonia's approach to empowerment goes beyond traditional professional development. They've created a system where employees at every level can initiate environmental and social impact projects. This isn't just about corporate social responsibility - it's about creating alignment between individual values and organisational purpose.

The company recognized that its employees weren't just looking for jobs - they were looking for meaning. Many Patagonia employees are passionate about environmental issues, but traditional corporate structures don't provide outlets for that passion. The company decided to turn this passion into a competitive advantage.

The Empowerment Model:

- 1% for the Planet Program: Employees can nominate and champion environmental causes, with budget allocation decisions made at the regional level. This isn't just a donation program - it's an empowerment program that allows employees to drive meaningful environmental impact.

Employees can propose causes, build business cases, and lead implementation efforts.

- Activism Training: Managers learn to support employee activism, even when it creates operational challenges. This training helps managers navigate the tension between business needs and employee values. It provides frameworks for making decisions when activism might conflict with business operations.
- Emotional Authenticity: Employees are encouraged to bring their whole selves to work, including their environmental anxieties and social concerns. The company has created space for employees to express their fears about climate change, their frustration with political inaction, and their hope for positive change. This emotional authenticity creates deeper engagement and stronger performance.
- Time for Change: Employees can dedicate work time to environmental and social causes they care about. This isn't just volunteer time - it's recognition that employee passion can drive business innovation and social impact.

The Results: Patagonia consistently ranks among the best places to work while maintaining fierce customer loyalty. Employees report feeling empowered not just professionally, but personally and ethically. The company's activism has become a competitive advantage, attracting both customers and employees who share their values.

Your Turn: Building Your Empowerment Model

The organisations that thrive in our volatile world aren't those with the smartest leader at the top - they're those with the most emotionally intelligent Empowerment Model throughout.

Empowerment completes the CARE cycle and sustains it. When you empower others to Connect, Analyse, Respond, and Empower, you create self-reinforcing emotional intelligence that strengthens over time – the CARE Turbine spins and spins and spins...

Your legacy won't be measured by what you accomplished, but by what others accomplished because of the systems you built. The careers you launched, the leaders you developed, and the culture you established.

Most powerfully, legacy lives in countless quiet moments when someone in your organisation decides with emotional intelligence, connects with empathy, responds with care, and empowers others to do the same - all because you created the systems that made it possible.

The empowerment question isn't whether you can lead with emotional intelligence. It's whether you can build systems that ensure emotional intelligence leads long after you're gone.

This is the ultimate expression of caring leadership - creating something bigger than yourself, something that will continue to serve people long after you've moved on, something that allows people to grow at a stretched but well-calibrated pace for themselves.

It's about building not just a successful organisation, but a sustainable one. Not just a profitable business, but a meaningful one. Not just a place where people work, but a place where people grow.

Your Chapter Challenge: This week, identify one person ready for more responsibility. Don't just give them authority - give them the emotional tools to use it wisely. Create their support system first, then watch them soar.

Empowerment is how your CARE legacy becomes culture. Start today - with one person, one decision, one system. Then step back - and watch the CARE Turbine spin.

When you empower people with the emotional tools to lead, something extraordinary happens: the space opens up - not just for performance, but for imagination.

So, we've connected. We've understood. And likely, your Care footprint on the Compass has increased. Now the question becomes:

what will we do with what we know? CARE illuminated the emotional map. DARE is where we choose a direction - boldly, bravely, and with strategic intent. And that's where we go next, chapter 6, to DARE, which starts with dreaming bigger.

Your Development: As you progress from CARE to DARE, consider taking stock of your evolution in the CARE, DARE, SHARE Compass (Chapter 1).

Chapter 5 Takeaways & Reflection

Empowerment is the moment leadership becomes legacy.

◇ **Key Takeaways**

- **Empowerment isn't delegation - it's distributed emotional intelligence**: True empowerment happens when others can lead with empathy, clarity, and care even in your absence.
- **From hero to orchestrator**: The leader's role shifts from emotional bottleneck to capability builder. Power isn't lost when shared - it multiplies.
- **Emotional intelligence must scale**: It's not enough for the CEO to "get it." The entire system needs to embody it - through structures, systems, and shared norms. We call that the Empowerment Model, which is an integral part of your Business Model
- **The CARE Turbine drives sustained performance**: When leaders model empathy, others feel seen, take ownership, and perform better - creating a virtuous cycle of growth.

◇ **Reflection Prompts**

- *Where in your organisation are you still the emotional gatekeeper?*
- *Who around you is ready for more - and what support would help them thrive?*
- *How will you know emotional intelligence is working - without you?*
- *What is your Empowerment Model?*
- *What's one process you could redesign this month to embed empowerment into your business model?*

Chapter 6: Dream - Envisioning Bold Possibilities (DARE: D)

Tomorrow is shaped by those who dare to imagine boldly - and act with the heart to make it real.

In a big grey building, the room was silent except for the hum of laptops and the distant sound of the city traffic far below. I was sitting with about 20 people from credit cards, daily banking, and digital teams at the European bank I was helping for their ambitious transformation. We were staring at a problem that felt like David facing Goliath. They had a fraction of the branches of other large banks - and their digital presence was equally fragmented, with multiple apps, ranging from banking to credit cards that confused rather than served customers.

The head of daily banking could not see how to change that trajectory. "It's really difficult. We see an opportunity to accelerate our current account growth. Without the branch footprint of larger competitors or a unified app, we need an innovative approach to win current accounts and increase our client base."

The investment in time and money required to build a sleek, world-class banking app from scratch to be able to compete with the fully digital banks in this country? Years and years, and millions and millions.....

"What if we're asking the wrong question?" one of the attendees said, breaking the tension. "Who says you need to start with current accounts to build banking relationships?"

The silence that followed wasn't empty - it was electric with possibility.

This bank was already among the leaders in credit cards, growing faster than most other players. They had a first version of Zaya, a customer service chatbot coupled with an underpinning credit card servicing platform that customers loved using because it was simple and effective. "No frills, does what it says on the tin" they would say.

Although clearly, at that moment, it was still a simple early version, powered by very elementary AI.

We looked at each other and we wondered: "Instead of following the traditional playbook, what if we flipped it entirely?" interjected another attendee.

And another continued: "What if we start from the strength - credit cards - and use Zaya to create a revolutionary conversational banking service?"

And finally, someone said aloud what had become obvious to all: "Instead of trying to outspend the giants on a new app, what if we use what we have and AI to revolutionize how customers interact with us?"

That moment changed everything. The realization that Zaya, the AI chatbot combined with a credit cards app, could be used to not just offer some simple functionalities (like checking credit cards balances, making payments) and answering questions, but to actually complete real tasks for customers. And it could do even better: try to detect the emotional state of customers, anticipate needs, and guide conversations that build deeper relationships, and help customers select the right product for them, when appropriate. Support teams wouldn't be replaced - they'd be empowered to connect more meaningfully because AI handled the routine inquiries and surfaced the moments that mattered most, whereas humans, the support specialists, could bring their time and talent to focus on the more complex tasks and make the difference to other humans, the customers.

The saying goes, "Necessity is the mother of all virtues".... In this case, indeed, constraints forced creativity. And creativity plus AI equals competitive advantage.

This is the power of **Dream** - the first pillar of DARE. But here's what makes this different from abstract visioning: You're not dreaming in a vacuum. You're building on everything you've discovered about your people, your clients, and your stakeholders in your CARE journey.

The breakthrough at the European bank didn't happen in isolation. It built on months of listening - to customers painstakingly navigating multiple apps, to support agents who knew they could provide better service if they had the right tools, to market realities that demanded innovation within constraints.

And a few months later, an improved version of Zaya, offering a quantum leap in conversational banking, was live. It won a major award for being one of the best AI applications around. And the current accounts growth climbed to almost double that of the year before.

The DARE Framework: Your Roadmap to Bold Leadership

Before we dive deep into Dream, let's establish the complete journey ahead. DARE isn't just about having bold visions - it's about systematically transforming them into reality through four connected phases:

DREAM *(This Chapter)* – Envision bold possibilities grounded in real human needs. Choose wisely your AI strategy based on the problems that matter most to your stakeholders.

ALIGN *(Chapter 7)* – Build coalitions around your vision and develop strong use-cases. Turn your bold dream into a shared mission that energizes rather than threatens your organisation.

REFINE *(Chapter 8)* – Deploy AI strategically while keeping humans at the centre. Transform vision into measurable impact through disciplined implementation.

EXECUTE *(Chapter 9)* – Iterate and scale based on real-world feedback. Continuously refine your approach as you learn what works and what doesn't.

Each phase builds on the last. You can't align people to a fuzzy vision. You can't execute without buy-in. And you can't evolve what you haven't systematically implemented.

Why Dream Comes First

Through CARE, you know where the pain points are. You've felt the frustration of talented employees trapped in bureaucratic processes. You've heard customers describe what they truly need, not just what they say they want. You've seen the cracks in your systems, the gaps in your knowledge, the missed opportunities.

Now it's time to dream solutions that matter - where your Human Intelligence (HI) takes centre stage, drawing from that deep understanding, then gets amplified by AI's analytical capabilities to transform bold possibilities into grounded strategies.

Dream is not about reckless dreaming; it's about strategic imagination grounded in human need. This is how you break free from the trap of incrementalism, which can only optimize what already exists, never create what is truly new.

From Understanding to Transformation

Before you can dream boldly, you need to dream specifically. The CARE work you've done has revealed the truth about your organisation:

- **Your people's real frustrations** – Where are they burning out? Where are their deepest pain points? What meaningful work gets buried under administrative noise?

- **Your clients' unspoken needs** – What do they struggle with that your industry hasn't solved? What would turn them into ambassadors of appreciation for your company?

- **Your stakeholders' hidden concerns** – What keeps your investors, partners, and board members awake at night? What do your regulators worry deeply about?

These insights become the raw material for your dreams.

But now comes the crucial question: Where should AI make your biggest impact?

Your vision must be grounded in one of five fundamental AI-powered strategies. Each represents a different path to transformation, a different way AI can solve the real problems you've uncovered, at an accelerated pace. And the more focused your goals, the more achievable great success becomes:

1. Operational Streamlining

The Dream: Enable your people to focus on what only humans can do - creativity, relationship-building, strategic thinking - while AI automates the soul-crushing bureaucracy, the clunky processes, the frequent and simple requests that clog call-centres.

The Reality: Employees spend a large amount of time on admin tasks. Customers wait weeks for simple approvals that they expect should be immediate. Costs spiral because every process has unnecessary steps.

The Vision: What if AI could cut waste so dramatically that your people become energized, your customers get instant value, and your margins improve by double digits?

2. Outcome Optimization

The Dream: Become a beacon of reliability. Every decision is informed by intelligence your competitors don't have. Clients know exactly what to expect and can count on it will always work. Your accuracy improves, quality soars, and client satisfaction becomes your unfair advantage.

The Reality: Teams make decisions based on incomplete data. Quality issues surface too late. Outcomes vary from one salesperson to the other, from one support specialist to the other. Client needs and expectations evolve faster than your ability to adapt. Social media is full of horror stories of when your service faltered.

The Vision: What if AI could predict problems before they happen, optimize outcomes in real-time, and help every team member make expert-level decisions, with the consistency of a metronome?

3. Empowered Workforce

The Dream: Equip your people to become humans that engage and connect. AI handles the routine while humans tackle the complex, creative, and deeply personal work that creates lasting value.

The Reality: Your best talent is trapped in repetitive tasks. Performance indicators turn everyone into adopting a robotic behaviour. Burnout is rising. People feel disconnected from meaningful impact.

The Vision: What if AI could liberate human potential so completely that engagement scores soar, innovation accelerates, and people actually love coming to work or interacting with clients?

4. Knowledge at Scale

The Dream: Foster the deep and instant sharing of your organisation's collective wisdom to everyone in your business. Expert knowledge stops walking out the door with retiring employees.

The Reality: Institutional knowledge lives in people's heads. New employees take months to get up to speed. Best practices don't spread effectively.

The Vision: What if AI could capture, organise, and democratize expertise so that every team member has access to your organisation's best thinking?

5. Growth Acceleration

The Dream: Make AI a central tenet of your value proposition. AI, not just to improve what you do - but as a core product in itself, a new source of value. Your offerings evolve, new revenue streams emerge, and market opportunities multiply.

The Reality: Most businesses are still looking at AI as a tool to automate existing products and services. Very few are yet asking themselves: what can AI do that is a completely different aspect of our value proposition?

The Vision: What if AI could become the core differentiator in your offerings, opening up entirely new business models and market possibilities?

The Courage to Dream Big

Dreaming in leadership isn't wishful thinking - it's strategic imagination. Your Human Intelligence brings irreplaceable strengths to this process: the ability to synthesize unrelated insights, to sense the emotional undercurrents of change, and to envision a future that data alone cannot forecast.

Consider Sara Blakely's story with Spanx. Her Human Intelligence was shaped by personal frustration, door-to-door sales experience, and an intuitive grasp of what women truly wanted. No AI could have predicted that cutting the feet off pantyhose would launch a billion-dollar brand. Her creative leap was born from lived emotion and first-hand knowledge - something data couldn't manufacture.

This practice of temporarily setting aside current limitations is a form of what is known as 'First-Principles Thinking.' Popularized by innovators like Elon Musk and rooted in the philosophy of Aristotle, it involves breaking down a problem to its most fundamental, irreducible truths. Instead of reasoning by analogy ('this is how other banks have done it'), you reason from the ground up ('what does a customer fundamentally need from a financial relationship?'). The insights from your CARE journey provide these first principles - the deep human needs that your bold new vision must address.

But here's where today's leaders have an unfair advantage: You don't have to rely solely on intuition. AI now acts as a multiplier - turning inspired human visions into scenarios, models, and validated strategies. While Sara Blakely tested her hunch through trial and error, you can test hundreds of variations instantly.

The new leadership equation: Emotional understanding + Inspired vision + AI validation = Competitive advantage.

Your Human Intelligence: The Irreplaceable Visionary

Human Intelligence in the Dream phase operates on dimensions AI cannot replicate:

- Strategic Intuition – Built from years of navigating uncertainty, you sense patterns that algorithms miss. You've lived through market cycles, felt the emotional weight of difficult decisions, and developed an internal compass for what feels right.
- Emotional Resonance – You understand the 'why' behind behaviour - the aspirations, fears, and values that drive people. You know that behind every purchase is a human story, behind every complaint is an unmet need.
- Creative Synthesis – You fuse insights across disciplines, connect the unrelated, and generate innovations born from friction and diversity. This is jazz improvisation in business form.
- Values-Driven Vision – Your moral compass helps define not just what's possible, but what's responsible and meaningful. You don't just ask "can we?" but "should we?"

Pause and reflect: Where have you dismissed in the past a bold idea because it felt "unrealistic"? What if that idea was actually ahead of its time?

AI as Your Vision Amplifier

AI is not here to replace your creativity - it's here to supercharge it:

- Scenario Modelling – Run thousands of potential futures to test assumptions and reveal hidden risks or pathways. What used to take months of market research now takes hours.
- Market Intelligence – Process millions of data points to uncover early trends, weak signals, and white spaces. AI spots the patterns hiding in plain sight.

- Pattern Recognition – Surface correlations and emerging clusters that enrich your intuition. Your gut instinct gets backed by statistical confidence.
- Resource Optimization – Help you prioritize ideas based on feasibility, readiness, and strategic alignment. Dream big, but build smart.

The magic lies in the symbiosis: Your HI provides vision; AI provides validation and velocity.

Case Study: The Netflix Revolution - Growth Acceleration in Action

Reed Hastings' dream of a world without late fees catalysed Netflix's transformation from DVD-by-mail to streaming giant. But what's often missed is how this aligned with deeper customer frustrations he'd uncovered - the inconvenience, the limited selection, the social awkwardness of returning adult movies.

His chosen path? Growth Acceleration - making AI the core of an entirely new offering.

The execution revealed the power of this strategy. Netflix's recommendation engine wasn't just an add-on - it became their content creation oracle. By understanding viewer behaviour at scale, Netflix could predict not just what shows people would watch, but what shows to create. They didn't just eliminate late fees; they eliminated the entire trip to the video store and the guesswork in movie ideation.

The results: A platform that reshaped global entertainment, sparked the streaming wars, and turned "Netflix and chill" into common vernacular.

The key insight: Hastings didn't just improve the video rental business - he redefined entertainment itself. That's Growth Acceleration working at its highest level.

But here's what most people miss: Netflix's boldest bet wasn't technology - it was believing people would binge-watch entire seasons. That insight came from understanding human psychology, not data analytics. It came from the understanding of customers that the CARE framework gives. The dream was human; the delivery was an HI-AI collaboration.

The Four Dimensions of Strategic Dreaming

To fully harness your Human Intelligence in this phase, develop these capabilities and apply them to the outcomes of your CARE journey that have revealed to you the deep unmet needs:

1. Future-Back Thinking

Start with your ideal future, then trace back the necessary steps. This isn't forecasting - it's back casting. You're not predicting tomorrow; you're creating it.

AI Enhancement: Test scenarios and illuminate pathways from the future to the present. Model different routes to your vision.

2. Cross-Industry Inspiration

Apply lessons from other sectors. What if you brought the empathy of hospitality into healthcare? The user-centricity of gaming in education? The community-building of churches into corporate culture?

AI Enhancement: Validate transferability and model hybrid solutions. Scan patents and business models across industries.

3. Human-Need Archaeology

Look beneath customer requests to find unspoken needs. Your emotional radar detects the desire for connection, dignity, or control - needs people can't always articulate.

AI Enhancement: Quantify and segment those needs at scale through sentiment analysis and behavioural data.

4. Constraint-Free Ideation

Give yourself freedom to imagine, unbounded by today's limitations. Budget, regulations, technology - park those for now.

AI Enhancement: Later, stress-test and ground the most promising ideas in operational reality.

Reflection question: Where has fear or feasibility thinking limited your vision?

Case Study: The Airbnb Impossibility - Empowered Workforce Strategy

When Brian Chesky and Joe Gebbia pitched Airbnb, investors called it impossible. "Strangers won't stay in strangers' homes."

But their Emotional Intelligence, their process through the CARE framework, had uncovered something deeper through their own struggles as broke design students: people craved authentic connection, and hosts needed income. Their chosen strategy? Empowered Workforce - but with a twist. Their "workforce" was millions of hosts who needed AI to succeed.

Their dream wasn't about lodging - it was about belonging anywhere. But to make hosts successful, AI became essential: managing trust through reviews, detecting fraud, optimizing pricing, and matching guests with hosts based on subtle compatibility signals.

The insight: They didn't replace human hospitality with AI - they amplified it. Every host became empowered by intelligent tools that helped them provide better experiences while protecting their interests.

The dream was human. The platform was human-scaled by AI.

Today, Airbnb has more rooms than Hilton, Marriott, and Hyatt combined - without owning a single property. That's the power of choosing the right AI strategy for your specific human insights.

Try this: Schedule a 90-minute "What If" session. No sceptics allowed. Dream like a child, then validate like a CEO.

Your turn: The Four Steps to Your Dream Framework

Step 1: Ground Your Vision in Real Problems

Don't start with technology - start with the insights from your CARE work:

- **Employee Pain Points** – Where are your people frustrated, burnt out, or underutilized?

- **Client Struggles** – What do customers complain about, work around, or accept reluctantly?

- **Stakeholder Concerns** – What systemic issues threaten long-term success?

Step 2: Choose Your AI Strategy

Based on those real problems, pick the strategy with the highest impact:

- **Operational Streamlining** if bureaucracy and inefficiency are killing morale

- **Outcome Optimization** if quality, accuracy, or decision-making gaps hurt results

- **Empowered Workforce** if your people need liberation from routine work

- **Knowledge at Scale** if expertise silos limit organisational capability

- **Growth Acceleration** if you need AI as a core differentiator

Step 3: Vision Workshop

Now dream within your chosen strategy:

- **Future Headlines** – Draft news stories about your transformation success

- **Customer Journey Mapping** – Reimagine the ideal experience your AI strategy enables

- **Employee Day-in-the-Life** – Visualize how work changes with your AI approach

Step 4: Reality Testing with AI Intelligence

- **Impact Modelling** – Quantify potential improvements in your chosen area

- **Feasibility Analysis** – Assess technical and organisational readiness

- **Resource Planning** – Map investment requirements and success metrics

Ask yourself the courage question: "What would I attempt if I knew I could not fail?"

This question isn't about fantasy - it's strategic reframing. It bypasses internal scepticism and invites expansive, possibility-driven thinking. AI then helps you refine that vision with data, not diminish it.

The most transformative leaders don't just dream - they dream publicly, unapologetically, and with conviction.

When Jeff Bezos dreamed of a store that sold "everything," people called him crazy. When he said Amazon would be "Earth's most customer-centric company," sceptics laughed.

They're not laughing now.

Your Dream, Your Legacy

The future doesn't just happen - it's authored by the bold. Your Emotional Intelligence and your Human Intelligence, when paired with the analytical clarity of AI, become a generative force for change.

AI alone cannot dream. But it can be the research team that helps make your dreams real. And the bolder your dream, the greater the legacy.

As we move forward in DARE, remember this: Vision without execution is just fantasy. But execution without vision is just busy work.

Your Chapter Challenge: at this point in your CARE, DARE, SHARE journey, I dare you to:

1. *Problem Audit: Review insights from your CARE journey. List the top 3 pain points that you want to solve.*

2. *Strategy Selection: Match each pain point to one of the 5 AI strategies. Which path offers the biggest transformation potential?*

3. *Vision Session: Spend 2 hours dreaming within your chosen strategy. What would success look like in 3 years?*

4. *Reality Check: Use AI tools to validate your vision against market data and competitive landscape.*

In the next chapter, we'll explore how to Align others to your vision - making sure bold dreams become shared missions, not just solitary ambitions.

The leader who shapes tomorrow starts by solving the problems that matter today.

What will your legacy begin with?

Chapter 6 Takeaways & Reflection

Dream boldly - not blindly. Insight fuels imagination. AI fuels momentum.

◇ **Key Takeaways**

- **Strategic dreaming starts with pain, not fantasy**: The most transformative visions emerge from deep listening - use your CARE insights as the launchpad for bold, human-centred innovation.
- **Fit AI in a precise strategy**: Focus your vision around one of five distinct strategies - Operational Streamlining, Outcome Optimization, Empowered Workforce, Knowledge at Scale, or Growth Acceleration.
- **Human Intelligence is the irreplaceable spark**: Emotional resonance, strategic intuition, and values-driven imagination allow leaders to dream what AI can't see - but AI can validate, scale, and refine those dreams.
- **Constraint is a catalyst**: Limitations in budget, structure, or tech can unlock radical creativity. Imagination thrives within boundaries.
- **HI + AI = Competitive Advantage**: Dreaming becomes powerful when intuition meets data. Visionary leadership today requires both emotional acuity and technological fluency.

◇ **Reflection Prompts**

- *Where in your organisation have you accepted stagnation?*
- *What recurring stakeholder frustrations could become fuel for a bold new value proposition?*
- *What new value propositions fuelled by AI could you offer to clients with offerings close but radically innovative to current?*
- *Which of the five AI strategies best aligns with where you think AI can bring you the most?*
- *Have you dismissed a bold idea recently - and what did you miss by doing so?*
- *How might you create space for strategic dreaming in your leadership rhythm - individually and with the team?*

Chapter 7: Assess – Evaluating With AI Insights (DARE: A)

Intuition can guide. But data must decide.

The energy in the room at the European bank, which I was helping with a CARE, DARE, SHARE transformation, was electric after we flipped the strategy to focus on conversational banking. But a bold dream is not a business case. We now had a dozen exciting ideas, but the resources to pursue only a few. The next challenge was daunting: how do we separate the game-changing opportunities from the expensive distractions? Intuition can guide, but data must decide.

This critical step of assessing a bold vision with data is what separates successful transformations from costly failures.

Unilever faced a similar moment when its traditional advertising approach was failing. It was early 2019, and Chief Marketing Officer Keith Weed faced a problem that would have been unthinkable just a decade earlier: Unilever's traditional advertising approach was haemorrhaging effectiveness while its sustainability promises felt increasingly hollow to younger consumers.

The data was clear. Brand loyalty among millennials and Gen Z had plummeted 30% over five years. Meanwhile, competitor brands with authentic sustainability messaging were stealing market share at an alarming rate. But here's what made the challenge even more complex: Unilever had over 400 brands across 190 countries. Any strategic shift needed to work for Dove in Detroit, Knorr in Lagos, and Ben & Jerry's in Amsterdam.

Imagine the conference room at Unilever's London headquarters buzzed with nervous energy, and Keith concluding, "We need to fundamentally rethink how we connect with consumers, but I'm not willing to bet £8 billion in annual marketing spend on intuition alone."

That's when Unilever deployed something revolutionary: AI-powered consumer sentiment analysis across 15 languages and 40 countries, combined with predictive modelling of purchasing behaviour linked to sustainability messaging. The results shocked even the data scientists.

The AI revealed that consumers weren't just saying they cared about sustainability - their purchasing patterns showed they would pay premium prices for brands that delivered authentic environmental impact. But here's the crucial insight that only AI could surface at scale: the definition of "authentic" varied dramatically by region, age group, and even seasonal timing.

Armed with this intelligence, Unilever launched its "Sustainable Living Brands" strategy. Brands that embedded genuine sustainability into their core purpose - not just marketing messaging - grew 69% faster than the rest of their portfolio. The AI hadn't just validated Keith's instinct; it had shown exactly how to execute it profitably across hundreds of markets simultaneously.

This is the power of Assess - the second pillar of DARE. Your Human Intelligence provided the vision. Now AI provides the intelligence to make that vision unstoppably strategic.

From Dream to Data-Driven Strategy

In the previous chapter, you learned to Dream with strategic intent, choosing one of five AI strategies based on real human needs uncovered through your CARE journey. But bold visions without rigorous identification and assessment of use-cases become expensive fantasies.

Your Emotional Intelligence through the CARE journey helps you sense opportunities that others miss, and the DARE journey helps you evaluate which opportunities deserve your limited resources, attention, and political capital.

The most successful leaders don't just dream bigger; they assess smarter where to deploy their efforts.

The 8-Question Filter: Assessing AI Opportunities

As soon as you start listing which AI use-cases to develop within the broad strategy you have identified in the Dream phase, my experience is that you will soon be overwhelmed by the sheer number of ideas that your teams will come up with.

But the truth is, not every use-case is worth investing in. Even for a very large company, at this point in the development of technology, there are only a few, like 10-20, use-cases that make a real difference to the bottom line, achieving a healthy ROI in the 10-20% after 18-36 months of deployment. The rest will either never be scalable enough or will be stuck in negative or marginal ROI-land.

To bring discipline to our dream, we needed a rigorous way to Assess each opportunity. This is why I developed the 8-Question Filter - a super simple, powerful tool to force clarity and make data-driven choices, ensuring our boldest dares were also our smartest bets. It is a tool designed to outsmart the Rationality Mirage, forcing an assessment of value far beyond mere financial ROI. And crucially, this filter is designed to be a bridge for the empathy sceptics. When you ask, 'How does this build our brand?' you can now bring in the data collected in the CARE phase, showing, for example, how human-centric solutions drive customer loyalty. When you ask, 'How does this energise our people?' you can reference, for example, the retention numbers and productivity gains you've already proven are linked to psychological safety.

The 8-Question Filter allows to perform a first ranking of what is worth considering to deploy. The beauty of this tool is its comprehensiveness, coupled with its simplicity, by design. Such that it can be used by any level of seniority, both during, for example, a live session, like a workshop with the Board, or a more in-depth analysis, for example, a report for the executive team. It fosters discussions and participation by everyone, and as such, becomes a great tool of engagement and buy-in.

Before we dive into these questions, it's important to understand *why* such a framework is necessary. Our brains are wired to take mental shortcuts, or 'biases,' that can derail even the most well-intentioned innovation. The pioneering work of Nobel laureate Daniel Kahneman and his partner Amos Tversky identified dozens of these, from **Confirmation Bias** (we seek data that confirms our beliefs) to the **Planning Fallacy** (we consistently underestimate the time and cost of projects). This 8-question framework is not just a checklist; it is a disciplined system for overriding our innate biases and making decisions based on reality, not just intuition.

All you need to do is take the list of use-cases you are considering and score them along these 8 questions. And to make things starkly clear, we force only "Yes" or "No" answers, no wishy-washy "Maybe".

1. Impact (+2 if yes, -2 if no)

Will it grow revenue, cut costs, improve quality, or solve a real daily pain point?

The highest-value AI applications address genuine business bottlenecks, not theoretical improvements. Look for initiatives that remove friction from critical workflows, eliminate constraints that limit growth, or provide pressure relief for overwhelmed roles. To answer this one well, you may want to challenge yourself as to which one of these you can really answer positively:

- Does it amplify our people's best skills? (Y/N)

- Does it eliminate a source of human friction or frustration? (Y/N)

- Does it deepen our understanding of our customers' needs? (Y/N)

- Does it create a new form of value? (Y/N)

- Does it build our brand's reputation for innovation and care? (Y/N)

- Does it energize our people and attract new talent? (Y/N)

Example: Maersk's AI-powered port optimization system reduced container ship waiting times by 30%, directly improving customer satisfaction while cutting operational costs.

2. Complexity (+1 if yes, -2 if no)

Can you buy/subscribe to an AI tool that's >90% trained?

Favor solutions you can implement quickly over custom-built systems that require months of development. The AI landscape now includes sophisticated platforms that handle most use-cases out of the box.

Example: Shopify's Magic AI assistant was deployed across their entire platform using pre-trained language models, requiring minimal custom development.

3. Team (+1 if yes, -2 if no)

Do you have the multi-disciplinary team to develop it, and can they be removed from their current duties?

AI success requires business domain experts, technical implementation specialists, and compliance/legal oversight working together. If these people are already maxed out, your AI initiative will struggle.

Example: ING Bank created dedicated AI development teams pulled from their highest performers, ensuring both technical competence and business understanding.

4. Data (+1 if yes, -6 if no)

Is your data >80% clean and structured, and can it be ring-fenced to avoid risk?

This is often the make-or-break factor. AI is only as good as the data feeding it. Inaccurate, inconsistent, or vulnerable data will doom even the most sophisticated AI system.

Example: JPMorgan Chase spent 18 months cleaning customer data before launching their AI-powered investment advisor, but the preparation enabled rapid scaling across millions of clients.

5. Integration (-4 if complex, +1 if simple)

Does it require deep integration into legacy systems that can't be easily automated?

AI systems that require extensive integration with fragile legacy infrastructure introduce massive risk and delay. Look for AI applications that can operate independently or through simple APIs.

Example: American Express implemented AI fraud detection as an overlay system, requiring minimal changes to existing payment processing infrastructure.

6. Reputation (-5 if high risk, +1 if low risk)

If the AI hallucinates or performs inconsistently, will this cause significant embarrassment?

Customer-facing AI or AI that makes critical decisions carries higher reputation risk. Internal process optimisation typically offers safer starting points.

Example: Deutsche Bank started with AI-powered document processing for internal operations before deploying customer-facing AI advisory services.

7. Explainability (-5 if required, +1 if not required)

Is it necessary to explain every outcome due to regulations or business requirements?

Highly regulated industries or critical decisions may require explainable AI, which is more complex and expensive to implement than pattern-recognition systems.

Example: Ping An Insurance uses explainable AI for underwriting decisions to meet regulatory requirements, while using black-box AI for customer service optimization.

8. Influence (+2 if broad, -2 if narrow)

If successful, will it be relevant for more than 30% of your company?

Prioritize AI initiatives that can scale across departments, geographies, or business units. Narrow applications may deliver local value, but won't transform your organisation.

Scoring Your AI Initiatives

Total Score Interpretation:

- **8+**: Green light - high probability of success with significant impact

- **4-7**: Proceed with caution - good potential but address weak areas first

- **0-3**: Yellow light - requires significant risk mitigation before proceeding

- **Below 0**: Red light - find a different approach or abandon the initiative

Pause and reflect: Try to run a few use-cases you have in mind for your business through this list. What scores are you getting? Are your use-cases likely winners?

Once you have identified your likely winner use-cases, you can start a deeper level of assessment along essentially the same dimensions.

This will allow us to go deeper into the identification of difficulties, solutions, and to develop a blueprint for development. However, here as well, AI can give you an extraordinary helping hand.

The AI-Powered Deep Assessment

Traditional assessment of initiatives relies on historical data, competitor analysis, and expert opinions. These approaches worked when change was gradual and predictable. But in today's world:

- Historical patterns break down when AI transforms entire industries overnight
- Competitor analysis lags reality - by the time you've studied their success, the market has shifted
- Expert opinions reflect personal biases and past experience that may no longer apply
- Focus groups lie not intentionally, but because people can't predict their own future behaviour

AI changes everything. Once you have identified the use-cases you want to focus on using the 8-question framework, you can leverage AI to help you refine your initiative along the same eight dimensions. Depending on the use-case at hand, you can tap into millions of data points - consumer interactions, market signals, operational metrics - simultaneously to help you really validate things.

But here's the crucial insight: AI doesn't replace human judgment - it elevates it. Your intuition guides what questions to ask; AI provides answers at a superhuman scale and speed.

Deep Assessing Along the 8 Dimensions

Here are some of the in-depth assessment you can perform thanks to AI. They are constructed along the exact same dimensions of the quick assessment. Of course, not all will be equally relevant for different use-cases. And as always, judgment should be exercised. If you can keep things simple to back your first answer to the 8-question list presented above, then do keep things simple. However, if the level of resources to be committed warrants a higher, deeper level of scrutiny, then these assessment techniques that leverage AI for speed and insight can be very helpful.

1. Impact Validation at Scale

Use AI to validate whether your use-case truly addresses business bottlenecks:

- **Revenue Impact Modelling**: Predictive analytics platforms (Palantir, DataRobot, H2O.ai) that process millions of market signals to forecast revenue effects
- **Cost Reduction Analysis**: AI-powered process mining tools that identify exactly where costs can be cut
- **Quality Improvement Metrics**: Real-time performance monitoring that shows quality gains
- **Pain Point Mapping**: Consumer sentiment analysis (Brandwatch, Sprout Social) that reads emotional undertones across customer interactions to validate daily frustrations

2. Complexity and Solution Availability Assessment

AI helps you honestly evaluate implementation complexity:

- **Market Solution Analysis**: Automated scanning of AI vendor capabilities using competitive intelligence systems (Crayon, Klue) to identify pre-built solutions
- **Build vs. Buy Optimisation**: Cost-benefit modelling that compares custom development against existing platforms
- **Implementation Timeline Prediction**: Project complexity algorithms that forecast development time with 85%+ accuracy

3. Team Readiness and Capability Mapping

Deploy AI to evaluate your human resources honestly:

- **Skills Gap Analysis**: Platforms like LinkedIn Learning or Coursera that map current capabilities against future needs using AI matching
- **Team Availability Modelling**: Resource optimisation algorithms that show realistic capacity for new initiatives
- **Multi-disciplinary Team Formation**: AI-powered talent matching that identifies optimal team compositions

4. Data Quality and Risk Assessment

This is often the make-or-break factor that AI can evaluate comprehensively:

- **Data Quality Scoring**: Automated data profiling tools that assess cleanliness, consistency, and completeness across systems
- **Data Structure Analysis**: Machine learning algorithms that evaluate how structured your data really is
- **Security and Compliance Modelling**: AI-powered risk assessment that identifies data vulnerabilities and regulatory exposure
- **Data Availability Forecasting**: Predictive models that show what data you'll need and when

5. Integration Complexity Simulation

AI excels at modelling system integration challenges:

- **Legacy System Mapping**: Automated architecture analysis that identifies integration points and dependencies
- **API Compatibility Assessment**: AI-powered system analysis that predicts integration difficulties
- **Change Impact Modelling**: Simulations that show how AI implementation will affect existing workflows

6. Reputation Risk Modelling

Use AI to assess and mitigate reputational exposure:

- **Failure Mode Analysis**: Monte Carlo simulations that model different AI failure scenarios and their business impact
- **Brand Sentiment Monitoring**: Real-time social listening that shows how AI initiatives affect brand perception
- **Crisis Simulation**: Predictive modelling that shows reputation recovery timelines for different failure types
- **Customer Trust Scoring**: Algorithms that predict customer acceptance of AI applications

7. Explainability Requirement Analysis

AI can help determine regulatory and business explainability needs:

- **Regulatory Compliance Mapping**: Legal AI that analyses industry requirements for algorithmic transparency
- **Stakeholder Explainability Needs**: Sentiment analysis of internal stakeholders to understand explanation requirements
- **Explainable AI Solution Assessment**: Evaluation of available interpretability tools and their costs

8. Influence and Scalability Prediction

Model how your AI initiative can scale across the organisation:

- **Cross-Department Applicability Analysis**: Organisational data mining that identifies where use-cases can be replicated
- **Geographic Scalability Modelling**: Cultural and operational analysis that predicts international deployment success
- **Network Effect Simulation**: Algorithms that model how AI benefits compound as adoption spreads
- **Resource Scaling Requirements**: Predictive models that forecast investment needs across different expansion scenarios

The AI Advantage

This AI-amplified assessment process provides something traditional methods cannot: simultaneous evaluation across all eight dimensions with real-time data updates. Instead of sequential analysis that takes months, you get comprehensive insights in weeks.

More importantly, the AI assessment helps you honestly confront the dimensions where you're weakest before you commit resources. If your data quality scores poorly, you know to address that first. If integration complexity is high, you can architect around it from the start.

Your Human Intelligence identifies which use-cases align well with your strategic vision. AI Intelligence shows you exactly how to make those use-cases successful by addressing each critical dimension systematically.

The leaders who shape the future don't wait for certainty. They assess rapidly across all dimensions, act decisively where they're strong, and iterate continuously where they're learning.

Case Study: Netflix's Data-Driven Content Revolution

When Netflix announced they were investing $15 billion annually in original content, traditional Hollywood executives called it reckless. "You can't algorithm your way to great storytelling," they scoffed.

But Netflix's assessment process revealed something profound. Their AI analysed viewing patterns across 200+ million subscribers, identifying micro-genres that traditional studios never recognised: "Critically Acclaimed Emotional Movies with a Strong Female Lead" or "Quirky British Comedies for Late-Night Viewing."

More importantly, their predictive models showed that subscribers who found content matching their specific taste profile were 70% more likely to remain subscribers and 40% more likely to recommend Netflix to friends.

Chief Content Officer Ted Sarandos didn't just trust his creative instincts - he amplified them with AI intelligence. The result? Original series like "Stranger Things," "The Crown," and "Squid Game" weren't accidents. They were strategically designed to match unmet viewer needs that AI had identified.

Netflix's content assessment process now includes:

- Audience demand forecasting for different story concepts

- Cast optimisation modelling based on global appeal data

- Genre performance prediction across different markets

- Cultural relevance scoring for international content

The outcome: Netflix originals now drive 80% of viewing time, compared to 20% when they started creating original content. Their assessment framework turned a $15 billion gamble into the foundation of their global dominance.

Case Study: Starbucks' Operational Intelligence Revolution

Howard Schultz's return as CEO in 2008 faced a crisis: Starbucks had lost its soul, customers were defecting to competitors, and same-store sales were declining for the first time in company history.

But instead of relying on gut instinct alone, Starbucks deployed AI-powered assessment across three dimensions:

- Customer Experience Analysis: Using Deep Brew (their AI platform), Starbucks analysed millions of purchase patterns, app interactions, and customer feedback to understand exactly why people were leaving. The AI revealed that wait times over 4 minutes triggered a 60% probability of customer defection, and personalisation increased purchase frequency by 25%.
- Operational Efficiency Assessment: AI modelling showed that optimising staff scheduling could reduce labour costs by 15% while improving customer satisfaction scores. The system predicted busy periods with 85% accuracy, allowing for proactive staffing adjustments.
- Product Innovation Intelligence: By analysing purchasing combinations and seasonal patterns, AI identified opportunities for new products and personalised recommendations that increased average transaction value by 12%.

The results were staggering. Same-store sales recovered, customer satisfaction scores reached all-time highs, and Starbucks' stock price increased 8,000% during Schultz's tenure.

But here's the key insight: Schultz's emotional intelligence identified the core problem (loss of customer connection), while AI provided the precise roadmap for solution implementation at scale across 32,000 stores globally.

Case Study: Domino's Digital Transformation Assessment

When Patrick Doyle became CEO of Domino's in 2010, the company was a punchline. Their pizza was widely mocked, their stock price had collapsed, and delivery times were unacceptable. But instead of incrementally improving operations, Doyle made a bold assessment-driven bet on AI and digital transformation.

Domino's used predictive analytics to model customer behaviour and discovered something counterintuitive: customers cared more about delivery predictability than absolute speed. This insight redirected their entire AI strategy from "fastest delivery" to "most reliable delivery."

They deployed AI across multiple fronts:

- Order prediction algorithms that pre-staged ingredients during high-demand periods

- Route optimisation AI that reduced delivery times by 25%

- Quality control systems using computer vision to ensure consistent pizza appearance

- Customer sentiment analysis that identified and resolved issues before they escalated

The Results: Domino's stock price increased by over 7,000% during Doyle's tenure, making it one of the best-performing stocks of the decade. More importantly, customer satisfaction scores increased from among the worst in the industry to consistently top-rated.

But here's the assessment insight that made the difference: Doyle's AI strategy focused on solving the daily pain points of both customers and employees rather than pursuing flashy technology for its own sake. Every AI initiative scored high on impact and influence while remaining relatively simple to implement.

Your Assessment Action Plan

Phase 1: Use-Case Identification and Initial Scoring (Week 1)

Generate Your AI Use-Case Portfolio:

- Based on your Dream phase strategy, brainstorm 15-25 potential AI use-cases with your team

- Don't filter yet - capture everything from obvious applications to wild possibilities

- Document each use-case in one sentence that describes the business problem it solves

Apply the 8-Question Framework:

- Score each use-case across all 8 dimensions using the framework

- Be brutally honest - optimistic scoring leads to expensive failures

- Focus on use-cases scoring 4+ for deeper assessment

- Identify your top 5-10 candidates for Phase 2

Quick Reality Check:

- If most use-cases score below 0, revisit your Dream phase strategy - you may need a different approach

- If everything scores 8+, you're probably being too optimistic - challenge your assumptions

Phase 2: AI-Powered Deep Assessment (Weeks 2-5)

For your top-scoring use-cases, deploy AI tools to validate and refine your assessment:

Weeks 2-3: Impact and Market Validation

- Deploy consumer sentiment analysis tools (Brandwatch, Sprout Social) to validate customer pain points

- Use predictive analytics platforms (DataRobot, H2O.ai) to model potential revenue impact

- Implement competitive intelligence monitoring (Crayon, Klue) to understand market dynamics

- Analyse internal data to quantify current costs of the problems you're solving

Weeks 4-5: Implementation Reality Check

- Conduct automated data quality assessment on systems that would feed your AI

- Use skills gap analysis platforms to honestly evaluate team readiness

- Deploy system architecture analysis to understand integration complexity

- Run Monte Carlo simulations to model different failure scenarios and their business impact

Assessment Refinement:

- Re-score your use-cases based on AI-generated insights

- Some "winners" may drop out when reality hits - this saves you from expensive mistakes

- Others may score higher as you discover hidden benefits or simpler implementation paths

Phase 3: Blueprint Development (Week 6-10)

Create Detailed Implementation Roadmaps: For your highest-scoring use-cases (typically 2-4 initiatives):

- Use project management AI tools to optimise implementation timelines

- Deploy resource optimisation modelling to plan team allocation

- Create scenario planning models for different implementation approaches

- Develop success probability analysis for various strategic paths

Risk Mitigation Planning:

- For each weak dimension in your 8-question scoring, create specific mitigation strategies

- If data quality is poor (scored -6), plan a data cleaning initiative first

- If integration is complex (scored -4), architect API-based solutions

- If reputation risk is high (scored -5), start with internal pilots

Resource Allocation Strategy:

- Use AI-powered portfolio optimisation to balance risk and impact across initiatives

- Plan for 70% of resources on your highest-scoring use-cases

- Reserve 30% for learning initiatives that could become tomorrow's winners

Phase 4: Stakeholder Alignment and Launch Preparation (Ongoing)

Executive Buy-In:

- Present your assessment results using the 8-question framework - it's designed for board-level discussions

- Show the AI-generated market intelligence that validates your approach
- Demonstrate how assessment data addresses the specific concerns different stakeholders have

Team Preparation:

- Use the skills gap analysis to plan training programs
- Deploy employee sentiment analysis to gauge readiness for change
- Create cross-functional teams based on AI-powered talent matching insights

Continuous Assessment:

- Set up real-time monitoring of the market signals and competitive moves that could affect your initiatives
- Plan quarterly re-assessment using the same framework to adapt as conditions change
- Build feedback loops that automatically update your scoring based on implementation learnings

The Courage to Act on Data

Remember: Assessment is not a one-time activity - it's an ongoing discipline that separates successful AI leaders from those who chase every shiny new technology.

Assessment without action is analysis paralysis. The goal isn't perfect information and perfect prediction - it's sufficient confidence to act boldly while managing risk intelligently and continuous calibration of where to deploy your limited attention, resources, and political capital for maximum impact.

Your Human Intelligence provides the vision and values that guide what to assess. AI provides the scale and speed to evaluate options that would be impossible through traditional methods. But ultimately, leadership means making decisions with incomplete information and adapting as you learn.

The leaders who shape the future don't wait for certainty. They assess rapidly, act decisively, and iterate continuously.

Your Chapter Challenge: What are the 5-10 likely significant use-cases that fit the strategy you have identified in the Dream phase for your business and that you should consider deploying?

In our next chapter, we'll explore how to Refine your organisation around your assessed vision - transforming individual insights into collective momentum.

The future belongs to leaders who dream boldly and assess wisely. Your AI-amplified intelligence gives you both capabilities.

What will you build with this unfair advantage?

Chapter 7 Takeaways & Reflection

Bold vision requires sharp evaluation. Human insight asks the right questions - AI answers at scale.

◇ **Key Takeaways**

- **Analysing separates fantasy from feasibility**: Great ideas are only as powerful as their fit with the strategic focus you have selected. The 8-Question Filter helps leaders cut through hype and prioritize what truly matters.
- **AI elevates human judgment - not replaces it**: Your intuition spots patterns. AI helps validate, scale, and sharpen them with speed and rigor across all critical dimensions.
- **Not all use-cases are created equal**: Even the most innovative companies succeed by focusing on only a handful of high-impact, high-confidence AI initiatives. Success lies in disciplined selection.
- **Simplicity drives alignment**: The 8-question yes/no format fosters shared understanding across seniority levels, departments, and regions – turning complexity into clarity.
- **Deep Analysis unlocks strategic advantage**: AI-powered tools help assess ROI, risk, scalability, and readiness across functions - giving the confidence to act fast and learn faster.

◇ **Reflection Prompts**

- *Which AI use-cases in your pipeline feel exciting - but haven't yet been rigorously analysed?*
- *What dimensions (data quality, integration risk, explainability, etc.) are you most likely to underestimate - and why?*
- *How often do you pause to ask: "Should we build this?" instead of just "Can we?"*
- *Where could a simple yes/no evaluation bring clarity to a team stuck in endless debate?*
- *What process, platform, or tool could help your organisation shift from intuition-only to insight-backed decisions - without losing its soul?*

Chapter 8: Refine - Iterating With Experience (DARE: R)

Mastery is earned by those who fall often - and rise more times than most even begin.

One of the events that has most shaped me as a leader and crystallized the need to combine Care with Dare and Share, happened to me more than fifteen years ago. It was a moment of profound personal crisis that, in retrospect, became a masterclass in the difference between a transaction and a relationship.

My former husband and I had agreed to buy a house. With very small children, it was a home we were dreaming of, a place to build our future. We had done everything by the book, securing a loan from a major bank. The contracts were signed, the wheels were in motion. But then, just before the mortgage was due to be paid out, the world shuddered. The great financial crisis of 2008 swept across the globe, and in that unprecedented environment of extreme market volatility, the shockwaves hit our lives with brutal force.

The bank retracted the loan. Their reasoning was cold, corporate logic: my husband was an entrepreneur, and I was working in finance in London, therefore most likely to be exposed, in their view, to the Lehman Brothers collapse. On paper, for them, we were simply a risk to be avoided. But in real life, away from credit models, we felt the devastating brunt of this decision: we were a young family on the verge of ruin. We were legally committed to buying the house; backing out meant personal bankruptcy. The strain was immense, further compounded when my husband's own companies were hit by the crisis, and he informed me he could no longer keep up with his half of the purchase.

I was left alone to face the abyss. So, I gathered my payslips, swallowed my pride, and, cap in hand, went to every other relevant bank. One by one, they said no. Finally, one bank agreed to grant me a loan. The price was high, the terms were steep, but in those circumstances, I thought, "beggars can't be choosers."

That bank saved my children and me. To this day, we have happy family moments in the house they enabled us to buy.

But here is the lesson that has stayed with me, the one that informs my work every single day. That bank that did give us the loan never truly understood what they had done. They had saved a young mother and her small kids from what would have been a disaster, earning a loyalty she was desperate to give. As my career progressed and my savings grew, I repaid the mortgage and I remained faithfully their client for years. Yet, throughout that entire time, they treated me politely, professionally, but always as a number.

They had a treasure trove of information about my life, my financial journey, my resilience. But they never used it to connect. They never reciprocated the relationship I was willing to have with them, never offered products or advice that were both financially AND emotionally relevant to the evolutions of my life. When I recently told them I was moving a significant part of my savings to another bank, they were shocked. They offered meetings with their investment specialist and their senior managers. But by then, it was too late. The connection had never been forged.

They had dared to take a risk on me, but they had failed to care about the human story behind the loan. They had shared a service, but never a relationship.

This experience is my constant reminder that even the most functional, life-altering service is incomplete without an emotional connection. And so, whenever I work with a company and we get feedback like the one we recently got, at a consumer lending company I am helping, from a customer named Sarah, who told us,: *"Your bot knows everything about consumer loans, but nothing about my life. I'm a single mother working two jobs. I don't need more options - I need someone who understands that I'm scared of making the wrong choice",* it strikes a deep chord. Sarah had used a consumer lending app that is technically perfect but emotionally hollow.

Her message, like my own history, is the North Star for the most crucial phase of daring: Refinement.

Because bold visions and rigorous assessments get you launched. But Human Intelligence, refined through real-world experience, is what transforms good solutions into truly transformational, inspirational ones.

Sarah put the finger on something no amount of user testing pre-launch could have revealed: as AI-enabled solutions become more sophisticated and capable, emotional context isn't a nice-to-have in AI solutions – it is something customer expect. They can't understand that AI can do so many things, and yet not consider who they are as a human. So being able to factor in the emotional context meaningfully becomes the difference between adoption and abandonment.

From Launch to Legacy: The Art of Intelligent Refinement

Through the Dream and Assess phases, you've built something remarkable. Your AI initiatives are live, delivering measurable value, and generating the success metrics that validate your strategic choices. But if you stop here, you've missed the most powerful opportunity in leadership: turning initial wins into enduring transformation.

The Refine phase is where your Human Intelligence becomes most valuable. While AI excels at processing feedback and identifying patterns, only your lived experience can interpret what those patterns mean for human beings navigating complex, emotional realities of life.

This isn't about fixing bugs or tweaking parameters. It's about evolving your solutions from functionally correct to emotionally resonant, from organisationally accepted to culturally transformative.

This process of transforming a good solution into a great one through real-world experience is the organisational embodiment of what Stanford psychologist Carol Dweck calls a 'Growth Mindset.' An organisation with a 'fixed mindset' would have defended its initial solution, viewing Sarah's feedback as an outlier or a criticism. But an organisation with a growth mindset sees feedback not as a verdict on its past performance, but as invaluable fuel for its future evolution. The Refine phase is where a leader's commitment to a growth mindset becomes a tangible, value-creating process.

The Four Dimensions of Strategic Refinement

Refinement operates across four critical dimensions, each requiring the unique synthesis of AI insights and human wisdom:

1. Emotional Calibration

- **The Challenge:** AI solutions often optimize for efficiency while missing emotional context.
- **The Refinement:** Use real user stories to infuse emotional intelligence into functional systems, to make them evolve to become emotionally more relevant.
- **AI's Role:** Pattern recognition in feedback, sentiment analysis at scale.
- **HI's Role:** Interpreting emotional undertones, understanding unspoken needs.

2. Cultural Integration

- **The Challenge:** Solutions that work technically may clash with organisational culture or social norms.
- **The Refinement:** Adapt AI behaviour to align with human values and cultural expectations.
- **AI's Role:** Analysing adoption patterns, identifying resistance points.
- **HI's Role:** Understanding cultural dynamics, navigating sensitive change management.

3. Scalability Design

- **The Challenge:** Pilot successes often fail when scaled due to hidden complexity and resistance by users.
- **The Refinement:** Build solutions with reuse, documentation, and transfer of ownership in mind.
- **AI's Role:** Modelling scaling scenarios, optimizing resource allocation.
- **HI's Role:** Anticipating organisational dynamics, designing for sustainable adoption.

4. Impact Amplification

- **The Challenge:** Good solutions remain isolated instead of becoming catalysts for broader transformation.
- **The Refinement:** Connect AI initiatives to create network effects and compound value.
- **AI's Role:** Identifying connection opportunities, measuring systemic impact.
- **HI's Role:** Orchestrating organisational alignment, building a coalition for change.

The magic happens when these dimensions work together. My own personal story and Sarah's feedback spurred us to start developing empathy-based engagement. It made us realize that every AI touchpoint needed emotional context awareness, e.g. cultural sensitivity to financial anxiety, scalable empathy training, and connection to our broader customer relationship strategy.

Case Study: Spotify's Human-AI Harmony Revolution

When Daniel Ek founded Spotify, the music industry was imploding. Piracy was rampant, CD sales were collapsing, and artists were struggling to reach audiences. But Spotify's initial solution - unlimited music streaming for a monthly fee - was just the beginning of their transformation story.

The real revolution came through relentless refinement driven by a simple Human Intelligence insight: People don't just want access to music; they want music that understands their emotional journey.

The Initial Success: Spotify's recommendation algorithm was technically impressive, using collaborative filtering to suggest music based on similar users' preferences. Early users loved the vast catalogue and fair pricing.

The Refinement Challenge: But Daniel Ek noticed something in user data that algorithms couldn't explain: engagement would spike and then plateau. People would discover great new music, but their listening patterns suggested they were still searching for something more personal.

The HI Insight: Through customer interviews and his own experience as a music lover, Ek realized that mood and context mattered more than genre preferences. People didn't want "music you might like" - they wanted "music that fits how you feel right now."

The AI-HI Solution: Spotify refined its approach by combining AI pattern recognition with human curation:

- Emotional Calibration: They created mood-based playlists (Focus, Chill, Energy) that adapted to time of day, weather, and user behaviour patterns

- Cultural Integration: Local human curators worked with AI to ensure playlists resonated with regional cultural contexts

- Scalability Design: They built a system where successful playlist strategies could be replicated across markets while maintaining local relevance

- Impact Amplification: They connected music discovery to social sharing, creating viral loops that amplified both user engagement and artist exposure

The Results: Spotify didn't just survive the music industry collapse - they transformed it. Today, they have over 500 million users, and their

Discover Weekly feature alone generates 40 million personalized playlists every week. More importantly, they've become the primary discovery engine for new artists, fundamentally changing how music culture evolves.

The Refinement Lesson: The initial AI was functionally correct, but human insight revealed that emotional resonance was the missing ingredient for transformational impact. The refined solution combined the scale of AI with the intuition of human curators to create something neither could achieve alone.

Case Study: Starbucks' Third Place Evolution

Howard Schultz's vision of Starbucks as the "third place" between home and work was emotionally compelling but operationally challenging. How do you create intimate community feelings in thousands of locations while maintaining consistency and efficiency?

The Initial Success: Starbucks grew rapidly by standardizing the coffee shop experience - consistent products, predictable service, recognizable atmosphere. Their early success was built on reliability.

The Refinement Challenge: By 2008, the soul of Starbucks was fading. Efficiency had replaced connection; the aroma of burnt cheese from breakfast sandwiches overpowered the smell of fresh coffee. When Howard Schultz returned as CEO, he didn't start in the boardroom; he started on the front lines.

For weeks, he worked in stores, talking to baristas and listening to customers. He heard their stories - the frustration with long lines, the feeling that Starbucks had become another faceless corporation. One barista told him, "We're not making coffee anymore; we're just processing orders." That single human insight was more powerful than any sales report.

Back in a tense meeting with executives, Schultz didn't present a chart. He shared what he heard. "We've lost our way," he declared, his voice filled with the emotion of what he'd witnessed. "We're not in the coffee business, serving people; we're in the people business, serving coffee. And we've forgotten that." This was the CARE phase in its purest form: his Human Intelligence revealed that the core problem wasn't operational, but emotional. People came to Starbucks not just for coffee, but for moments of human connection in their increasingly digital lives. The path back to success wasn't just about efficiency; it was about restoring moments of human connection.

The AI-HI Solution: Starbucks refined its approach by using AI to enable, rather than replace, human connection:

- Emotional Calibration: Their Deep Brew AI system learned individual customer preferences not just for drinks, but for interaction style - some customers wanted quick efficiency, others craved personal conversation

- Cultural Integration: AI helped optimize store layouts and staffing to create more opportunities for meaningful barista-customer interactions while reducing wait times

- Scalability Design: They created training programs that could teach emotional intelligence skills to baristas across thousands of locations, using AI to personalize coaching for individual employees

- Impact Amplification: The mobile app became a tool for deepening relationships rather than avoiding them, allowing baristas to prepare personalized greetings along with personalized drinks

The Results: Same-store sales recovered and reached record highs. Customer satisfaction scores improved dramatically. More importantly, Starbucks redefined what a technology-enabled service experience could feel like - efficient and personal, scaled and intimate.

The Refinement Lesson: The initial focus on operational efficiency was necessary but insufficient. Human insight revealed that emotional connection was the core value proposition, and AI became most powerful when it enabled human moments rather than replacing them.

Case Study: Microsoft's Cultural Renaissance

When Satya Nadella became CEO of Microsoft in 2014, the company was technically proficient but culturally stuck. Their products worked well, but the internal culture of competitiveness and know-it-all attitudes was alienating customers and limiting innovation.

The Initial Success: Microsoft had dominant market positions in operating systems, office productivity, and enterprise software. Their technical capabilities were world-class.

The Refinement Challenge: But Nadella sensed something deeper through his experience leading diverse teams: Microsoft's culture was becoming a competitive disadvantage. Employees were afraid to take risks, collaboration was limited, and customer feedback often felt dismissive rather than curious.

The HI Insight: Through employee listening sessions and his own leadership journey, Nadella realized that Microsoft needed to evolve from a "know-it-all" culture to a "learn-it-all" culture. This wasn't just about being nicer - it was about unleashing innovation by changing how people thought about failure and learning.

The AI-HI Solution: Microsoft refined its approach by using AI to support cultural transformation:

- Emotional Calibration: They deployed sentiment analysis tools to measure cultural change in real-time, but used human insights to interpret what the data meant and how to respond

- Cultural Integration: AI-powered coaching systems helped managers have more effective one-on-one conversations, but the content was designed around human psychology and growth mindset principles

- Scalability Design: They created culture change playbooks that could be adapted across different business units while maintaining core principles of empathy and growth

- Impact Amplification: The cultural transformation became a competitive advantage in recruiting, customer relationships, and partnerships - creating virtuous cycles that reinforced the changes

The Results: Microsoft's stock price increased by about 1000% during Nadella's tenure. Employee satisfaction scores reached all-time highs. More importantly, they became a company that others wanted to partner with, transforming their ecosystem relationships.

The Refinement Lesson: Technical excellence without cultural resonance creates fragile success. Human intelligence identified that culture was the constraint limiting everything else, and AI became most valuable when it supported human transformation rather than replacing human judgment.

Your Refinement Action Plan: The SCALE Approach

Based on patterns from successful refinements across industries, I've developed the SCALE approach for systematically improving AI initiatives through Human Intelligence-guided iteration. The name is not random. This is an essential step to prepare for the future scaling up of your successful initiatives:

S - Signals: Listen for What Data Can't Capture

- **Deploy Real-Time Feedback Loops:** Use AI to capture quantitative patterns, but design qualitative feedback mechanisms that reveal emotional context

- **Customer Journey Archaeology:** Map the complete emotional experience, not just the functional touchpoints

- **Employee Sentiment Intelligence:** Understand how AI changes daily life for humans, be they clients, employees, or other stakeholders, not just productivity metrics

- **Cultural Pattern Recognition:** Identify where AI solutions clash with organisational or social values

C - Context: Interpret Signals Through Human Wisdom

- **Story Behind the Numbers:** Use your leadership experience to understand why patterns emerge, not just what they are

- **Emotional Needs Translation:** Convert customer, employee, or other stakeholders' frustrations into design requirements that AI can address

- **Organisational Dynamic Mapping:** Anticipate how changes will ripple through different teams and stakeholders

- **Cultural Lens Adjustment:** Adapt AI behaviour to align with human values and social expectations

A - Adaptation: Design Changes That Honor Both Efficiency and Humanity

- **Emotional Intelligence Integration:** Build empathy and context awareness into AI responses

- **Human-AI Handoff Optimization:** Create seamless transitions between automated and personal interactions

- **Cultural Sensitivity Programming:** Ensure AI behaviour aligns with cultural norms and individual preferences

- **Values-Based Decision Logic:** Program AI to make choices consistent with organisational values, not just optimal outcomes

L - Learning: Codify Insights for Systematic Improvement

- **Experience Documentation:** Create detailed case studies that capture both what worked and why it worked

- **Pattern Playbooks:** Develop reusable frameworks that can be applied to new AI initiatives

- **Failure Analysis Reports:** Document what went wrong and the human insights that led to solutions

- **Best Practice Libraries:** Build searchable knowledge bases that help teams avoid reinventing solutions

E - Evolution: Scale Refined Solutions Across the Organisation

- **Pilot-to-Production Pathways:** Design scalable processes for taking refined solutions organisation-wide

- **Cross-Functional Integration:** Connect AI improvements to broader business transformation initiatives

- **Change Management Orchestration:** Use refined solutions as catalysts for larger cultural shifts

- **Success Metric Evolution:** Expand measurement systems to capture both functional and emotional impact

Designing for Scalability, Not Just Delivery

Before we scale, we must refine. But how do you know what's truly ready? That's where the Scalability Assessment comes in. One of the most common refinement failures happens when successful AI pilots can't scale beyond their original context. Your Human Intelligence becomes crucial in designing solutions that can replicate success across different teams, geographies, and use-cases.

To help you foster scalability, we have developed **The Scalability Assessment Questions:**

Reusability Design (Score 1-5 per question):

- Are AI solutions built with templates and documentation that other teams can adapt?

- Can non-technical business users understand and modify AI behaviour for their context?

- Are successful approaches documented with enough detail that others can replicate them?

- Do AI systems include configuration options that allow customization without re-development?

Learning Codification (Score 1-5 per question):

- Is learning from each initiative systematically captured and shared across the organisation?

- Are failure patterns documented so other teams can avoid similar mistakes?

- Do success stories include the human insights that made the difference, not just technical details?

- Are there regular forums for sharing AI refinement learnings across business units?

Business Ownership (Score 1-5 per question):

- Do business units, not IT teams, take primary ownership of AI adoption and refinement?

- Are business leaders equipped to make decisions about AI modifications without technical gatekeeping?

- Do teams have access to AI modification tools that don't require programming skills?

- Are AI success metrics owned and tracked by business stakeholders rather than technical teams?

Success Playbooks (Score 1-5 per question):

- Are there clear, step-by-step guides for replicating successful AI implementations elsewhere?

- Do playbooks include both technical setup and change management approaches?

- Are successful use cases documented with enough contextual detail that others can adapt them?

- Do teams have access to expert consultation when adapting playbooks to new contexts?

Scoring Your Scalability:

- **16-20:** Your refined solutions are designed for organisational transformation

- **12-15:** Good foundation, but some scalability gaps need attention

- **8-11:** Successful pilots may struggle to scale without additional design work

- **Below 8:** Focus on scalability design before investing in new AI initiatives

The most successful leaders don't just refine individual AI solutions - they use refinement learnings to build organisational capabilities that compound over time.

Your Turn: Choose one AI initiative currently running in your organisation and apply the SCALE framework:

1. *Signals: What quantitative metrics show success, but what qualitative feedback suggests missing emotional or cultural elements?*

2. *Context: Based on your leadership experience, what human truths might explain the gap between functional performance and user satisfaction?*

3. *Adaptation: How could you modify the AI to address both efficiency and emotional resonance?*

4. *Learning: What insights from this refinement could be applied to other AI initiatives?*

5. *Evolution: How could this refined solution become a catalyst for broader organisational transformation?*

Case Study: The Sarah Refinement – A Deeper Connection

As a direct result of the retracted mortgage experience I just shared at the beginning of this chapter, I have made a specific form of refinement a non-negotiable part of every transformation I advise on. It's a process I call the "Sarah Refinement," named after the customer whose feedback so perfectly mirrored my own life lesson. It ensures that we never forget the human context behind the data.

The Sarah Refinement takes the principles we've discussed and broadens them, insisting on a deliberate and continuous effort to refine the link between an offering and the emotional reality of the customer (even, when it is a corporate customer, because even at corporate customers the decision-makers are human, and as we saw in Chapter 2 emotional biases always play a role – pure rationality is a mirage).

Let's look at how this played out at the consumer lending company I was helping. We had launched a new, AI-powered consumer credit app which could pre-screen eligible customers and grant a consumer loan in one click. The initial quantitative data showed it was performing well, with very accurate risk predictions and great customer satisfaction scores. But Sarah's feedback revealed something the metrics missed: emotional context was the difference between a customer that would take a loan (and hopefully pay it over time) but who would over-time regret having taken it, versus someone for whom the loan really fitted all their circumstances and would come back for further loans in their life.

This led us to deploy deeper listening mechanisms, which we called Empathy-Based Engagement, partly inspired from the "emotional engagement scoring" developed by Netflix and outline in Chapter 3:

- **Emotional Journey Mapping:** We moved beyond tracking what customers accomplished to mapping how they *felt* during and after interactions.

- **Stress Signal Detection:** We used tools like voice analysis and conversation flow patterns to identify when customers were feeling overwhelmed or anxious.

- **Context Awareness:** We began capturing environmental clues, time of day, urgency indicators, previous interaction history, that revealed a customer's likely emotional state.

My own experience as a single mother who had faced financial stress helped me and the team interpret Sarah's feedback. She wasn't criticizing our technical capabilities; she was telling us that financial decisions feel scary when you're responsible for others. The Human Intelligence insight was clear: for many customers, efficiency without empathy feels cold when the stakes are high.

Once we had analysed this in depth, we began to adapt. We changed the customer journeys within the app to make them dynamically responsive to the emotions displayed by the customer, all while fulfilling the necessary compliance and consumer duty obligations.

Our enhanced customer journeys would now not only provide correct and appropriate information but would also recognize and respond to emotional context:

- **Emotional Calibration:** The AI learned to detect stress signals and adjust its communication style, providing reassurance and simplification when customers seemed overwhelmed or even proposing a period of reflection for a few days.

- **Cultural Integration:** We trained the AI to understand that different customers need different types of emotional support alongside technical information.

- **Values Alignment:** Every interaction was redesigned to reinforce the consumer lender's tone of voice and brand values of transparency, fairness, and putting customers first.

The Sarah insight didn't just improve one app - it became a template for all customer-facing AI across the other business lines of the group. We documented these new approaches, creating Empathy Design Patterns and Context Awareness Protocols that could be scaled. The refined consumer lending platform became the foundation for the group's broader AI strategy, leading to a new core marketing theme around the idea: "We understand your life."

The results were profound. Customer satisfaction and retention improved, and cross-selling increased significantly in a short amount of time. Technical correctness is table stakes. The Sarah Refinement proves that emotional resonance is what creates loyalty, advocacy, and sustainable competitive advantage.

Your Personal Refinement Practice

Refinement is ultimately a discipline led from the top - a systematic approach to evolving good solutions into great ones through the strategic application of your accumulated wisdom. Here's how to develop this capability:

Weekly Refinement Reviews

Every Friday, spend 30-60 minutes reviewing AI initiative performance through two lenses:

- **Quantitative Performance:** What do the metrics tell you about functional success?

- **Qualitative Insights:** What are people saying about the experience, both customers and employees?

Look for the gaps between quantitative success and qualitative satisfaction - these gaps are where your Human Intelligence creates the most value.

Monthly Human Intelligence Sessions

Once a month, gather the people closest to your AI solutions - customer service representatives, sales teams, implementation specialists - and ask them, as relevant:

- What are customers really struggling with that the AI isn't addressing?

- Where do you see opportunities to make the AI more helpful or intuitive?

- What would happen if we designed this solution for emotional impact, not just functional efficiency?

Quarterly Refinement Sprints

Every quarter, choose one AI initiative for intensive refinement using the SCALE framework:

- Week one - gather signals that reveal the human story behind the data

- Week two - use your leadership experience to interpret what those signals mean

- Week three - design adaptations that honour both efficiency and humanity

- Week four - codify learnings and plan broader evolution

Annual Strategic Refinement Review

Once a year, assess your entire AI portfolio through the scalability lens:

- Which refined solutions are ready to scale across the organisation?

- What patterns in successful refinements should become standard practices?

- Where are the biggest opportunities to connect AI initiatives for compound impact?

- How has your Human Intelligence evolved, and what new refinement capabilities do you want to develop?

The Compounding Power of Intelligent Refinement

The leaders who create lasting transformation don't just implement AI solutions - they evolve those solutions through systematic application of hard-earned wisdom.

They BUILD, SUCCEED, SHOWCASE, REPEAT. And in so doing, they apply SCALE repeatedly until their AI-use-cases become organisation-wide examples of transformation in action.

They understand that the first version is never the final version, and that the difference between good and transformational lies in the quality of refinement, progressive, repeated, and iterative.

Your Human Intelligence provides something AI cannot: the ability to sense what success should feel like, not just what it should measure like. When you combine this intuitive wisdom with AI's analytical power, you create solutions that don't just work - they inspire.

Sarah's message taught us that customers don't want perfect technology - they want technology that perfectly understands their human experience and that is relevant to their own existence, not the generic life of a generic person.

That insight didn't come from data analysis or user testing. It came from the accumulated wisdom of leadership experience applied to the specific challenge of creating a relevant and engaging customer experience at scale.

This is the power of Refine - elevating functional success into human transformation through the strategic application of your accumulated wisdom.

That one message from a mother trying to make the right financial choice, which resonated with my own painful experience is not just important to improve the CARE, DARE, SHARE underpinning methodologies. For me, it acts as a daily reminder for how I need to exercise my leadership, keeping always in mind that if you solve a real problem for a real person, you become unstoppable.

Your Chapter Challenge: Assess your current AI portfolio using the Scalability Design questions. Are you building solutions that can compound impact across your organisation, or isolated successes that will require individual reinvention?

In our next chapter, we'll explore how to Share these refined insights - transforming individual AI success into organisational intelligence that elevates everyone's capability.

The future belongs to leaders who don't just deploy AI, but who continuously evolve AI through the lens of human wisdom. This refinement is the practical work of defeating the Rationality Mirage, turning a potentially cold algorithm into a tool of genuine connection and service. Your refined solutions become the foundation for transformation that endures.

What human insight will guide your next refinement?

Chapter 8 Takeaways & Reflection

Refinement turns good into great and prepares for successful scaling. When data meets lived wisdom, AI becomes human-centric.

◇ **Key Takeaways**

- **Refinement is leadership in action**: The boldest visions only become reality when leaders remain present, humble, and responsive to real-world experience.
- **Feedback is a goldmine - when emotionally decoded**: What customers *feel* often matters more than what they say. Emotional calibration transforms usability into loyalty.
- **Scaling without refining creates shallow wins**: Functionally sound pilots can crumble at scale without cultural alignment, user trust, and emotional intelligence baked in.
- **Human intelligence interprets what AI observes**: AI detects patterns, but only your experience can translate signals into meaningful, actionable adjustments.
- **The SCALE framework builds sustainable transformation**: Signals, Context, Adaptation, Learning, and Evolution ensure that what you refine today becomes tomorrow's advantage.

◇ **Reflection Prompts**

- *What "Sarah moments" have surfaced recently in your projects - and have you truly listened?*
- *Where are you scaling solutions that haven't been emotionally or culturally refined?*
- *How do you make space - personally and organisationally - for reflection and iteration?*
- *Are you codifying what works (and why), or reinventing from scratch every time?*
- *What emotional blind spots might your AI initiatives be missing - and how can your leadership surface them?*

Chapter 9: Execute - Driving Impact With Confidence (DARE: E)

Even the sharpest plan can collapse when we forget that execution succeeds not through perfection, but through people.

At the logistics company I have been helping, one morning, Anne stared at the whiteboard covered in metrics, timelines, and stakeholder maps. Six months after her AI initiative had been approved, the pilot program was finally ready to launch. But as she looked at the complex deployment plan, a familiar anxiety crept in. She had dreamed boldly, assessed thoroughly, and aligned her stakeholders - but now came the moment of truth. Would her vision translate into real impact for real people?

Her phone buzzed with a message from Marcus, her head of operations: "Anne, we had a meeting this morning with the team heads, and their big question was whether this AI thing is going to make their jobs harder or easier. What should we tell them?"

Anne realized that all her strategic frameworks meant nothing if she couldn't answer that simple, human question with confidence and truth.

The Execution Gap: Where Vision Meets Reality

The transition from strategic alignment to tactical execution is where most AI initiatives stumble. Not because of technical limitations, but because leaders forget that execution is fundamentally about people navigating and accepting change together.

The most sophisticated deployment plan, AI and non-AI, in the world fails if the humans implementing it don't understand why they should care, how they fit in, or what success looks like for them personally.

This is where the final pillar of DARE - Execute - transforms strategic potential into measurable impact. But execution in the AI age requires a new kind of leadership discipline: one that balances the precision of data-driven monitoring with the nuance of human-centred adaptation.

The IMPACT Framework: Execution with Intelligence

Through my experience of implementing AI solutions across industries, I've observed that successful execution follows a predictable pattern. The most effective leaders use what I call the IMPACT framework - a systematic approach that keeps human intelligence at the centre while leveraging AI for real-time optimization:

I - Intentional Communication

M - Measured Implementation

P- People-First Adaptation

A - Agile Monitoring

C- Continuous Calibration

T- Transparent Results

In your organisation, some people will be believers (i.e. positively inclined towards the adoption of AI and naturally seeing it as an opportunity), some people will be at the opposite end of the spectrum, i.e. sceptics, and they will be difficult to sway, and then a vast majority will be undecided. Progressively turning some of the undecided into believers will be the key to adoption and success. According to psychology practice, the critical threshold for adoption of an idea is 30%, i.e. you need to target the believers to account for 30% or more of your population in order to sway enough undecided.

This is where this framework is particularly important. According to a recent study by IBM, 70-80% of AI adoptions fail precisely because they do not sufficiently take the human dimension on board, and therefore end up being the shiny new toy abandoned on the shelf.

Your turn: During your recent AI implementations, can you tell who was a believer, who was a sceptic, and who was undecided? Any sense of which proportion of your audience they represented?

Let's explore how each element transforms good intentions into great outcomes that bring the people from undecided to believers.

Intentional Communication: Starting with People, Not Projects

The first rule of AI execution is deceptively simple: start every conversation with an impact on people, not the capability of technology.

When Anne finally responded to Marcus about the warehouse team, she didn't begin with algorithm specifications or efficiency metrics. She started with this: "They'll spend less time on repetitive data entry and more time solving problems that actually matter to customers."

This also means that the AI project, particularly for the first ones, must be seen as CEO or Business Leader-led. One of the biggest mistakes organisations make is to entrust it to the Chief Technology Officer and to see it as a technological deployment.

Yes, there is some technological component in it, of course, but in the same way that you would not have the tech team champion the launch of a new service or product to your customers just because it uses a computer to deliver it, you should not see AI as purely a technological deployment.

You need to see it as a catalyst for business redesign, and therefore, it must be seen and perceived as led by the CEO or a senior business leader.

This shift from "project-speak" to "CEO-led people-speak" isn't just good change management - it's strategic communication that builds the emotional foundation for success at scale.

Part of the success of Zaya is that the team consistently positioned it as a member of the team, i.e. a help and support to the colleagues in the support team, not a replacement. So Zaya was helpful to both customers and internal teams, which enabled its very quick acceptance.

Case Study: Target's AI-Powered Supply Chain Transformation

When Target embarked on its AI-driven supply chain overhaul in 2019, it faced a challenge familiar to any leader implementing large-scale AI: how do you get thousands of distribution centre workers to embrace technology that fundamentally changes their daily work?

Target's approach began with something radical: they didn't start with the technology. They started with listening tours.

Supply chain VP Sarah Gallagher spent three months visiting distribution centres, not to explain the coming AI systems, but to understand the daily frustrations of workers. What she discovered changed their entire implementation strategy. Workers weren't afraid of AI taking their jobs - they were frustrated by inefficient processes that made their jobs harder than necessary.

The insight led to a reimagined communication strategy. Instead of announcing "AI implementation," they framed it as "solving the problems you've been telling us about." The AI system that optimized inventory placement wasn't presented as algorithmic efficiency - it was positioned as the tool "helping you find products faster so you can focus on quality checking."

This human-centred approach led to a very high employee approval rating for the new AI systems and, most importantly, voluntary uptake of additional AI tools by workers who initially showed the most resistance. The company also saw a double-digit improvement in processing speed and a 15% reduction in carrying costs, and achieved a 98% in-stock rate through its AI-driven inventory management.

Target's key lesson: "We learned that people don't resist AI - they resist being treated like they're irrelevant to AI's success."

Measured Implementation: The Power of Intelligent Pilots

The most successful AI executions begin with intelligent pilots that serve as both proof of concept and learning laboratory, not grand rollouts. But here's what separates effective pilots from expensive experiments: they're designed from the start to generate insights for scaling, not just validate initial assumptions. Build, Succeed, Showcase, Repeat is the mantra to pursue in deploying these pilots and progressively scaling them up.

Case Study: Starbucks' Deep Brew Rollout Strategy

When Starbucks decided to implement its Deep Brew AI platform across 30,000+ locations, it faced a complexity that would overwhelm most organisations. How do you deploy personalized customer experience AI across diverse markets, cultures, and operational contexts?

Their answer was what CEO Kevin Johnson called "measured deployment with intelligent feedback loops."

Phase 1 started with just 100 stores, but these weren't randomly selected. Starbucks chose locations that represented their full spectrum of challenges: urban and suburban, high-volume and intimate, tech-savvy markets and traditional communities. Each pilot location was equipped with both AI monitoring systems and human intelligence gathering protocols.

The AI tracked traditional metrics: order accuracy, wait times, and sales conversion. But human district managers were trained to capture what AI couldn't see: customer emotional responses, barista confidence levels, and cultural adaptation needs.

Three months into the pilot, the data revealed something unexpected. The AI was performing beautifully in high-volume urban stores but creating friction in smaller community locations where customers valued personal recognition over algorithmic efficiency.

This insight led to a crucial execution pivot: instead of one uniform AI deployment, Starbucks developed three different implementation models, each calibrated for different store personalities and customer expectations.

The measured approach paid off. By the time Deep Brew reached full deployment, all metrics had significantly improved: customer engagement grew by 15%, barista job satisfaction grew by double digits, and same-store sales by single digits (a feat in retail!), and ROI reached 30%. But perhaps most importantly, voluntary adoption of additional AI features by baristas was almost unanimous - a clear signal that the technology was enhancing rather than replacing human connection.

People-First Adaptation: When Humans Override Algorithms

The most sophisticated AI execution plans must remain humble in the face of human wisdom. The leaders who achieve lasting impact understand that their role isn't to ensure perfect adherence to the original plan, but rather to recognize when human intelligence reveals opportunities for better outcomes.

Your Turn: What human wisdom has emerged during your recent project implementations that your monitoring systems might have missed?

Case Study: Domino's AI-Driven Quality Revolution

Domino's Pizza faced a brutal reality in 2019: despite massive investments in delivery technology, customer satisfaction scores were plateauing. Their AI systems could optimize routes and predict demand, but something was missing from the execution equation.

The breakthrough came from an unexpected source: a store manager in Phoenix named Maria Santos, who noticed that their AI was optimizing for speed but ignoring quality signals that human workers intuitively recognized.

"The AI would push us to get pizzas out fast during rush times," Maria explained, "but experienced pizza makers could feel when the oven temperature was slightly off or when dough consistency wasn't quite right. The AI couldn't sense these things, but they made the difference between a good pizza and a great one."

Rather than dismissing this feedback as resistance to change, Domino's operations team saw it as crucial execution intelligence. They adapted their AI implementation to include what they called "craftsperson override protocols" - systematized ways for experienced workers to input quality signals that AI could learn from.

The adaptation process was as much cultural as it was technical. Domino's positioned experienced pizza makers as "AI trainers," elevating their status while expanding the system's capabilities. Workers who had been nervous about AI displacement became excited about AI collaboration.

Results validated the people-first adaptation approach: quality scores improved 14-15%, while speed metrics continued climbing. But the real victory was cultural - employee engagement scores hit all-time highs as workers felt valued as partners in technological advancement rather than obstacles to efficiency.

Agile Monitoring: Real-Time Intelligence for Dynamic Execution

Traditional project monitoring tracks whether you're executing the plan. Intelligent AI monitoring tracks whether the plan is still worth executing. This distinction separates leaders who deliver projects from those who drive lasting impact.

The most effective AI execution monitoring combines three intelligence streams:

Performance Intelligence: Traditional metrics enhanced by AI pattern recognition

Human Intelligence: Emotional signals and cultural adaptation indicators

Strategic Intelligence: Early indicators of market shifts or competitive responses

Case Study: Unilever's AI-Powered Sustainability Execution

When Unilever committed to making all its brands sustainable by 2030, it needed execution monitoring sophisticated enough to track progress across 190 countries, 400 brands, and thousands of suppliers. Traditional quarterly reviews weren't adequate for the complexity and urgency of their commitment.

Their solution combined AI monitoring with human intelligence gathering in what Chief Sustainability Officer Hanneke Faber called "intelligent accountability systems."

AI dashboards tracked quantitative sustainability metrics in real-time: carbon emissions, water usage, waste reduction, and supply chain compliance. But human intelligence networks gathered qualitative signals: supplier relationship health, consumer response to sustainability messaging, and employee engagement with green initiatives.

The integration of both intelligence streams proved crucial during the pandemic. While AI detected supply chain disruptions and shifting consumer priorities, human intelligence revealed emotional context:

consumers weren't just changing what they bought, they were changing why they bought it.

This insight led to a mid-execution pivot that traditional monitoring would have missed. Instead of pausing sustainability investments during economic uncertainty, Unilever doubled down - reframing sustainability from environmental responsibility to economic resilience.

The agile monitoring approach delivered results that exceeded original projections: 75% of their brands achieved sustainable sourcing ahead of schedule, customer loyalty to sustainable brands increased 28%, and employee engagement with sustainability initiatives reached 94%.

Continuous Calibration: Learning While Doing

The most successful AI executions evolve capabilities instead of just implementing plans. Leaders who achieve lasting impact understand that each execution cycle should leave their organisation more intelligent than when it started.

This requires what I call "execution with learning intent" - systematically capturing what worked, why it worked, such that insights can be applied to future challenges.

Anne had experienced this firsthand during her warehouse AI implementation. Three months into execution, her team discovered that the AI was correctly predicting demand patterns but missing cultural nuances that affected local customer behaviour.

Instead of viewing this as a failure, Anne's team treated it as intelligence. They established "cultural calibration sessions" where local team members could input context that refined the AI's predictions. Within six weeks, prediction accuracy improved 34%, but more importantly, the team had developed a replicable process for cultural adaptation that would benefit future AI implementations.

Transparent Results: Building Trust Through Truth

The final element of intelligent execution is transparent communication about results - both successes and setbacks. Leaders who achieve lasting AI impact understand that transparency is much more than ethical communication - it's strategic trust-building that enables future innovation.

The final element of intelligent execution is transparent communication about results - both successes and setbacks. Leaders who achieve lasting AI impact understand that transparency is much more than ethical communication - it's deep trust-building that enables future innovation. But transparency without intelligent measurement is merely storytelling. True AI leadership requires a sophisticated approach to measuring and sharing results that captures the full spectrum of value creation.

Traditional project measurement focuses on single-dimension success: did we achieve the intended outcome on time and within budget? AI execution requires what I call "three-dimensional measurement" - tracking indicators across performance, learning, and strategic impact simultaneously. This is how I advise you to construct your performance indicators (of course, choose the indicators that are relevant for your type of AI project, e.g. revenue-focused versus cost-focused versus....):

1. **The Foundation Layer**

These are the metrics that justify initial investment and demonstrate immediate value:

- **Financial Returns:**

  o Traditional ROI calculations (cost savings ÷ implementation investment)

  o Time-to-value metrics (weeks from deployment to measurable impact)

  o Productivity gains (output per hour, error reduction rates)

- o Revenue enhancement (new opportunities enabled by AI capabilities)

- **Operational Excellence:**

  - o Quality improvements (defect reduction, accuracy gains)

  - o Process efficiency (cycle time reduction, resource optimization)

  - o Customer satisfaction (service quality, response times)

  - o Risk mitigation (compliance improvement, error prevention)

2. **The Growth Layer (Learning Indicators)**

These metrics capture how AI implementation builds organisational capability:

- **Capability Development**

  - o Skill acquisition rates (employees gaining AI-adjacent competencies)

  - o Cross-functional collaboration improvements

  - o Problem-solving sophistication (complexity of challenges teams can tackle)

  - o Innovation velocity (ideas generated and tested per quarter)

- **Adaptation Intelligence**

  - o Speed of response to changing conditions

  - o Cultural shift indicators (attitudes toward experimentation, technology adoption)

  - o Knowledge retention rates (lessons learned and successfully applied)

- o Change resilience (organisation's capacity to absorb future AI implementations)

3. **The Future Layer: Strategic Indicators**

These forward-looking metrics reveal whether AI investments are building sustainable competitive advantage:

- **Market Position**
  - o Competitive differentiation strength
  - o Innovation pipeline robustness
  - o Customer loyalty and retention improvements
  - o Market share growth in AI-enhanced service areas

- **Future Readiness**
  - o Organisational learning velocity
  - o Technology absorption capacity
  - o Strategic option value (new possibilities created by current AI capabilities)
  - o Ecosystem resilience (ability to adapt to market disruptions)

- **Intelligent ROI:** To win over a culture trapped in the Rationality Mirage, we need to expand our definition of value. I developed the 'Intelligent ROI' formula to do just that. It's a way to make a quantitative case for the qualitative, human elements we've discussed. It respects the need for data but insists on a more complete, more intelligent set of inputs. This formula allows you to present a business case that a purely 'rational' leader can understand, proving that the 'soft' stuff is often where the real value lies.
  It's calculated as:

Intelligent ROI = (Performance Value + Learning Value + Strategic Option Value) / (Implementation Investment + Ongoing Learning Investment)

Where:

- **Performance Value** = immediate cost savings + revenue enhancement + efficiency gains. This is what you find in a classical ROI in the nominator.

- **Learning Value** = capability development + cultural capital + knowledge assets created. This value can be estimated using methods like human capital appreciation, training cost avoidance, or by measuring the increase in innovation velocity (increase in the number of new ideas).

- **Strategic Option Value** = future opportunities enabled + competitive positioning + innovation potential. This can be quantified by analysing potential market expansion or the value of the innovation pipeline created.

- **Implementation Investment** = technology costs + training + change management. This represents the initial, upfront costs required to launch the initiative.

- **Ongoing Learning Investment** = continuous improvement + capability maintenance + adaptation costs. This captures the costs required to maintain and evolve the initiative, ensuring its long-term value.

This formula recognizes that AI implementations should be evaluated not just on immediate returns, but on their contribution to organisational intelligence and future capability.

How to measure Learning value and Strategic Option Value?

Learning Value represents the organisational capability enhancement that AI implementations create. While harder to measure than direct cost savings, it can be quantified through several approaches:

1. Human Capital Appreciation Method

Formula: Learning Value = (Number of employees × skill enhancement factor × average salary × capability multiplier)

Example Calculation:

- 200 employees gained AI-adjacent skills
- Average skill enhancement: 15% (measured through competency assessments)
- Average salary: $75,000
- Capability multiplier: 1.2 (ability to take on more complex tasks)
- **Learning Value = 200 × 0.15 × $75,000 × 1.2 = $2,700,000**

2. Training Cost Avoidance Method

Formula: Learning Value = Cost of equivalent external training + opportunity cost of time saved

Measurement approach:

- Compare internal AI-driven learning outcomes to external training costs
- Include saved time value (employees learning on-the-job vs. attending courses)
- Factor in retention value (skills developed internally vs. hiring externally)

Example:

- External AI training would cost $5,000 per employee for 200 employees = $1,000,000
- Time saved: 40 hours per employee × $50/hour × 200 = $400,000

- **Learning Value = $1,400,000**

3. Innovation Velocity Method

Formula: Learning Value = (Increase in ideas generated × conversion rate × average value per innovation)

Measurable indicators:

- Ideas submitted to innovation programs (before vs. after AI implementation)
- Cross-functional collaboration projects initiated
- Time from idea to prototype/implementation
- Success rate of new initiatives

Example:

- Pre-AI: 50 ideas/quarter, 10% conversion rate, $50,000 average value = $250,000 / quarter
- Post-AI: 120 ideas/quarter, 15% conversion rate, $75,000 average value = $1,350,000 / quarter
- **Annual Learning Value = ($1,350,000 - $250,000) × 4 = $4,400,000**

4. Cultural Capital Method

Formula: Learning Value = Improved employee engagement × retention cost savings + productivity gains

Measurement framework:

- Employee engagement scores (pre/post implementation)
- Voluntary turnover reduction
- Internal mobility and promotion rates
- Collaboration effectiveness metrics

Strategic Option Value quantifies the future opportunities that current AI investments create. This draws from real options theory, which values the flexibility and future choices that investments provide.

1. Market Expansion Approach

Formula: Option Value = (Probability of expansion × Expected market value × Market share potential) - Exercise cost

Practical measurement:

- Identify new markets/services enabled by AI capabilities

- Estimate market size and growth potential

- Calculate the probability of successful entry

- Determine investment required to "exercise" the option

Example:

- AI chatbot capability enables expansion into 24/7 customer service

- Market opportunity: $10M additional revenue potential

- Probability of success: 70%

- Exercise cost (full implementation): $2M

- **Option Value = (0.7 × $10M) - $2M = $5M**

2. Innovation Pipeline Approach

Formula: Option Value = Σ(Future innovation probability × Expected innovation value)

Measurement approach:

- Catalog potential innovations enabled by current AI infrastructure

- Assign probability and value estimates to each

- Assign a weight factor, e.g. 1 if the innovations can be implemented within 6 months, 0.5 for 12-24 months, 0 beyond

- Sum across all identified options, for example

  - Market opportunity: $15M revenue potential

  - Success probability: 60%

  - Exercise cost: $3M

  - Option Value = (0.6 × $15M) - $3M = $6M

Case Study: Microsoft's AI Ethics Execution

When Microsoft launched its AI for Good initiative, it made a commitment that many tech companies avoid: complete transparency about both successes and failures in their AI implementations. But their approach went beyond simple reporting - they developed a comprehensive measurement framework that tracked all three dimensions of AI success.

Their approach, led by Chief Responsible AI Officer Natasha Crampton, involved quarterly public reports that detailed not just positive outcomes, but challenges, setbacks, and lessons learned from AI deployments that didn't meet expectations.

Microsoft's Three-Dimensional Measurement Approach:

Performance Tracking: Traditional metrics showed $2.1B in cost savings and 34% improvement in service delivery speed across their AI implementations.

Learning Indicators: More importantly, they tracked cultural shifts: 78% of employees reported increased confidence in working alongside AI systems, and cross-functional collaboration on AI projects increased 156%.

Strategic Measures: They quantified strategic option value by measuring new service possibilities enabled by AI capabilities, which opened $800M in new market opportunities within 18 months.

Their Intelligent ROI Calculation:

- Performance Value: $2.1B (cost savings) + $400M (efficiency gains) = $2.5B

- Learning Value: $300M (estimated value of capability development and cultural capital)

- Strategic Option Value: $800M (new market opportunities)

- Total Value: $3.6B

- Total Investment: $1.2B (implementation) + $200M (ongoing learning) = $1.4B

- Intelligent ROI: 257%

This transparency initially felt risky - why publicize your failures and share your measurement methodology? But the approach generated unexpected benefits. Academic researchers began collaborating on solutions to Microsoft's published challenges. Other companies shared their own experiences, creating industry-wide learning networks. Most importantly, Microsoft's employees developed deeper trust in leadership's commitment to responsible AI development.

The transparent results approach proved strategically powerful. When Microsoft faced regulatory scrutiny over AI bias concerns, its documented history of transparent reporting and continuous improvement became evidence of good faith efforts rather than defensive damage control.

Your Execution Assessment

To help you evaluate your current execution capabilities, rate your organisation on these key dimensions (1 = Not started, 5 = Fully embedded):

1. Start with People, Not Projects

- Have you mapped your internal AI stakeholders (believers, sceptics, undecided)? ___

- Have listening tours or stakeholder interviews been conducted pre-project? ___

- Do quiet subject-matter experts have a platform to contribute? ___

- Is there a cross-functional AI council with representation from different levels and different areas (ranging from tech to business to legal to comms)? ___

2. Build Cross-Functional AI Literacy

- Have non-technical teams been trained on AI fundamentals? ___

- Is AI part of regular upskilling programs for product, operations, etc.? ___

- Is prompt engineering or data reasoning part of common curricula? ___

- Are leaders trained to spot and evaluate good AI opportunities? ___

Your Execution Readiness Score: ___/40

If you scored 30+: You're ready for ambitious AI execution with confidence.

If you scored 20-29: Focus on strengthening stakeholder alignment before launching major initiatives.

If you scored below 20: Invest in foundational AI literacy and change readiness before proceeding.

Executing Your Next AI Initiative

Based on the IMPACT framework, here's your action plan for executing AI initiatives that deliver lasting value:

Phase 1: Pre-Launch Intelligence (2-4 weeks)

1. **Map Your Human Ecosystem**: Identify champions, sceptics, and undecided who will determine success

2. **Establish Listening Protocols**: Create formal channels for capturing human intelligence throughout execution

3. **Design Learning Systems**: Build feedback mechanisms that generate insights for scaling, not just problem-solving

Phase 2: Intelligent Pilot (8-12 weeks)

1. **Launch with Learning Intent**: Implement your pilot with explicit goals for capability building, not just outcome achievement

2. **Monitor Multiple Intelligence Streams**: Track AI performance, human adaptation, and strategic context simultaneously

3. **Practice Adaptation Protocols**: Use early signals to refine approach while maintaining strategic direction

Phase 3: Scaling with Wisdom (Ongoing)

1. **Codify Human Intelligence**: Document insights that AI can't capture but humans consistently recognize

2. **Build Cultural Integration**: Embed AI as an enhancement to human capab lity, not a replacement of human judgment

3. **Establish Continuous Calibration**: Create systems for ongoing refinement based on changing context and new learning

Pause and reflect: How might your current execution approach change if you prioritized learning capability over delivering outcomes?

The Execute Mindset: Confidence Through Discipline

As I learned during my own transition from technical expert to CEO, confidence in execution doesn't come from having perfect plans - it comes from having systematic approaches to learning and adapting when plans encounter reality.

The Execute phase of DARE isn't about flawless implementation of predetermined strategies. It's about disciplined responsiveness to emerging intelligence, whether that comes from AI systems detecting patterns or human wisdom recognizing context that algorithms miss.

Anne discovered this six months after her warehouse AI implementation. When asked what made the difference between her successful AI execution and others she'd observed, her answer was simple: "We never forgot that we were implementing AI to help humans do better work, not to replace human judgment with fancy algorithms."

This mindset - AI as amplification of human intelligence rather than automation of human decisions - transforms execution from a technical deployment challenge into a leadership development opportunity. And it is key to achieving success.

As Anne looked back six months later, it wasn't the AI dashboard metrics she remembered - it was the moment her most sceptical team lead called to say, 'This is actually making us better.' That's when she knew: execution had worked - not because it was perfect, but because it stayed human.

Linking Execute to Share

The Execute phase completes the DARE cycle, but it also creates the foundation for what comes next: Share. Every successful AI execution generates three forms of value that can be shared across your organisation:

1. **Capability Value**: The specific AI tools and processes that solved problems

2. **Intelligence Value**: The human insights that made AI implementations successful

3. **Cultural Value**: The trust and collaboration patterns that enabled human-AI partnership

Your Chapter Challenge: Choose one current initiative and apply the IMPACT framework.

Your Development: You have now completed the DARE part of your journey. If you were to take again the Compass questions of Chapter 1, how different would your score be versus when you started this book?

As we'll explore in the next section, the ability to SHARE these forms of value determines whether your AI leadership creates isolated successes or organisational transformation.

The discipline of Execute teaches us that AI implementation succeeds not through perfect technology, but through intelligent leadership that remains centred on human flourishing while leveraging AI for amplified impact.

Your leadership drives DARE from strategic potential to measurable results. But your wisdom in execution determines whether those results become stepping stones to greater transformation or isolated victories that fade with time.

So, now, you've dared. You've moved from insight to bold action. But transformation doesn't stick until it becomes collective. Now begins the real test: Can your courage scale through culture? Can your leadership ripple through others? SHARE is about sustaining momentum through trust, transparency, and rhythm.

Your Development: As you progress from DARE to SHARE, consider taking stock of your evolution in the CARE, DARE, SHARE Compass (Chapter 1).

Chapter 9 Takeaways & Reflection

AI execution doesn't succeed through perfection - it succeeds when people are equipped, engaged, and emotionally onboard.

◇ **Key Takeaways**

- **Execution is emotional before it is operational**: This truth is systematically ignored by the Rationality Mirage, which believes a good plan is enough. A leader who masters Care, Dare, Share knows that a plan is only as good as the belief it inspires.
- **Your believers, sceptics, and undecided determine your trajectory**: A 30% tipping point of engaged advocates can transform hesitation into momentum.
- **Execution is a leadership manifestation - not a technical rollout**: CEO-led, human-centred communication shifts AI from a "project" to a culture-changing force.
- **Pilot for learning, not validation**: Intelligent pilots should reveal what needs refining, not just prove what already works.
- **Human intelligence strengthens AI outcomes**: When human insight is valued as "data," organisations unlock a deeper layer of executional success.
- **Measurement must evolve too**: The most successful leaders track not just ROI, but capability growth and strategic readiness - what you learn is as important as what you deliver.

◇ **Reflection Prompts**

- *Are you leading your AI execution with people-first language - or tech-first updates?*
- *What percentage of your team would you say are true believers? What would it take to tip the undecided?*
- *What frontline signals might your dashboards be missing?*
- *Are your execution metrics capturing learning, growth, and future readiness - or just performance?*

Chapter 10: Synthesize - Aggregating Collective Knowledge (SHARE: S)

The wisdom of the many always exceeds the intelligence of the few - but only if someone knows how to listen.

We were sitting in our regular reviews of Zaya, the conversational banking AI-powered app of the European bank I was helping to execute their CARE, DARE, SHARE transformation. 6 months into the deployment of the new and enhanced Zaya, all seemed going well: marketing automation showing promising engagement metrics, operations streamlining improving by the day, customer satisfaction increasing, the empathy-based-engagement, even if simple, was running well. On paper, Zaya was winning. But only in isolated pockets. It was not yet quite achieving the deep transformation of all the business lines of this bank.

Then Pier, from the customer experience team, made an offhand comment that really highlighted what was going on: "It's funny – Zaya keeps escalating the same types of complaints that operations could easily prevent, but those insights never make it back to them. And at the same time, marketing generates leads and ideas that do not seem to fully factor in what Zaya has learned about customer pain points."

In that moment, the team realized it had fallen into the classic trap of AI implementation (or actually any implementation) - optimizing individual functions while accidentally fragmenting collective intelligence. I call it "knowledge islands" - brilliant AI solutions, like Zaya, or AI-powered anti-fraud systems, or AI-powered marketing systems, that can't talk to each other, and more importantly, can't learn from each other.

The 'knowledge islands' are a classic symptom of what management thinker Peter Senge, in his landmark book *The Fifth Discipline*, described as the failure of 'Systems Thinking.' Senge argued that organisations consistently fail not because of individual incompetence, but because they cannot see the interconnected patterns that govern their success. Each department optimizes its own function, blind to how its actions impact the whole. The act of Synthesizing, therefore, is the first and most critical step in developing the discipline of systems thinking. It is the practice of making the invisible connections visible, so the organisation can begin to learn and act as a cohesive whole.

The first and most crucial element of the **SHARE** framework has to be **Synthesize**. Because here's what I've learned: AI doesn't just help you aggregate data. When guided by empathic intelligence, it becomes the nervous system that connects your organisation's scattered wisdom into something far more powerful than the sum of its parts. This is an incredibly powerful feature that was so much harder to realise before the advent of generative AI.

Why Synthesize Matters More Than Ever

Paradoxically, we live in the age of information abundance and insight scarcity. Your organisation generates thousands of data points daily - customer feedback, employee sentiment, market signals, operational metrics. AI can process this volume at unprecedented speed. But without intentional synthesis, this creates what MIT's Sherry Turkle calls "data-rich, insight-poor" organisations.

The traditional approach treats knowledge like inventory - collect it, categorize it, store it. But knowledge isn't static. It's dynamic, iterative, contextual, and most valuable when it connects across boundaries. Real synthesis requires what I call Human Intelligence-guided aggregation - using your empathic intelligence to ask the right questions and AI to find patterns you'd never spot alone. The goal of Synthesize is to create a solution that no single individual, or silo, could have created alone. This collaborative act directly attacks the foundations of the Rationality Mirage, which creates silos as a natural byproduct of its focus on narrow, functional optimization.

Consider this: Netflix doesn't just use AI to recommend movies. They synthesize viewing patterns, rating behaviours, and even pause-and-rewind data to inform content creation, marketing strategies, and global expansion decisions. When they noticed audiences in 190+ countries pausing at similar emotional moments in *Stranger Things*, they didn't just file that insight in their entertainment analytics. They shared it with their marketing team, who used it to create more emotionally resonant trailers. They shared it with their content teams, who applied the insight to greenlight *Dark Crystal* and *The Witcher*. One synthesis became multiple breakthroughs.

But here's the crucial difference: Netflix's success wasn't just about smart algorithms. It was about leaders who asked empathic questions - *Why do people pause there? What does that tell us about human connection? How might this insight serve our global community?*

The SHARE Framework: Your Legacy of Leadership

CARE taught you to lead with emotional intelligence. DARE taught you to act with strategic boldness.

SHARE is where it all comes together - where your leadership shifts from being the smartest voice in the room to the one that orchestrates everyone else's brilliance.

If CARE is the heart and DARE the spine, SHARE is the nervous system. It's not about collecting more knowledge, but about connecting the wisdom that already exists - across departments, systems, and people.

This is where you shift from being the expert with the answers to the leader who enables powerful connections. Where leadership isn't about how much you know, but how well you help others integrate what they know - so the whole system becomes smarter, faster, and more alive.

Before we dive into Synthesize, let me introduce the SHARE framework that will guide the final section of your leadership transformation journey:

S – Synthesize: Aggregate collective knowledge with AI-enhanced empathic intelligence

H – Harness: Channel synthesized insights into coordinated action

A – Align: Create coherence across people, systems, and priorities

R&E – Radiate and Engage: Amplify belief, energy, and learning beyond boundaries

In other words, SHARE moves from sensing to impact: **Synthesize** helps you surface meaningful insights from fragmented data and emotion, **Harness** converts those insights into focused intent and direction, **Align** ensures that people, systems, and strategies move in cohesion, **Radiate and Engage** extend your impact - by amplifying clarity, energy, and belief across and beyond the organisation. Together, these arcs transform disconnected intelligence into collective momentum.

Unlike CARE (focused on your personal emotional intelligence) and DARE (on strategic boldness), SHARE positions you as the architect of collective intelligence. You shift from being the smartest person in the room to the one who helps the room become smarter - by connecting, amplifying, and activating the wisdom around you.

This is where your journey from a self and individual discovery progressively moves you to a system-wide, organisation-wide embrace. This is about multiplying your leadership.

The Architecture of Intelligent Synthesize

Effective Synthesize requires three layers of intelligence integration. While this sequence may resemble the one in Chapter 4, the Respond chapter in CARE, here it is applied at a different, wider enterprise-wide level, to affect not just one country, one department, one function, but to affect the entire company or community:

Layer 1: Signal Detection

AI excels at pattern recognition across vast datasets. It can identify emerging trends, anomalies, and correlations that human analysis would miss. But it can't interpret *meaning*. That's where your empathic intelligence becomes essential. You provide the context that transforms data points into human insights.

Layer 2: Context Integration

This is where human and artificial intelligences (HI+AI) become genuinely collaborative. AI can map relationships between disparate information sources - customer complaints, employee engagement scores, market trends, competitive moves. Your empathic intelligence interprets these relationships through the lens of human needs, organisational culture, and strategic intent.

Layer 3: Wisdom Synthesis

The highest level combines analytical insights with experiential wisdom. AI provides the "what" and "when." Your human intelligence provides the "why" and "how." Together, they generate actionable wisdom that neither could achieve alone.

Your turn: What patterns is your organisation missing because insights remain isolated? How might Synthesize change not just what you know, but how you act on what you learn?

Case Study: Unilever's Sustainable Living Synthesize

When Unilever committed to its Sustainable Living Plan, it faced a classic Synthesize challenge. They had sustainability data scattered across 190 countries, 400 brands, and thousands of suppliers. Each region was generating valuable insights about consumer behaviour, supply chain innovations, and environmental impact. But these learnings remained isolated, limiting their collective impact.

CEO Alan Jope and his team implemented what they called their "Living Insights Platform" - an AI-powered system designed not just to collect sustainability data, but to synthesize it into actionable organisational intelligence.

Here's how they applied the three-layer approach:

Signal Detection: AI algorithms continuously scanned sustainability metrics, consumer sentiment, regulatory changes, and supply chain data across all markets. The system identified patterns like the correlation between packaging innovation in their Brazilian operations and consumer loyalty increases in similar emerging markets.

Context Integration: Regional leaders provided human intelligence about cultural, economic, and social factors that shaped consumer behaviour. When AI detected increased demand for plastic-free packaging in Kenya, local leaders explained how this connected to community values around environmental stewardship and local manufacturing capabilities.

Wisdom Synthesis: The global leadership team used these synthesized insights to make strategic decisions that no single region could have reached alone. They discovered that sustainability innovations in one market often solved business challenges in completely different markets. A water-saving manufacturing process developed for drought-stricken India became a cost-saving opportunity in water-abundant Netherlands.

The results were remarkable: Unilever's sustainable living brands grew 69% faster than the rest of their business, contributing 75% of their total growth. But the deeper transformation was organisational. They had created a learning system where every market's innovation contributed to global intelligence.

Jope later reflected: "AI helped us see patterns we'd never spot. But human wisdom helped us understand what those patterns meant for real families buying our products. The combination became our competitive advantage."

Case Study: Shopify's Merchant Success Synthesize

Shopify processes over $175 billion in annual merchant sales, serving millions of entrepreneurs worldwide. Each merchant generates unique data about customer behaviour, product performance, and business challenges. The traditional approach would be to provide each merchant with its own analytics. But Shopify realized they could create exponentially more value through intelligent Synthesize.

They developed what they call their "Commerce Intelligence Engine" - a system that synthesizes insights across their entire merchant ecosystem while protecting individual merchant privacy. Here's how they did it:

Anonymous Insight Aggregation: AI systems identify successful patterns - which product descriptions drive conversions, what pricing strategies work in different markets, how seasonal trends vary by category - without exposing individual merchant data.

Contextual Pattern Recognition: Human intelligence from Shopify's merchant success teams interprets these patterns through the lens of business fundamentals, industry expertise, and entrepreneurial psychology. They understand that a successful strategy for a luxury brand won't work for a volume retailer, even if the data looks similar.

Actionable Synthesis: The platform provides each merchant with insights that combine their individual data with synthesized intelligence from millions of similar businesses. A new merchant launching handmade jewellery doesn't just see their own limited data - they benefit from anonymized insights about what's worked for thousands of other jewellery entrepreneurs.

The impact has been profound. Merchants using Shopify's synthesized insights show double-digit higher revenue growth and double-digit better customer retention rates. But beyond metrics, they've created something more valuable: a platform where every entrepreneur's learning contributes to everyone's success.

President Harley Finkelstein explained their philosophy: "AI helps us find the signal in the noise of billions of commerce transactions. But empathy helps us translate those signals into guidance that feels personally relevant to each entrepreneur. We're not just providing data - we're sharing collective wisdom."

The Synthesize Toolkit: Practical Implementation

Based on these cases and my own experience, here's your practical framework for implementing Synthesize in your organisation:

1. Map Your Knowledge Ecosystem

Start by auditing where valuable insights currently live in your organisation. Most leaders are shocked to discover how much intelligence exists in silos. Create a visual map that includes:

- **Formal data sources**: CRM systems, analytics platforms, performance dashboards

- **Informal intelligence networks**: Customer-facing teams, field operations, support channels

- **External insight streams**: Market research, customer feedback, partner intelligence

- **Hidden wisdom repositories**: Project retrospectives, failed experiment learnings, veteran employee knowledge, subject-matter experts sitting at their desks....

2. Design Your Synthesize Architecture

Choose dedicated AI tools that can aggregate insights across these sources while preserving human context. The best synthesis platforms include:

- **Knowledge Repositories**: Tools like Confluence, Notion, or SharePoint enhanced with AI-powered search and pattern recognition. These should capture not just what happened, but why it mattered and what was learned.
- **Insight Aggregation Platforms**: Systems like Tableau, Power BI, or custom dashboards that can pull data from multiple sources and identify cross-functional patterns.
- **Collaborative Intelligence Tools**: Platforms like Slack with AI-powered insights, Microsoft Teams with automated meeting

summaries, or custom systems that capture informal knowledge sharing.

3. Establish Synthesize Rituals

Technology enables synthesis, but human intelligence guides it. Create regular practices that combine AI capabilities with empathic insight:

- **Monthly Cross-Functional Synthesize Sessions**: Bring together leaders from different departments to review AI-generated insights and provide human context. Ask questions like: "What patterns surprise us? What context is missing? How might these insights change our approach?"
- **Quarterly Strategic Synthesize Reviews**: Use AI to identify longer-term patterns and human intelligence to interpret their strategic implications. Focus on questions like: "What are we learning about our customers/employees/market that we didn't know six months ago? How should this change our priorities?"
- **Annual Wisdom Capture Projects**: Systematically document and synthesize the year's key learnings in formats that can inform future decisions. This isn't just data reporting - it's organisational memory creation.

4. Build Synthesize Skills Across Your Organisation

Synthesize isn't just a leadership capability - it's an organisational competency. Invest in developing these skills throughout your teams:

- **AI Literacy Training**: Help your people understand how to work with AI tools for insight aggregation, not just task automation.
- **Pattern Recognition Development**: Train teams to identify meaningful connections between seemingly unrelated information.

- **Context Integration Skills**: Develop your organisation's ability to interpret AI insights through human wisdom, cultural understanding, and strategic context.

Your Synthesize Assessment

To evaluate the current Synthesize capabilities of your organisation or community, score yourself on these questions (1-5 scale, where 1 is rarely/low and 5 is very frequently/very much):

Knowledge Integration

1. Does our organisation systematically capture insights from failed experiments and near-misses? (___/5)

2. Can we quickly identify patterns across different departments, regions, or customer segments? (___/5)

3. Do our AI tools help us discover unexpected connections between different business areas? (___/5)

4. Are insights from customer-facing teams regularly integrated with strategic decision-making? (___/5)

Cross-Functional Learning

5. Do we have regular processes for sharing learnings across departmental boundaries? (___/5)

6. Can our teams easily access relevant insights from other parts of the organisation? (___/5)

7. Are our collaboration tools designed to capture and share institutional knowledge? (___/5)

8. Do we treat organisational learning as a strategic capability, not just an operational necessity? (___/5)

Synthesize Leadership

9. Do leaders actively ask questions that connect insights across different business areas? (___/5)

10. Are we using AI to identify patterns that inform strategic decisions, not just operational efficiency? (___/5)

11. Do we have systems that turn individual insights into organisational intelligence? (___/5)

12. Are we better at Synthesize today than we were six months ago? (___/5)

Scoring Guide:

- **45-60**: You're ready to build sophisticated Synthesize capabilities that can drive competitive advantage

- **30-44**: You have solid foundations but need to strengthen cross-functional integration and strategic application

- **Below 30**: Focus on basic knowledge capture and AI literacy before advancing to complex Synthesize

The Synthesize Challenge: Your Next 30 Days

Here's your immediate action plan to begin building Synthesize capabilities:

Week 1: Map your knowledge ecosystem. Identify where valuable insights currently exist in isolation.

Week 2: Choose one AI-powered tool that can help aggregate insights across at least two different data sources. Implement it with a specific use-case.

Week 3: Conduct your first cross-functional Synthesize session. Bring together leaders from different departments to review patterns and provide human context to AI insights.

Week 4: Document what you've learned and design your ongoing Synthesize rituals. Create a plan for monthly and quarterly Synthesize practices.

The Bridge to Harness

Synthesize creates the foundation for the rest of the SHARE framework, but synthesis without action is just sophisticated information hoarding.

In our next chapter, we'll explore Harness - the second arc of SHARE, where you turn synthesis into strategy. It's where collective insight begins to shape collective direction.

The question isn't whether your organisation generates valuable insights. It's whether you can synthesize them into wisdom that drives better decisions, stronger relationships, and more meaningful impact.

Your Chapter Challenge: Select one business challenge your organisation is currently facing:

1. *Identify at least three different sources of information related to this challenge that currently exist in isolation (different departments, systems, or stakeholder groups).*

2. *Think about how ideally you would like to connect insights across these sources.*

3. *Challenge your tech team to give you two ideas of tools/setups to achieve this connection*

Synthesize starts with your leadership. It scales with AI. It succeeds through empathic intelligence. In Synthesize, your leadership becomes the bridge between scattered intelligence and collective wisdom.

That bridge is where real change begins. Because, as Pier so simply put it, what use is smart insight if no one else hears it? Synthesize isn't about data - it's about making sure that every voice, every learning, every signal gets where it needs to go to make a difference.

Chapter 10 Takeaways & Reflection

AI-powered knowledge isn't enough - transformation begins when insights connect, resonate, and inform action across boundaries.

◇ **Key Takeaways**

- **Synthesize turns scattered intelligence into strategic wisdom**: AI finds patterns, but only human empathy can shape them into decisions that matter.
- **Knowledge islands stall transformation**: Even the best insights lose power if they're trapped in silos. Connectivity multiplies impact
- **Great leaders ask integrative questions**: Insight isn't just found in data - it's unlocked by the questions leaders choose to ask and the people they choose to involve so as to expand the learning through the organisation or community.
- **Synthesize must be intentional and ongoing**: It's not a one-off analysis but a continuous leadership habit of meaning-making.
- **AI is your amplifier, not your replacement**: Collective intelligence emerges when AI's analytical speed meets human context and curiosity.
- **Organisations must build rituals and tools for synthesis**: Without deliberate structure, shared learning fades - wise systems keep wisdom alive.

◇ **Reflection Prompts**

- *Where is your organisation "data rich, insight poor", not fully building on the learnings?*
- *What valuable learnings are hiding in plain sight across departments or systems?*
- *Are your teams synthesising intelligence - or just storing information?*
- *What rituals or tools do you have in place to regularly bring insights together?*
- *What's one question you could ask this week to connect dots others haven't yet seen?*

Chapter 11: Harness - Leveraging AI For Collaboration (SHARE: H)

The only real way to know if trust is possible - is to offer it first.

In the orchestra of transformation, alignment and collaboration don't happen by accident – they are designed. This chapter invites a new leadership shift: from managing collaboration through control to enabling it through intelligent connection. Collaboration in the age of AI isn't about more tools - it's about designing systems where human insight and machine intelligence move together, in rhythm.

At 11:47 PM, Sarah Chen stared at her laptop, drowning in fragments: 17 Slack channels, 12 email threads, 3 project dashboards - and no clarity. Singapore was waiting for London. London for New York. New York for Bangalore. Everyone was brilliant. Everyone was working hard. But together, they were stuck. Despite having every collaboration tool money could buy, Sarah's team functioned like isolated islands - each holding a piece of the puzzle, but no shared picture.

Sounds familiar?

This is the collaboration paradox of our AI age: we have more connectivity than ever, yet our collective intelligence remains fragmented. We synthesize insights beautifully within our silos, but struggle to harness that synthesis across the human complexity of real organisations.

The second pillar of SHARE – Harness - transforms synthesized intelligence into coordinated action through AI-powered collaboration that honours both human wisdom and organisational reality.

When you harness collective energy, you are no longer just managing resources; you are leading a movement. The Rationality Mirage is built for a world of optimising a few machines on a factory floor; whereas SHARE, as a whole, and Harness, in particular, is how you build an army of co-creators, bursting the mirage.

The Hidden Cost of Fragmented Intelligence

Before we explore how to harness AI for collaboration, let's acknowledge what poor collaboration actually costs us. It's not just delayed projects or missed deadlines - it's the systematic underutilization of our collective intelligence.

At a consumer lending firm I have advised, we had discovered that the customer service team had developed incredible insights about customer financial stress patterns during the pandemic. Meanwhile, the product development and risk management teams were designing new lending algorithms based on historical data that completely missed these emotional signals.

Brilliant teams, all serving the same customers, operating with fragmented intelligence despite sharing the same building and mission.

The breakthrough comes when we realize that collaboration isn't just about better communication, it's about creating shared intelligence systems where AI amplifies human connection rather than replacing it.

Pause and Reflect: Where is collaboration in your team currently breaking down - information, emotion, or energy?

Beyond Shared Dashboards: The Intelligence Orchestra

Most organisations approach AI-powered collaboration as if they're buying better sheet music when what they really need is a conductor who can help the orchestra play together.

To have true collaboration, you must simultaneously harness the three types of intelligence:

1. Distributed Intelligence: AI systems that aggregate insights obtained through the Synthesize framework presented in Chapter 10, across teams and time zones

2. Contextual Intelligence: Human wisdom that interprets AI insights through organisation-wide cultural and emotional lenses

3. Orchestrated Intelligence: Leadership frameworks that coordinate both into coherent action

The magic happens at the intersection of all three.

The Principles of Collaborative FLOW

After studying successful collaborations across dozens of organisations, and leading it myself at Aegon NL across thousands of colleagues scattered throughout the Netherlands, turning fragmented teams into collaborative intelligence networks requires focusing on four key principles that create **FLOW**:

- **F - Find the Connective Tissue**
- **L - Listen Across Boundaries**
- **O - Orchestrate Shared Learning**
- **W - Weave Intelligence into Action**

And this approach can nowadays be turbo-boosted thanks to the impressive AI tools that exist and can be deployed for this purpose. Let me show you how this works in practice.

F-Find the Connective Tissue

The first step isn't deploying new tools - it's mapping the invisible connections that already exist between your teams' work.

At Spotify, Chief Technology Officer Gustav Söderström faced a challenge familiar to many scaling organisations: their famous "Squad Model" was producing incredible innovation within teams, but cross-squad collaboration was breaking down as they grew beyond 3,000 employees.

Rather than restructuring teams or mandating collaboration, Söderström's team created what they called the "Intelligence Web" - an AI system that identifies natural connection points between different squads' work by analysing code commits, user feedback patterns, and feature interactions.

The AI didn't tell teams what to collaborate on. Instead, it surfaces hidden interdependencies and shared opportunities, then facilitates human-to-human connections based on actual work overlap.

The result? Cross-squad collaboration increased by 147% within six months, leading to product innovations that no single squad could have created alone - like their AI-powered playlist collaboration features that emerged from connections between the social, recommendation, and audio engineering squads.

Your Connective Tissue protocol

1. List your team's top three current initiatives

2. For each initiative, identify what other teams' work it depends on or impacts

3. Map where shared data, insights, or decisions create natural collaboration points

4. Look for patterns: Where does fragmented intelligence cost you speed or quality?

L - Listen Across Boundaries

Once you've mapped the connective tissue, the next step is creating systematic listening that crosses organisational boundaries - not just geographic or departmental ones, but hierarchical and functional ones too.

Microsoft's transformation under Satya Nadella provides a masterclass in AI-enhanced cross-boundary listening. When Nadella became CEO in 2014, Microsoft had brilliant teams working in parallel on cloud, productivity, and AI initiatives, but little meaningful collaboration between them.

The breakthrough came through what they called "Intelligence Bridges" - AI-powered systems that don't just share information across teams, but actively listen for collaboration opportunities and emotional signals that indicate when teams are ready to work together.

Here's how it works: Microsoft's AI systems continuously analyse communication patterns, project timelines, customer feedback, and even team sentiment data to identify moments when cross-team collaboration would be most valuable and most welcome.

For example, the AI detected that the Azure team was receiving customer requests for AI capabilities right as the Cognitive Services team was looking for real-world application testing. But more importantly, the system recognized that both teams were at similar points in their development cycles and had complementary skills gaps.

Instead of mandating collaboration, Microsoft's people development team received AI-generated insights about this opportunity, then facilitated organic connections through shared workshops and joint customer meetings.

The result was the development of Azure Cognitive Services - a $2 billion product line that neither team could have created independently. More importantly, this collaborative success created organisational muscle memory for future AI-enabled partnerships.

Your Cross-Boundary Listening Protocol:

1. Weekly Intelligence Pulse: Use AI tools to analyse communication patterns and identify where teams are discussing similar challenges

2. Quarterly Collaboration Readiness Assessment: Survey teams about their collaboration capacity and interests

3. Monthly Opportunity Bridges: Host facilitated sessions where AI-identified collaboration opportunities are explored by relevant teams

4. Continuous Sentiment Monitoring: Track emotional signals that indicate when teams are open to collaboration versus when they need to focus internally

O - Orchestrate Shared Learning

The third element of FLOW moves beyond information sharing to coordinated learning - using AI to help teams learn from each other's experiences in real-time rather than through quarterly retrospectives or annual conferences.

Unilever's approach to orchestrating shared learning across its 190-country operation illustrates this beautifully. Chief Learning Officer Leena Nair (now CEO of Chanel) faced the challenge of helping local teams learn from each other's AI experiments without creating bureaucratic knowledge-sharing processes that would slow innovation.

Their solution: the "Living Learning Network" - an AI system that identifies successful patterns across different markets and automatically connects teams working on similar challenges, regardless of geographic or business unit boundaries.

Here's what makes it powerful: instead of creating a knowledge repository where teams deposit learnings for others to discover, Unilever's AI actively seeks out teams facing similar challenges and creates dynamic learning cohorts.

For example, when Unilever's team in Brazil developed an AI system for predicting demand spikes during local festivals, the AI identified that teams in India, Indonesia, and Nigeria were facing similar seasonal demand volatility challenges. Rather than sharing a case study, the system connected these teams for real-time learning exchanges.

The Brazilian team shared not just their technical approach, but the cultural insights that made their AI successful - like understanding that festival demand patterns were driven as much by social media sentiment as by calendar dates. The Indonesian team contributed insights about religious holiday patterns. The Nigerian team provided learnings about regional supplier reliability during high-demand periods.

The result was a collaborative AI approach that was stronger than any single team's solution, now deployed across 47 countries with local adaptations that account for cultural context.

Your Shared Learning Orchestra protocol:

1. Learning Pattern Recognition: Use AI to identify successful approaches within your organisation that could apply elsewhere

2. Dynamic Cohort Creation: Instead of static communities of practice, create temporary learning groups around specific challenges

3. Real-Time Wisdom Exchange: When teams face similar challenges, connect them for collaborative problem-solving rather than after-the-fact knowledge sharing

4. Cultural Intelligence Integration: Ensure AI identifies not just technical solutions, but the human insights that made them successful

W - Weave Intelligence into Action

The final element of FLOW is where collaborative intelligence becomes collaborative impact - translating shared insights into coordinated action across multiple teams and timelines.

Domino's Pizza provides an unexpected but powerful example of weaving intelligence into action. When CEO Russell Weiner took over in 2022, Domino's was facing intensifying competition from third-party delivery platforms. The challenge wasn't just operational - it was collaborative.

Their stores had deep intelligence about local customer preferences. Their technology teams had sophisticated AI capabilities for demand prediction and routing optimization. Their marketing teams understood broad consumer trends. But these insights weren't flowing together into coordinated action.

Domino's created what they call "Intelligence Action Loops" - AI-enhanced processes that don't just share information between teams, but coordinate their responses to create amplified impact.

Here's how it works: When AI systems detect a pattern (like increasing demand for plant-based options in college towns), three things happen simultaneously:

1. Store Intelligence: Local stores receive AI-enhanced insights about customer preferences, including emotional context about why these preferences are emerging

2. Supply Chain Coordination: AI systems automatically coordinate with supply chain teams to ensure ingredient availability matches predicted demand patterns

3. Marketing Activation: Marketing teams receive customer sentiment data and local context to create targeted campaigns that feel authentic to each market

But here's the key innovation: instead of each team responding independently, Domino's AI systems coordinate the timing and messaging of responses to create what they call "synchronized customer experiences."

For example, when the AI detected growing interest in plant-based options among college students, stores in college towns began offering samples during high-traffic periods. Simultaneously, supply chains ensured these stores had adequate inventory. Marketing teams created campus-specific campaigns that acknowledged students' environmental concerns without being preachy.

The result was an 18% increase in trial rates for new products and a 23% improvement in customer satisfaction scores in test markets - outcomes that no single team could have achieved independently.

Your Intelligence Action Weaving protocol:

1. Synchronized Response Planning: When AI identifies opportunities or challenges, coordinate team responses for amplified impact

2. Timing Intelligence: Use AI to optimize when different teams take action for maximum collaborative effect

3. Feedback Loop Integration: Ensure each team's actions generate data that improves other teams' AI systems

4. **Impact Measurement**: Track collaborative outcomes, not just individual team metrics

Case Study: The Challenge at Shopify

To see FLOW in action across a truly complex global organisation, let's examine how Shopify transformed its approach to serving millions of merchants across 175 countries.

By 2023, Shopify was processing over $200 billion in gross merchandise volume annually, but its merchant support was struggling with the complexity of serving businesses ranging from individual creators to enterprise companies across vastly different markets, regulations, and cultures.

Each regional team had developed deep expertise about its local merchants' needs. The product development teams had sophisticated AI capabilities. The merchant success teams had rich relationship intelligence. But these insights weren't being harnessed collectively to serve merchants better.

The Transformation: Intelligence Without Boundaries

Shopify's Chief Operating Officer Kaz Nejatian led the development of what they called "Merchant Intelligence Fabric" - an AI-enhanced collaboration system that harnesses collective intelligence while respecting local autonomy.

Phase 1: Find the Connective Tissue

Rather than assume they knew where collaboration opportunities existed, Shopify used AI to analyse two years of merchant interactions, support requests, feature usage patterns, and success outcomes across all regions.

The AI identified surprising connection points: merchants in rural Australia faced similar fulfilment challenges as merchants in small-town America. E-commerce businesses in Lagos had payment processing needs that mirrored those in Mexico City. Fashion brands in Toronto were using marketing strategies that would resonate with fashion merchants in Copenhagen.

Most importantly, the AI identified that successful merchants across all regions shared certain behavioural patterns - but different regions had developed different solutions for nurturing these behaviours.

Phase 2: Listen Across Boundaries

Instead of creating top-down collaboration mandates, Shopify established "Intelligence Listening Posts" - AI-enhanced systems that continuously identified natural collaboration opportunities between regions and functions.

For example, when merchants in Brazil began requesting inventory management features that didn't exist in Shopify's standard platform, the AI identified that merchants in Southeast Asia had been solving similar problems using third-party integrations. Instead of building new features from scratch, Shopify connected the regional teams to learn from each other's approaches.

The Brazilian team learned about specific technical solutions. The Southeast Asian team gained insights into Portuguese-language user interface considerations. The product development team received requirements that reflected actual merchant needs across multiple markets.

Phase 3: Orchestrate Shared Learning

Shopify created "Dynamic Learning Clusters" - AI-facilitated groups that form around specific merchant challenges rather than geographic or functional boundaries.

When the AI detected that merchants across multiple regions were struggling with social media marketing integration, it automatically created a learning cluster that included:

- Regional merchant success teams who understood local social media preferences

- Product teams working on social commerce features

- Marketing teams that understood platform-specific best practices

- High-performing merchants who had solved these challenges successfully

These clusters weren't permanent committees - they formed around specific challenges, collaborated intensively for 60-90 days, then dissolved while maintaining their collective intelligence for future reference.

Phase 4: Weave Intelligence into Action

The final phase transformed shared learning into synchronized action across Shopify's global operations.

When AI systems identified opportunities or challenges affecting merchants, responses were coordinated across regions and functions to create amplified impact. For example, when the system detected growing merchant interest in sustainability features, three things happened simultaneously:

1. **Regional Adaptation**: Local teams received culturally contextualized insights about why sustainability mattered to merchants in their markets

2. **Product Coordination**: Development teams prioritized sustainability features based on comprehensive global intelligence rather than isolated regional requests

3. **Merchant Education**: Marketing and success teams created coordinated educational content that reflected both global trends and local values

The Results

After 18 months of harnessing collaborative intelligence, the results were spectacular: double-digit growth in merchant satisfaction scores, feature adoption rates as products better reflected global merchant needs, regional team efficiency increased by 28% as teams learned from each other's solutions, and time-to-market for new features decreased by 41% through coordinated development approaches, merchant retention. across all regions

But the most significant result was cultural: Shopify transformed from a company with smart regional operations to a globally intelligent organisation where local expertise enhanced global impact.

The Human Intelligence Factor

What made Shopify's approach successful wasn't just better AI tools - it was the recognition that collaborative intelligence requires emotional intelligence at scale.

Nejatian's team discovered that the most successful collaborative efforts happened when three human factors were present:

1. **Psychological Safety**: Teams felt safe sharing both successes and failures across regional boundaries

2. **Cultural Curiosity**: Team members actively sought to understand different approaches rather than defending their own methods

3. **Shared Purpose**: Everyone understood how collaboration served merchants better, not just organisational efficiency

The AI systems were designed to amplify these human factors, not replace them.

Your Harness Assessment Questionnaire: Collaborative Intelligence Readiness

Before implementing AI-powered collaboration tools, assess your organisation's readiness across four critical dimensions:

1. Intelligence Flow Assessment (Score 1-5 each, where 1 is rarely/low and 5 is very frequently/very much)

Knowledge Connectivity

- Our teams can easily identify who else is working on related challenges (___/5)

- Insights from one team regularly inform decisions in other teams (___/5)

- We have systems for surfacing unexpected connections between different areas of work (___/5)

- Teams actively seek out intelligence from other parts of the organisation (___/5)

Cross-Boundary Communication

- Teams regularly communicate about their work with other departments (___/5)

- We have established rhythms for cross-functional intelligence sharing (___/5)

- Teams feel comfortable asking for input from colleagues in other areas (___/5)

- Communication flows easily up, down, and across organisational boundaries (___/5)

Collaborative Learning Capacity

- Teams actively learn from each other's experiments and experiences (___/5)

- We have processes for identifying and sharing successful approaches (___/5)

- Teams are willing to adapt their methods based on others' insights (___/5)

- Learning from collaboration improves everyone's individual performance (___/5)

Coordinated Action Ability

- Teams can align their efforts when working toward shared objectives (___/5)

- We coordinate timing of initiatives for maximum collective impact (___/5)

- Teams adjust their plans based on other teams' activities and insights (___/5)

- Our collaborative efforts produce results no single team could achieve alone (___/5)

Partial Result Guide (sum the scores for these 16 questions pertaining to Intelligence Flow before scoring part 2. AI Collaboration Tool Readiness)

- 65–80: You are ready for AI-enhanced collaborative intelligence tools and orchestration frameworks.

- 50–64: Solid foundation; focus next on tightening rhythms and reinforcing cultural habits.

- 35–49: Fragmentation is holding you back; work on communication flow and mutual learning.

- Below 35: Start with cultural trust-building and basic intelligence-sharing rituals before layering AI.

2. AI Collaboration Tool Readiness

Technical Infrastructure

- We have reliable systems for sharing data across teams (___/5)

- Our communication platforms support integration with AI tools (___/5)

- Teams have adequate digital literacy for AI-enhanced collaboration (___/5)

- We have technical support for implementing and maintaining AI tools (___/5)

Cultural Readiness

- Teams are open to AI-enhanced collaboration approaches (___/5)

- Leadership actively supports cross-team collaboration (___/5)

- Teams trust each other to use shared intelligence responsibly (___/5)

- We have established norms for AI-assisted decision making (___/5)

Interpretation – Total Score (Max: 40)

- **32–40**: You're well-positioned to deploy advanced collaborative AI platforms - consider pilot scaling.

- **24–31**: Strong openness and tech backbone - focus now on refining team-level practices.

- **16–23**: Build up digital fluency and test lightweight AI integrations before wider rollout.

- **Below 16:** Begin with cultural preparation and trust-building; AI will only amplify what exists.

Implementing Your Collaborative Intelligence System

Based on your assessment results, here's your implementation roadmap:

Phase 1: Foundation Building (Weeks 1-4)

Week 1: Connective Tissue and Intelligence Mapping

- Map current collaboration patterns using the connective tissue exercise

- Identify 2-3 areas where better collaboration would significantly improve outcomes

- Survey teams about their collaboration experiences and preferences

Week 2: Listening Infrastructure

- Establish regular cross-team communication rhythms

- Implement basic AI tools for identifying collaboration opportunities (start with communication pattern analysis)

- Create psychological safety protocols for sharing insights and challenges

Week 3: Learning System Design

- Design dynamic cohort processes for specific challenges

- Establish shared learning repositories with AI-enhanced search

- Create protocols for rapid knowledge transfer between teams

Week 4: Action Coordination Framework

- Develop synchronized response planning templates

- Establish shared metrics for collaborative outcomes

- Create feedback loops that improve collaborative intelligence over time

Phase 2: AI Enhancement (Weeks 5-12)

Deploy Collaborative AI Tools

Based on your organisation's needs and readiness, prioritize these AI-enhanced collaboration capabilities:

For High-Readiness Organisations (Score 64+):

- Advanced pattern recognition across team communications and outcomes
- Predictive collaboration opportunity identification
- Automated learning cohort formation based on challenge similarity
- Synchronized action planning with AI-optimized timing

For Medium-Readiness Organisations (Score 48-63):

- Communication pattern analysis to identify collaboration gaps
- AI-enhanced knowledge sharing and search capabilities
- Basic opportunity identification for cross-team learning
- Simple coordination tools for aligned action planning

For Foundation-Building Organisations (Score below 48):

- Focus on human collaboration skills before adding AI enhancement
- Use basic AI tools only for communication analysis and simple knowledge management
- Prioritize trust-building and cultural development over technological solutions

Phase 3: Integration and Scaling (Weeks 13-26)

Continuous Improvement Loop

- Weekly: Review collaborative outcomes and adjust AI systems based on results

- Monthly: Assess team satisfaction with collaborative intelligence tools

- Quarterly: Expand successful collaborative approaches to additional teams

- Annually: Evolve your collaborative intelligence strategy based on organisational growth

The Leadership Mindset for Harnessing with Collaborative Intelligence

Successfully harnessing AI for collaboration requires a fundamental shift in how leaders think about their role. Instead of being the central hub through which all intelligence flows, you become the conductor who helps your organisation's collective intelligence create beautiful music together.

This means changing your perspective:

From Information Gateway to Intelligence Orchestrator: Rather than controlling information flow, you create systems where intelligence flows naturally, where it's needed most.

From Decision Maker to Decision Enabler: Instead of making all important decisions yourself, you ensure teams have the collaborative intelligence they need to make great decisions together.

From Performance Monitor to Collaboration Catalyst: Rather than just tracking individual and team performance, you actively cultivate the conditions where collaborative intelligence thrives.

From Problem Solver to Pattern Recognizer: Instead of solving every challenge yourself, you help teams identify patterns and connections that lead to collaborative solutions.

Connecting Harness to Your SHARE Journey

Harness builds directly on the Synthesize capabilities you developed in Chapter 10, while preparing you for the alignment and scaling phases ahead:

From Synthesize: You've learned to aggregate collective knowledge into actionable insights. Harness transforms those insights into coordinated action across multiple teams and contexts.

To Align: The collaborative intelligence systems you build through the FLOW framework of Harness create the foundation for organisational alignment around shared AI initiatives and strategic priorities. This is the focus of Chapter 12.

To Radiate and Engage: Effective internal collaboration becomes the launchpad for extending your organisation's intelligence and impact beyond your boundaries. The trust and collaborative capabilities you develop internally enable sustainable partnership and co-creation with internal and external stakeholders. This is the focus of Chapter 13.

Your Chapter Challenge: This week, implement one different element of the FLOW framework in your organisation, every day:

- *Day 1: Choose one current challenge or opportunity that involves multiple teams. Use the intelligence mapping exercise to identify natural connection points.*
- *Day 2: Implement a simple AI-enhanced listening system - this could be as basic as using communication analytics to identify collaboration opportunities, or as sophisticated as deploying specialized collaboration platforms.*
- *Day 3: Facilitate one cross-boundary learning session using AI insights to connect teams working on related challenges.*

- *Day 4: Design your first synchronized action experiment - coordinate how different teams respond to shared insights for amplified impact.*
- *Day 5: Document your experience: What worked? What surprised you? What would you adjust for broader implementation?*

As you develop your ability to harness AI for collaboration, remember that technology is only as powerful as the human relationships it enhances. The most successful collaborative intelligence systems don't replace human connection - they amplify it across the complexity of modern organisations.

In our next chapter, we'll explore how collaborative intelligence becomes the foundation for organisational alignment around shared AI strategies and cultural transformation - moving from smart collaboration to strategic coherence.

The future belongs to leaders who can orchestrate collective intelligence. Your role isn't to be the smartest person in the room - it's to help the room become smarter together.

Chapter 11 Takeaways & Reflection

AI doesn't make collaboration automatic - leaders do. Shared intelligence only creates impact when it's harnessed across teams, cultures, and contexts.

◇ **Key Takeaways**

- **Collaboration isn't about more tools - it's about more trust**: Fragmented systems drain energy. FLOW restores meaning by connecting intelligence, emotion, and execution.
- **FLOW also turns complexity into coherence**: When teams Find connective tissue, Listen across boundaries, Orchestrate shared learning, and Weave insights into action, collaboration becomes momentum.
- **AI amplifies - not replaces - connection**: From surfacing natural partnerships to coordinating synchronised action, AI works best when human intention leads the way.
- **Conflict can become contribution**: Tension between teams often signals unspoken intelligence - when harnessed, it becomes fuel for innovation.
- **Collaborative intelligence is cultural**: The most successful systems honour psychological safety, curiosity, and shared purpose - not just technical integration.

◇ **Reflection Prompts**

- *Where is collaboration breaking down in your team - information, emotion, or energy?*
- *Are your current systems promoting shared insight - or deepening silos?*
- *How often do your teams learn from each other's real-time experience - not just post-mortems?*
- *What simple rhythm or ritual could increase cross-boundary connection this month*
- *What part of the FLOW framework could you experiment with this week?*

Chapter 12: Align - Uniting Stakeholders With EI (SHARE: A)

You can't align a team by repeating the strategy louder. Alignment starts when people feel heard - emotionally, not just operationally.

When Marc Benioff stood before Salesforce's 73,000 employees in 2019, he faced a problem that no amount of data could solve alone. The company had grown exponentially, acquiring dozens of companies and expanding into new markets. But growth had created silos - engineering teams in San Francisco barely communicated with sales teams in New York, while customer success teams in Dublin operated with completely different priorities than their counterparts in Tokyo.

The quarterly employee engagement scores told the story in stark numbers: collaboration ratings had dropped 23% year-over-year, while "alignment with company priorities" hit an all-time low of 61%. But the real wake-up call came during a routine customer visit when a client asked, "Which Salesforce are we working with? We're getting different messages from every team."

This wasn't a technology problem - it was an emotional intelligence challenge at scale.

The solution didn't come from another reorganisation or process improvement initiative. Instead, Benioff and his leadership team embarked on what they called "Ohana Alignment" - a systematic approach to rebuilding stakeholder unity through emotional intelligence, enhanced by AI-powered insights. The results were remarkable: within 18 months, collaboration scores measurably improved, customer satisfaction jumped 35%, and cross-team innovation projects surged.

This is the power of Align - the third pillar of the SHARE framework. While Synthesize aggregates collective knowledge and Harness transforms insights into coordinated action, Align ensures that all stakeholders move forward with unified purpose and mutual understanding.

The Alignment Paradox

Modern organisations face an unprecedented alignment challenge. We have more communication tools than ever - Slack, Teams, Zoom, dashboards, collaboration platforms - yet teams often feel more disconnected than before. The problem isn't technological; it is emotional and cultural.

I witnessed this firsthand during my transition to CEO at Aegon NL. Despite having clear strategic priorities and regular communication, I discovered that different teams had different interpretations of our direction. Everyone was working hard, but we weren't working together.

The breakthrough came when I realized that alignment isn't about getting everyone to think the same way (and in fact they will never all think the same way as their jobs and responsibilities naturally lead them to different perspectives). Alignment occurs when everyone feels heard, understood, and valued in service of shared outcomes, shared purpose. This requires what I call Empathic Alignment: using emotional intelligence to build genuine understanding and trust among stakeholders, while leveraging AI to surface hidden disconnects and opportunities for unity. Does it sound similar to CARE? Yes, it is, but at a more organisational level instead of an individual or group of individuals level. And instead of being what you use the design the transformation, this is what you do to scale the behavioural learnings from the transformation and make it long-lasting.

The Architecture of Empathic Alignment

True people alignment operates on three interconnected levels:

1. Emotional Alignment: Building Trust and Understanding

At its foundation, alignment is an emotional process. People align with initiatives they feel connected to and leaders they trust. This requires systematic emotional intelligence applied at scale.

Before any strategic alignment initiative, successful leaders map the emotional landscape of their stakeholders; this is, in effect, emotion mapping. It involves understanding not just what people think, but what they feel, fear, and hope for.

Netflix provides a powerful example. When the company announced its transition from DVD-by-mail to streaming in 2011, the initial stakeholder reaction was overwhelmingly negative. Stock prices plummeted 77%, and customer cancellations spiked. The traditional approach might have been to push forward with data and rational arguments.

Instead, CEO Reed Hastings embarked on what Netflix internally called "The Listening Tour." Over six months, Hastings and his leadership team conducted hundreds of one-on-one conversations with employees, customers, investors, and partners. They weren't trying to convince; they were trying to understand the emotional reality behind the resistance.

The insights were revealing. Employees weren't just concerned about technology - they feared losing their identity as a company. Long-time customers weren't just worried about convenience - they felt abandoned by a brand they'd grown to love. Investors weren't just focused on financials - they questioned whether leadership truly understood the market.

Armed with these emotional insights, Netflix redesigned its alignment strategy. Instead of leading with technology capabilities, they led with shared values: "We love entertainment, and we want to bring joy to families everywhere." Instead of defending their timeline, they acknowledged the emotional difficulty of the transition: "This is hard for all of us, and we're going to figure it out together."

The result was remarkable. Within 18 months, Netflix had not only retained the overwhelming majority of its subscriber base but had grown by double-digits. More importantly, they had created a culture of emotional transparency that would serve them through multiple future transformations.

2. Cognitive Alignment: Creating Shared Understanding

Emotional alignment creates the foundation, but cognitive alignment ensures everyone understands the same reality. This is where AI becomes invaluable - helping leaders identify and bridge gaps in understanding that might not be visible to human intelligence alone.

AI can analyse communication patterns, meeting transcripts, and feedback data to identify if and when different stakeholders are operating from fundamentally different assumptions or information sets. The result is an integrated view of the different perspectives.

Unilever faced this challenge when launching its Sustainable Living Plan across 190 countries. Initial implementation attempts failed because teams in different regions had vastly different understandings of what "sustainability" meant practically. European teams focused on carbon reduction; Asian teams prioritized water conservation; African teams emphasized community economic development.

Rather than imposing a single definition, Unilever used AI-powered sentiment analysis and natural language processing to analyse thousands of hours of regional team discussions. The AI identified common themes and values across all regions, while human intelligence interpreted the cultural and contextual differences.

The breakthrough insight was that every region shared three common concerns: "Will this help our customers live better lives? Will this strengthen our communities? Will this create economic opportunity?" These became the universal alignment criteria, while allowing regional flexibility in implementation approaches.

The cognitive alignment process at Unilever involved three phases:

Phase 1: Understanding Mapping

- AI analysis of communication patterns to identify assumption gaps
- Human intelligence interpretation of cultural and contextual factors
- Stakeholder interviews to validate AI insights

Phase 2: Shared Framework Development

- Collaborative sessions to build common understanding
- AI-powered scenario modelling to test shared frameworks
- Iterative refinement based on stakeholder feedback

Phase 3: Implementation Alignment

- Role-specific implementation guides based on shared framework
- AI monitoring of early implementation for alignment drift
- Human intelligence coaching for teams struggling with alignment

The results were transformative: 89% of regional teams reported feeling "clearly aligned" with the Sustainable Living Plan, compared to 34% in the initial launch attempt.

3. Operational Alignment: Coordinating Action

The highest level of alignment occurs when emotional trust and cognitive understanding translate into coordinated action, i.e., that both your heart and mind feel in agreement with the decision to act and how to act. This requires systems that help people make consistent decisions even when leadership isn't present, a sort of decision integration model.

A decision integration model combines AI-powered decision support with human wisdom about stakeholder dynamics and cultural factors.

Microsoft's transformation under Satya Nadella provides a masterclass in operational alignment. When Nadella became CEO in 2014, Microsoft's different divisions operated almost like separate companies - Windows, Office, Azure, and Xbox teams had different strategies, success metrics, and even cultural values.

The alignment challenge wasn't just strategic; it was operational. Sales teams didn't know whether to lead with cloud solutions or traditional software. Engineers weren't sure whether to prioritize innovation or reliability. Customer support couldn't provide consistent guidance across Microsoft's expanding product portfolio.

Nadella's solution was what he called "One Microsoft Intelligence" - a combination of shared decision frameworks enhanced by AI-powered stakeholder analytics. The system worked on three levels:

Strategic Alignment: Every major decision was evaluated through three questions: "Does this empower our customers? Does this create a partner opportunity? Does this build our platform advantage?" AI analytics provided data on how different decisions would impact various stakeholder groups.

Cultural Alignment: Microsoft developed "empathy dashboards" that used AI to analyse employee sentiment, customer feedback, and partner concerns in real-time. Human intelligence interpreted this data to identify emerging alignment challenges before they became visible problems.

Operational Alignment: Teams received AI-powered "stakeholder impact" analysis for major decisions, showing how their choices would affect other teams, customers, and partners. Human coaches helped teams interpret and act on these insights.

The transformation was remarkable. Cross-division collaboration projects surged, customer satisfaction scores improved by double-digits, employee satisfaction by 23%, and Microsoft's market value grew from $300 billion to over $2 trillion during Nadella's tenure.

The Five Principles for Achieving Stakeholder UNITY

Bringing to life these components underpinning Empathic Alignment requires a systematic and practical approach built on five core principles that create stakeholder **UNITY**:

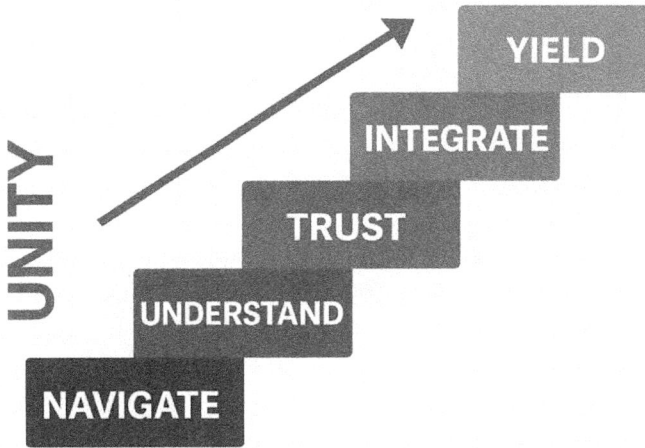

Fig. 5. The UNITY Staircase.

U - Understand the Emotional Landscape

Before attempting any alignment initiative, map the emotional reality of your stakeholders:

Stakeholder Emotion Mapping Process:

1. **Identify Primary Stakeholder Groups**: Not just formal roles, but emotional constituencies (sceptics, champions, fence-sitters)

2. **Map Emotional Drivers**: What do they hope for, fear, value, and need to feel successful?

3. **Surface Hidden Concerns**: Use both AI sentiment analysis and human intelligence conversations to uncover unspoken worries

4. **Identify Emotional Bridges**: Find shared values and concerns that can serve as alignment foundations

You can also use AI tools to help you with sentiment analysis of communications, predictive modelling of stakeholder reactions, and pattern recognition in feedback data.

Use human wisdom for cultural interpretation of AI insights, reading between the lines in conversations, understanding historical context, and relationship dynamics.

N - Navigate Different Perspectives

Alignment doesn't mean uniformity - it means coordinated diversity where different viewpoints strengthen rather than weaken collective action.

The Perspective Integration Process:

1. **Create Safe Spaces for Dissent**: Establish forums where stakeholders can express disagreement without fear

2. **Map Assumption Differences**: Use AI to identify where stakeholders are operating from different data or beliefs

3. **Find Common Ground**: Focus on shared outcomes even when approaches differ

4. **Design Flexible Implementation**: Allow for different paths to the same destination

Case Example: When Shopify expanded internationally, different regional teams had vastly different approaches to merchant onboarding. Rather than imposing one model, they used AI to analyse which elements were essential for success across all regions (trust-building, clear communication, responsive support) and which could vary by culture (communication style, relationship-building approach, decision-making processes).

I - Integrate Insights into Action

Transform understanding into coordinated behaviour through systems that help stakeholders make aligned decisions independently.

The Decision Integration Framework:

1. **Shared Decision Criteria**: Develop clear, emotionally resonant criteria that all stakeholders can apply

2. **AI-Powered Decision Support**: Provide real-time analysis of how decisions impact different stakeholder groups

3. **Human Wisdom Coaching**: Train leaders to interpret AI insights through stakeholder relationship dynamics

4. **Feedback Loops**: Create systems for rapid learning and course correction

T - Trust Through Transparency

Alignment requires ongoing trust-building through transparent communication about both successes and challenges.

The Transparency Protocol:

1. **Regular Alignment Check-ins**: Monthly stakeholder pulse surveys enhanced by AI analysis

2. **Open Challenge Sharing**: Acknowledge alignment difficulties and invite collaborative problem-solving

3. **Success Story Amplification**: Celebrate examples of effective alignment to reinforce positive patterns

4. **Course Correction Communication**: When alignment strategies need adjustment, explain the why and how

Y - Yield to Collective Wisdom

The strongest alignment comes when stakeholders feel their insights and concerns genuinely influence outcomes.

The Collaborative Intelligence Process:

1. **Stakeholder Advisory Systems**: Formal mechanisms for ongoing stakeholder input on strategic decisions

2. **AI-Enhanced Feedback Integration**: Use AI to identify patterns in stakeholder feedback that human intelligence might miss

3. **Shared Success Metrics**: Develop measures of success that reflect all stakeholder groups' core concerns

4. **Evolutionary Alignment**: Build systems that help alignment evolve as stakeholder needs and contexts change

Try this: Think of a recent transformation effort in your organisation that could have benefited from the UNITY approach? To what extent do you think it would have improved the outcome?

Case Study: Adobe's Creative Cloud Transformation

In 2012, Adobe's leadership team faced a revolt. Their bold vision for Creative Cloud was met with fury from their most loyal stakeholders: the creative professionals who had built careers on their software. The initial pitch was all about rational benefits - cost-effectiveness, continuous updates. But the response was pure emotion.

In a heated town hall, a veteran designer might have stood up and said, "You don't get it. I didn't 'rent' Photoshop. I felt like I owned it. It was my tool, my craft. Now you're turning me into a subscriber and taking away my control.". This wasn't a business objection; it was an identity crisis.

Instead of doubling down on data, CEO Shantanu Narayen launched the "Deep Listen Project". This was the start of their UNITY journey. They used AI to analyse thousands of comments, but they paired it with human-led "Creative Advisory Councils". By understanding the emotional landscape first, they navigated the different perspectives and discovered a crucial insight: their customers' greatest fear was losing creative freedom. This allowed them to reframe their entire strategy around empowerment, not just technology.

Understanding the Emotional Landscape

Adobe's initial approach focused on rational arguments - cost-effectiveness, feature updates, and cloud storage benefits. When adoption remained low and criticism mounted, CEO Shantanu Narayen initiated what Adobe called "The Deep Listen Project."

Using AI-powered sentiment analysis of social media, support tickets, and forum discussions, Adobe identified five primary emotional concerns:

1. **Control Anxiety**: Customers feared losing ownership of their tools

2. **Financial Uncertainty**: Worries about long-term cost implications

3. **Reliability Concerns**: Doubts about internet-dependent software

4. **Identity Threat**: Professional creatives feeling their expertise was being devalued

5. **Change Fatigue**: Exhaustion from constant technology evolution

Human intelligence research through focus groups and one-on-one interviews revealed deeper emotional drivers. Professional creatives didn't just use Adobe tools - they defined their professional identity through mastery of these tools. The subscription model felt like a threat to their creative autonomy.

Navigating Different Perspectives

Rather than fighting the resistance, Adobe embraced it as valuable feedback. They created "Creative Advisory Councils" in 12 major markets, combining professional designers, photographers, video editors, and students. These councils met monthly with Adobe leadership to share perspectives on the Creative Cloud transition.

AI analysis of these sessions revealed that different creative disciplines had different primary concerns:

- **Graphic Designers**: Focused on collaboration and file sharing

- **Photographers**: Prioritized image processing power and storage

- **Video Editors**: Needed rendering performance and project management

- **Students**: Required affordability and learning resources

Instead of one uniform Creative Cloud message, Adobe developed role-specific value propositions while maintaining a consistent emotional theme: "We're empowering your creativity, not controlling it."

Integrating Insights into Action

Adobe redesigned its alignment strategy around three emotionally resonant principles:

1. **Creative Freedom**: Position Creative Cloud as expanding rather than limiting creative possibilities

2. **Professional Growth**: Frame subscription model as investment in evolving creative capabilities

3. **Community Connection**: Emphasize how cloud features enable creative collaboration and learning

They used AI to personalize the transition experience based on user behaviour and stated concerns. Heavy Photoshop users received migration tools and tutorials. Collaboration-focused users got team feature previews. Cost-conscious users received detailed ROI calculators and flexible payment options.

Trust Through Transparency

Adobe implemented monthly "Transition Transparency Reports" that honestly addressed challenges alongside successes. When server outages affected users, Adobe proactively communicated not just technical fixes but emotional acknowledgment: "We know creative deadlines don't wait for technical problems, and we're investing $50 million in infrastructure improvements."

They also created "Feature Request Democracy" where users could vote on development priorities, with AI analysing voting patterns to ensure diverse creative disciplines felt heard.

Yielding to Collective Wisdom

The breakthrough moment came when Adobe's stakeholder feedback revealed an unexpected insight: many creative professionals wanted subscription benefits (latest features, cloud storage, collaboration tools) but needed the security of perpetual licenses for mission-critical work.

Adobe's response was Creative Cloud "Hybrid Plans" which combined cloud benefits with perpetual license options for core applications. This wasn't in their original roadmap, but stakeholder wisdom revealed a solution that served everyone's needs.

Results

The empathic alignment approach transformed Adobe's Creative Cloud adoption:

- **Customer Satisfaction**: Increased very significantly over 18 months

- **Employee Engagement**: Cross-functional collaboration scores improved by double digits

- **Revenue Growth**: Subscription revenue grew from $0 to $12.8 billion annually

- **Market Expansion**: Creative Cloud attracted 2.3 million new users who had never used Adobe products

- **Stakeholder Trust**: Net Promoter Score increased dramatically from deeply negative to deeply positive

Most importantly, Adobe created alignment that extended beyond their immediate stakeholders. The creative community began advocating for Creative Cloud, seeing Adobe as a partner in their professional growth rather than a vendor extracting subscription fees.

The AI-First Alignment Mindset

Modern stakeholder alignment can be made most effective and efficient with what I call an "AI-Native Empathy Approach" - building emotional intelligence capabilities from the ground up, with AI as an integral component rather than a bolt-on addition. This mindset shift transforms how leaders approach every aspect of stakeholder alignment.

The UNITY framework we just saw is how you operationalize the AI-native empathic mindset.

Having an AI-native approach entails adopting a new philosophy of alignment - one that begins with empathy, incorporates AI insight, and evolves through collaboration. UNITY translates that philosophy into action. Each step of the UNITY staircase is designed to combine human emotional intelligence with AI-powered insight:

- Understand the Emotional Landscape uses AI for wide sentiment sensing, and human EQ for depth and interpretation.

- Navigate Perspectives blends AI analysis of assumptions with inclusive, human-led dialogue.

- Integrate Insights puts AI and human wisdom side-by-side in decision-making.

- Trust Through Transparency ensures emotional signals from AI aren't just observed, but acknowledged and acted upon.

- Yield to Collective Wisdom turns AI pattern recognition into sustainable systems for co-creation and shared ownership.

You've already seen how the UNITY staircase creates empathic alignment. When viewed through an AI-native lens, each step becomes a platform where human and machine intelligence reinforce each other. UNITY is not just a framework - it's the operational scaffolding of the AI-native empathy approach.

In short, UNITY is the staircase that brings AI-native empathy from concept to capability - step by step.

Traditional Alignment vs. AI-Native Empathic Alignment

Traditional Approach:

- Communicate strategy, then address resistance

- Use data and mainly rationale-based arguments to convince sceptics

- Implement change, then manage stakeholder reactions

- Measure success through compliance metrics

AI-Native Empathic Approach:

- Map emotional landscape before strategic communication

- Use AI insights to design empathy-first stakeholder experiences

- Co-create change with stakeholder input and AI-powered feedback loops

- Measure success through stakeholder flourishing and collective intelligence growth

Your 26-Week Plan to Implement UNITY with an AI-Native Approach

Phase 0. Your Stakeholder Alignment Assessment

Before implementing the UNITY framework, assess your current alignment capabilities across five dimensions. This is q crucial step because it will provide essential information to build your phase 1, 2 3 of this 26-week plan:

- Foundation for Planning: The assessment results scoring determines how you approach Phase 1. A low-scoring organisation needs different infrastructure than a high-scoring one.

- Baseline Measurement: You need this baseline to measure progress throughout the 26 weeks and at the end.

- Resource Allocation: The assessment results help you allocate time and resources appropriately across the three phases.

Here is the assessment:

Emotional Intelligence Readiness (5 questions, 1-5 scale where 1 is Rarely/Low and 5 is Very frequently/Very high)

1. **Stakeholder Emotion Awareness**: How well do you understand the emotional drivers and concerns of your key stakeholder groups?

2. **Empathy Systems**: Do you have systematic ways to gather and interpret stakeholder emotional feedback?

3. **Trust Building Processes**: How effectively do you build and maintain trust across diverse stakeholder groups?

4. **Conflict Navigation**: How well do you navigate disagreement and resistance with empathy and understanding?

5. **Emotional Transparency**: How comfortable are you sharing challenges and uncertainties with stakeholders?

AI-Enhanced Insights (5 questions, 1-5 scale each)

6. **Stakeholder Analytics**: Do you use AI tools to monitor stakeholder sentiment and engagement across multiple channels?

7. **Pattern Recognition**: Can you identify stakeholder alignment trends and predict potential disconnects before they become problems?

8. **Personalization Capability**: How well do you tailor stakeholder communication and experiences based on AI-powered insights?

9. **Decision Impact Analysis**: Do you have systems that show how decisions will affect different stakeholder groups?

10. **Feedback Integration**: How effectively do you use AI to synthesize stakeholder feedback into actionable insights?

Collaborative Problem-Solving (5 questions, 1-5 scale each)

11. **Inclusive Decision-Making**: How well do you involve stakeholders in shaping solutions rather than just implementing predetermined plans?

12. **Perspective Integration**: Can you effectively synthesize different stakeholder viewpoints into stronger collective solutions?

13. **Shared Success Metrics**: Do you have alignment measures that reflect all stakeholder groups' core concerns?

14. **Collaborative Learning Systems**: How well do you create opportunities for stakeholders to learn from each other?

15. **Collective Intelligence Development**: Are you building your organisation's capacity for stakeholder wisdom, not just stakeholder management?

Scoring Guide:

- **60-75**: Ready for advanced AI-native alignment initiatives
- **45-59**: Strengthen foundation capabilities before scaling
- **30-44**: Focus on basic stakeholder relationship and AI literacy development
- **Below 30**: Begin with fundamental empathy and stakeholder awareness building

Pause and Reflect: If you were to run through these questions for your organisation or community, what do you think is your score, and where are the key strengths (high-scoring areas) vs key weaknesses?

Once you have completed and analysed the assessment, you can proceed with phase 1, 2, 3.

Phase 1: Foundation Infrastructure (Weeks 1-6)

In phase 1, there are four main activities:

- **Stakeholder Intelligence Systems**: Set up AI-powered listening across all stakeholder touchpoints - not just formal feedback, but social media mentions, support interactions, meeting transcripts, and informal communications. The key is combining breadth (AI can monitor thousands of conversations) with depth (human intelligence can interpret emotional subtext).
- **Empathy Enhancement Tools**: Implement sentiment analysis, emotional tone detection, and stakeholder journey mapping. But remember: AI provides the signals; human intelligence provides the meaning. Train your team to interpret AI insights through empathic lenses.

- **Decision Support Architecture**: Create systems that show stakeholder impact analysis for every significant decision. When proposing a new initiative, leaders should immediately see predictive models of how different stakeholder groups are likely to respond emotionally and practically.
- **Alignment Workshop**: Orchestrate a structured one-day intensive session that combines AI-powered stakeholder insights with human-centred dialogue to create genuine understanding and shared purpose among diverse stakeholder groups. Rather than imposing alignment from above, the workshop facilitates collaborative problem-solving where stakeholders co-create alignment approaches based on their shared emotional drivers and complementary expertise, building trust and commitment that sustains long-term unity.

Your Stakeholder Alignment Assessment results determine your Phase 1 focus:

Score 60-75 (Advanced Ready): Focus on sophisticated AI integration and cross-functional alignment systems. You can implement comprehensive stakeholder intelligence platforms immediately and move quickly to predictive analytics and personalized stakeholder experiences.

Score 45-59 (Foundation Strengthening): Begin with basic AI listening tools while simultaneously investing in relationship-building infrastructure. Prioritize simple sentiment tracking and stakeholder feedback systems, then gradually add complexity as your team's confidence grows.

Score 30-44 (Basic Development Focus): Start with manual stakeholder mapping and simple survey tools before introducing AI components. Spend extra time in weeks 1-3 building fundamental empathy skills and stakeholder relationship processes, then introduce basic AI insights in weeks 4-6.

Score Below 30 (Fundamental Building): Dedicate the full 6 weeks to human relationship foundations with minimal AI integration. Focus on establishing regular stakeholder communication rhythms, basic feedback collection, and trust-building processes. Plan to extend Phase 1 by 2-4 weeks if needed before moving to AI-enhanced capabilities.

Regardless of your starting score, all organisations should complete the stakeholder workshop in weeks 4-5, adapting the AI components to match your current capabilities while building toward more sophisticated integration in later phases.

Your Alignment Workshop

The most effective way to implement empathic alignment is through structured stakeholder workshops that combine human connection with AI-enhanced insights. Here's a proven framework:

- **Pre-Workshop Intelligence Gathering (2 weeks before)**
    1. **AI-Powered Stakeholder Analysis:**
        - Sentiment analysis of recent stakeholder communications
        - Pattern recognition in feedback, concerns, and engagement data
        - Predictive modelling of stakeholder responses to potential alignment topics
        - Identification of hidden connections and shared concerns across stakeholder groups
    2. **Human Intelligence Preparation**
        - One-on-one conversations with key stakeholders to understand the emotional context behind AI insights
        - Cultural and relationship dynamic analysis that AI might miss

- o Historical context research about previous alignment successes and challenges
- **Workshop Structure (1-day intensive to be delivered in week 4-5 of phase 1)**
    1. **Opening: Emotional Connection (90 minutes)**
        - o Begin with personal storytelling: each stakeholder shares what success means to them personally
        - o Use AI-generated insights to highlight unexpected commonalities in stakeholder hopes and concerns
        - o Create psychological safety through vulnerability modelling from leadership
    2. **Core Session: Perspective Integration (3 hours)**
        - o Present AI analysis of stakeholder landscape (anonymous insights, not individual data)
        - o Facilitate small group discussions where stakeholders explore different viewpoints
        - o Use human intelligence to guide conversations toward empathy and understanding
        - o Identify shared values and complementary concerns that can become alignment foundations
    3. **Solution Co-Creation (2 hours)**
        - o Collaborative problem-solving sessions where stakeholders design alignment approaches together
        - o AI-powered scenario planning: show how different alignment strategies might play out

- Human wisdom application: help stakeholders consider emotional and relationship factors that AI can't model

4. **Commitment and Next Steps (90 minutes)**

   - Stakeholder-designed success metrics that reflect everyone's core concerns
   - Clear roles and responsibilities for maintaining alignment
   - Scheduled follow-up processes combining AI monitoring with human check-ins

- **Post-Workshop Integration (ongoing, to be carried out throughout phases 2 and 3)**
  - **First 30 Days**: Weekly AI-powered alignment pulse checks combined with human intelligence interpretation and stakeholder coaching as needed.
  - **First 90 Days**: Monthly stakeholder alignment reviews using both quantitative AI metrics and qualitative human relationship assessment.
  - **Ongoing**: Quarterly alignment evolution sessions where stakeholders use both AI insights and collaborative wisdom to refine and strengthen alignment approaches.

Phase 2: Skill Development (Weeks 7-18)

In phase 2, there are 3 key activities:

- **AI-Enhanced Empathy Training**: Develop your team's ability to use AI insights to deepen rather than replace human connection. This includes interpreting sentiment data, identifying emotional patterns, and translating AI insights into empathic responses.
- **Stakeholder Scenario Planning**: Use AI to model different alignment strategies and their likely stakeholder impacts. Practice

responding to AI-predicted scenarios with human intelligence and emotional wisdom.

- **Collaborative Intelligence Development**: Train leaders to facilitate alignment conversations where AI insights inform but don't dominate the human connection and collaborative problem-solving process.

Organisations with scores of 60-75 in the Stakeholder Alignment Assessment can focus on advanced collaborative intelligence and complex stakeholder scenario planning, while those scoring below 45 should dedicate extra time to foundational empathy skills and basic AI interpretation before progressing to sophisticated alignment techniques.

Phase 3: Integration and Scaling (Weeks 19-26)

Phase 3 is where you truly embed regular injection of energy into the stakeholder alignment:

- **Organisational Alignment Rhythms**: Establish regular stakeholder alignment practices that combine AI monitoring with human connection. Monthly stakeholder pulse checks, quarterly alignment workshops, and annual stakeholder visioning sessions.
- **Cross-Functional Alignment Teams**: Create dedicated groups responsible for monitoring and nurturing stakeholder alignment across different organisational boundaries. These teams combine AI analysts with relationship managers and cultural interpreters.
- **Continuous Alignment Evolution**: Build systems that help alignment strategies evolve as stakeholder needs and contexts change. This requires both AI pattern recognition and human wisdom about relationship dynamics.

High-scoring organisations (60-75) can immediately implement sophisticated cross-functional alignment teams and automated stakeholder evolution systems, while lower-scoring organisations should focus on establishing basic alignment rhythms and simple monitoring processes before scaling to more complex organisational-wide integration.

The Ripple Effect of Empathic Alignment

When stakeholder alignment is built on emotional intelligence and enhanced with AI insights, the impact extends far beyond immediate project success. Organisations develop what I call "Alignment DNA" - the capability to create unity and coordinated action even in challenging circumstances.

At the European bank I was helping, this became visible during our digital transformation initiative. Initially, we faced typical stakeholder challenges: technology teams focused on innovation, operations teams prioritized stability, customer service emphasized usability, and compliance worried about risk management. Each group had valid concerns, but their competing priorities threatened to derail our progress.

Using the UNITY framework, we discovered that every stakeholder group shared a deeper emotional driver: pride in serving customers exceptionally well. Technology teams wanted to build innovative solutions that would delight customers. Operations teams wanted reliable systems that never let customers down. Customer service wanted tools that helped them solve problems quickly. Compliance wanted to protect customers from any potential harm.

This emotional common ground became our alignment foundation. Alignment on feeling and purpose is something that pure rationality assumed in the Rationality Mirage can neither understand nor create, making it a powerful source of competitive advantage.

Instead of debating technical specifications or process requirements, we started every conversation with customer impact. We then assessed how different technical approaches would affect customer experience, and human wisdom helped us interpret those insights through the lens of our service culture.

Preparing for Radiate and Engage

Empathic alignment creates the foundation for the final two elements of the SHARE framework. When stakeholders feel genuinely heard, understood, and valued, they become natural ambassadors for extending your organisation's impact beyond traditional boundaries (Radiate). When stakeholder relationships are built on emotional intelligence and mutual growth, they create sustainable systems for continuous collaborative learning (Engage).

The alignment you build today determines the reach and sustainability of the impact you'll create tomorrow. Stakeholders who feel aligned through empathy and enhanced by AI insights don't just implement your initiatives - they become co-creators of your organisation's evolving intelligence and expanding influence.

As we move into the final chapters of our SHARE journey, remember that alignment isn't a destination - it's a dynamic capability that grows stronger through practice and deeper through authentic relationship. The AI tools provide the insights; the human intelligence provides the meaning; but the alignment itself emerges from the space between technology and humanity, where trust, understanding, and shared purpose flourish.

Your stakeholders are waiting not just for your next initiative, but for the invitation to co-create something meaningful together. The question isn't whether you can align them around your vision - it's whether you can align yourself around the collective wisdom that emerges when empathy meets intelligence, when human hearts connect with technological insights, and when individual expertise serves collective flourishing.

The stage is set for a transformation that extends far beyond organisational boundaries. Your stakeholder alignment capabilities will determine how far and how sustainably that transformation can reach.

Your Chapter Challenge: select one alignment challenge in your organisation and design a workshop using the UNITY approach.

The goal is building your capability to create unity through emotional intelligence, enhanced by AI insights, and sustained through genuine stakeholder partnership.

Your alignment capabilities today determine your impact possibilities tomorrow.

Chapter 12 Takeaways & Reflection

You can't align a team by repeating the strategy louder. Alignment starts when people feel heard - emotionally, not just operationally.

◇ **Key Takeaways**

- **Alignment is emotional before it's operational:** People align with initiatives they feel connected to, leaders they trust. Data convinces minds; empathy moves hearts and creates unity.
- **The UNITY framework builds empathic alignment:** Understand the emotional landscape, Navigate different perspectives, Integrate insights into action, Trust through transparency, Yield to collective wisdom
- **AI-native empathy transforms stakeholder relationships:** Combine AI's pattern recognition with human emotional intelligence to map sentiment, predict concerns, and design experiences that make every stakeholder feel genuinely heard.
- **Alignment isn't uniformity - it's coordinated diversity:** Different viewpoints strengthen collective action when stakeholders feel valued for their perspectives while working toward shared goals.
- **Stakeholder workshops create collaborative alignment:** One-day intensive sessions that blend AI insights with human connection turn competing priorities into complementary strengths through co-creation.
- **Assessment-driven implementation prevents alignment failures:** Your current empathy and AI capabilities determine whether you need foundational relationship building or can immediately scale stakeholder intelligence systems.

◇ **Reflection Prompts**

- *What emotional concerns are your stakeholders carrying that you haven't fully acknowledged?*
- *Where could AI help you hear unheard stakeholder voices?*
- *Which stakeholder relationships would transform if built on empathy rather than compliance?*
- *What would change if your stakeholders felt like co-creators rather than implementers?*

Chapter 13: Radiate And Engage - Amplifying And Sustaining Collaboration (SHARE: R&E)

A leader's true power isn't in what they can do alone, but in what they inspire others to do together.

Six months into our transformation at Aegon NL, I found myself in our Leeuwarden office, facing circa 200 mortgage specialists who had become the unexpected heroes of our organisational change. These were the people who had embraced our new way of doing things at Aegon NL most enthusiastically; they had improved processing times by double digits, customer satisfaction as well, they had become significantly more efficient, and they were pioneering new technology to overcome their legacy IT issues. But that day, their faces reflected a different emotion entirely: uncertainty about their future under ASR's pending acquisition.

"Before we celebrate these wins," I began, looking directly at one of our key business leaders, M., who had led and pioneered our most innovative technology-human collaboration initiatives across the whole of Aegon NL, "I need to tell you about our failures - and what they teach us about our future."

The room went quiet. Everyone knew ASR already had a mortgage operation in Utrecht and other parts of the Netherlands. Everyone wondered if Leeuwarden would survive the integration.

"As you know, we have attempted to upgrade our legacy IT solutions in the mortgage business a few times, and we failed every time, for different reasons. We still don't have a perfect solution, and I am, we in the leadership team, are very sorry about that". A feeling of resigned acceptance floated through the room, but also a feeling of sympathy towards two leaders who were visibly taking accountability. "But," I continued, "despite that, what you have done is simply extraordinary: you have worked around those constraints to devise new processes and better products to enhance the performance of our mortgage business. Intermediaries are happier, customers are happier, employees feel deeply engaged, and financials are better. We feel proud, we feel great momentum. But, of course, we are contending with the real possibility, in a few months, to become part of the ASR group, and we are worried."

I paused, feeling the weight of their anxiety and the importance of this moment.

"Here's what should give us optimism. When we shared these failures transparently and engaged you in solving them, we didn't just fix problems - we built something truly special. Your expertise, combined with honest communication and sustained collaboration, has created capabilities that will define the future of both organisations, Aegon and ASR. And so I urge us to continue doing so, not to succumb to fear and worry, which we all share, but to continue working together to bring into ASR the best version of ourselves, the best version of this business. Because that is what will secure the best future for us, both collectively and individually." This notion of bringing into the company that is acquiring you the best version of yourself, instead of giving into fear and anxiety, is something that deeply resonated and inspired people to do their best. To the point that even one of the leaders of ASR commended us about it.

This is the power of the final two elements of the SHARE framework: Radiate and Engage. These aren't separate phases - they're interwoven practices that transform individual successes into organisational DNA and temporary initiatives into lasting transformation.

The Challenge of Sustained Impact

Most organisational transformations follow a predictable pattern: initial excitement, early wins, gradual momentum loss, and eventual regression to old patterns. Research shows that 70% of change initiatives fail not because of poor strategy or inadequate resources, but because organisations struggle to radiate success authentically and engage stakeholders sustainably.

The challenge becomes even more complex with AI initiatives. Success often happens in technical silos, benefits remain invisible to broader stakeholders, and the human stories behind the data get lost in dashboards and metrics. Without intentional efforts to radiate impact and engage people emotionally, even the most successful AI implementations become isolated victories rather than organisational capabilities.

This is where Human Intelligence becomes irreplaceable. While AI can track metrics and optimize processes, only human leaders can translate technical success into organisational meaning, build emotional connections to change, and create the cultural conditions for sustained collaboration.

Radiate: The Art of Transparent Amplification

Radiate means sharing outcomes, insights, and learning in ways that build trust, inspire action, and create organisational intelligence. It's not about corporate communications or public relations - it's about authentic transparency that honours both successes and failures while creating a shared understanding of what's possible. As a leader, this is where you take accountability for the mistakes, gratify the teams with the successes, and put things into a perspective that resonates with them.

The Three Dimensions of Radiate

1. Authentic Transparency True transparency means sharing the full story - successes, failures, and everything in between. It requires leaders to model vulnerability while maintaining confidence, showing that learning from failure is a strength, not a weakness.

2. Meaningful Translation Technical achievements must be translated into human impact. This means moving beyond metrics to stories, showing how improvements affect real people's lives, and connecting individual contributions to larger purposes.

3. Strategic Amplification Effective radiating creates momentum for future change by demonstrating what's possible, building credibility for next phases, and inspiring others to contribute their own innovations.

Pause and Reflect: What would change in your organisation if leadership shared failures as transparently as successes?

Case Study: Starbucks' "Partner Spotlight" Transformation

When Starbucks implemented its Deep Brew AI platform across 30,000 stores, it faced a critical challenge: How do you help 400,000+ partners (employees) understand and embrace AI-driven changes to everything from inventory management to personalized customer experiences?

Kevin Johnson, then-CEO, made a crucial decision: rather than communicating through traditional corporate channels, they would radiate success through their partners' (i.e., baristas') own voices.

The Challenge: Initial AI rollouts showed strong operational metrics - 15% reduction in waste, 23% improvement in customer wait times, and 18% increase in personalized recommendations. But partner surveys revealed confusion and concern. Many baristas felt disconnected from these improvements, worried about job security, and sceptical about AI's role in the Starbucks experience.

The Radiate Strategy: Starbucks created the "Partner Spotlight" system - a combination of AI-powered story aggregation and human-centred storytelling:

- Digital Story Walls: AI analysed thousands of partner feedback submissions to identify the most compelling human stories behind operational improvements

- Monthly Partner Town Halls: Regional managers shared specific examples of how AI helped partners serve customers better, with real names and locations

- "Behind the Numbers" Sessions: Leadership transparently shared both successes and failures, including a major AI recommendation error that initially suggested wrong inventory levels for 340 stores

The Human Intelligence Factor: What made this successful wasn't the technology - it was how leadership used emotional intelligence to interpret what partners really needed. They realized that partners didn't just want to understand AI; they wanted to see their own expertise valued and amplified by it.

Results:

- Partner engagement scores increased significantly

- Voluntary participation in AI training programs jumped from marginal to almost unanimous

- Customer satisfaction improved by double digits (partners felt confident explaining and personalizing the AI-enhanced experience)

- Most significantly: Partners began suggesting AI improvements, with hundreds of partner-generated ideas implemented in the first year

The Transformation: By radiating authentically, Starbucks transformed AI implementation from a top-down technology rollout into a partner-driven culture of innovation.

Case Study: Domino's "Honesty Revolution"

Perhaps no company better demonstrates the power of authentic Radiate than Domino's transformation under CEO Russell Weiner's leadership (building on Patrick Doyle's foundation).

It began with a painful, public truth. In 2010, Domino's was a punchline, with focus groups bluntly calling their pizza "cardboard". In a pivotal leadership meeting, then-CEO Patrick Doyle made a terrifying decision. The conventional wisdom was to rebrand with a slick marketing campaign. Doyle proposed the opposite.

"We have two choices," he likely told his sceptical team. "We can pretend these complaints aren't real, or we can look our customers in the eye and tell them, 'You're right. We messed up. And we're going to fix it.'"

This was the birth of their "Honesty Revolution." It was an act of corporate vulnerability that felt like a massive risk, but it was also a profound act of CARE - listening to and validating their customers' experience. It set the stage for a transformation where technology, like the DOM Pizza Checker, would become a tool for keeping their promise, radiating proof of their commitment with every order.

The Transparency Gamble: When Domino's began using AI to improve pizza quality, delivery optimization, and customer experience, they made an unprecedented decision: they would share everything publicly - including their failures - through real-time dashboards, customer communications, and media interviews.

The AI Integration: Their "DOM Pizza Checker" AI system could identify pizza quality issues with 97% accuracy, but early versions missed cultural preferences (New York customers wanted different sauce distribution than Chicago customers) and failed to account for local dietary restrictions.

The Radiate Approach:

- Public Quality Dashboard: Real-time display of quality scores, delivery times, and customer satisfaction by location

- "We Messed Up" Communications: Direct emails to customers when AI systems made errors, with specific explanations and corrective actions

- Employee Recognition System: AI-powered identification of exceptional service, shared through social media and internal communications

- Failure Analysis Sharing: Quarterly reports on what went wrong, what they learned, and how they improved

The Results:

- Customer trust scores increased dramatically, some sources even suggest it tripled, over three years

- Stock price grew from $11 to $400+ during the transformation period

- Employee Net Promoter Score jumped from deeply negative to staggeringly positive

- Most importantly: Competitors began copying their transparency approach, validating the model

The Key Insight: Domino's discovered that radical transparency about AI failures actually increased customer trust because it demonstrated authenticity and commitment to improvement.

Engage: Building Sustained Collaboration Systems

Engage means creating organisational systems that sustain collaboration, recognize contributions, and continuously evolve based on human and AI intelligence. It's about building culture, not just managing projects.

The Principles for Sustaining MOMENTUM

To sustain engagement effectively, we must focus on eight key principles that build **MOMENTUM**, addressing the unique challenges of AI-human collaboration:

M - Motivate Through Meaning: Connect initiatives (and in particular AI initiatives, as they are often the hardest to get accepted currently) to personal and organisational purpose, showing how technical improvements serve human flourishing.

O - Organise for Ongoing Learning: Create systematic opportunities for continuous skill development, feedback integration, and collaborative problem-solving.

M - Measure Human and Technical Success: Track both performance metrics and engagement indicators, using AI to identify patterns while relying on human intelligence for interpretation.

E - Evolve Recognition Systems: Develop AI-supported recognition that identifies contributions across technical and emotional intelligence dimensions.

N - Nurture Cross-Functional Relationships: Build connections between different organisational levels and departments, using AI insights to identify collaboration opportunities.

T - Trust Through Transparent Communication: Maintain open channels for feedback, concern-raising, and shared decision-making about AI implementation.

U - Unify Around Shared Outcomes: Keep focus on collective success rather than individual or departmental wins, using AI to track interdependent progress.

M - Multiply Leadership Capabilities: Develop AI-human collaboration skills across multiple organisational levels, creating resilience and sustainability.

Here are some AI tools you can consider to help you in the MOMENTUM framework application:

- Recognition: tools for collaboration patterns and exceptional contributions (e.g. Glint, Culture Amp)
- Learning: Personalized development paths and skill gap analysis tools (e.g. Degreed, LinkedIn Learning)
- Communication: Real-time sentiment analysis and transparency dashboards (e.g. Tableau, Slack Analytics)
- Measurement: Predictive engagement analytics and early warning systems (e.g. Microsoft Viva, Workday)

Case Study: Microsoft's "Culture Transformation Engine"

Under Satya Nadella's leadership, Microsoft faced the challenge of transforming from a competitive, know-it-all culture to a collaborative, learn-it-all organisation while implementing AI across all products and services.

The Engagement Challenge: With 180,000+ employees across 190 countries, how do you sustain cultural change while deploying AI technologies that fundamentally alter how work gets done?

The MOMENTUM Application:

Motivate Through Meaning: Microsoft connected AI initiatives to their mission of "empowering every person and every organisation on the planet to achieve more." Every AI project included an explicit discussion of human impact.

Organise for Ongoing Learning: They created "AI Learning Cohorts" - cross-functional groups of 12-15 people who met monthly to share AI experiences, challenges, and innovations. By 2023, over 140,000 employees participated in these cohorts.

Measure Human and Technical Success: Their "Culture Pulse" system used AI to analyse employee communications, feedback, and collaboration patterns while conducting quarterly human-centred culture surveys. They tracked both technical AI adoption rates and cultural indicators like psychological safety and cross-team collaboration.

Evolve Recognition Systems: Microsoft developed "Moments of Impact" - an AI-powered system that identified exceptional collaboration examples and shared them across the organisation. Unlike traditional employee-of-the-month programs, this recognized collective achievements and AI-human partnership examples.

The Results:

- Employee satisfaction increased significantly during the AI transformation period

- Internal collaboration metrics (measured through Teams and other platforms) increased 150+%

- AI adoption rates reached 80-90% voluntary participation

- External customer satisfaction with AI-enhanced products improved by double digits

- Revenue grew from $93 billion to $168 billion during the transformation period

The Key Innovation: Microsoft realized that sustaining AI transformation required building what they called "collective empathy" - the organisational ability to sense and respond to human needs while pursuing technical excellence.

Case Study: Unilever's "Living Learning Network"

Unilever's transformation under CEO Alan Jope provides another powerful example of sustained engagement around AI and sustainability initiatives.

The Global Coordination Challenge: With operations in 190 countries, 400+ brands, and 149,000 employees, how do you engage diverse stakeholders around AI-driven sustainability improvements while respecting local cultures and needs?

The Engagement System: Unilever created their "Living Learning Network" - a combination of AI-powered insight sharing and human-centred community building:

AI-Enhanced Insight Sharing: Machine learning systems identified sustainability innovations across different regions and automatically translated and contextualized them for other markets.

Human-Centred Community Building: Monthly virtual "Sustainability Circles" where teams from different regions shared challenges, solutions, and learning, facilitated by trained employee volunteers.

Recognition and Amplification: The "Sustained Living Champions" program used AI to identify employees making exceptional contributions to sustainability goals, then amplified their stories across the global organisation.

Transparent Progress Tracking: Real-time dashboards showing progress on sustainability metrics, with both successes and challenges visible to all employees.

The Sustained Engagement Results:

- Employee engagement with sustainability initiatives increased very strongly

- Cross-regional collaboration on sustainability projects increased manyfold

- AI-identified sustainability innovations were implemented 3x faster

- External stakeholder trust in Unilever's sustainability commitments improved significantly

- Sustained Living brands delivered 75% of total company growth

The Cultural Transformation: Unilever discovered that sustained engagement required what they called "purpose-driven AI" - ensuring that every AI system supported human flourishing and environmental regeneration, not just operational efficiency.

The Integration Challenge: Radiate and Engage Together

The most powerful transformation happens when Radiate and Engage work together as integrated practices. This requires leaders who can:

1. Share authentically while maintaining momentum - Being transparent about failures without undermining confidence in future success

2. Celebrate individual contributions while building collective capability - Recognizing personal achievements while emphasizing interdependent success

3. Use AI insights while honouring human wisdom - Leveraging data while respecting experiential knowledge and cultural intelligence

4. Scale successes while preserving local adaptation - Spreading what works while allowing for contextual modification

Building Your Radiate and Engage Systems

To implement effective Radiate and Engage practices in your organisation, follow this systematic approach:

Phase 1: Assessment (Weeks 1-2)

Radiate Readiness Assessment: Rate your organisation on a scale of 1-5 for each dimension:

Transparency Culture:

- Leaders regularly share both successes and failures (1-5)

- Employees feel safe raising concerns about AI initiatives (1-5)

- Information flows openly across organisational levels (1-5)

- Mistakes are treated as learning opportunities, not blame occasions (1-5)

Communication Effectiveness:

- Technical achievements are translated into human impact stories (1-5)

- Multiple communication channels reach diverse stakeholder groups (1-5)

- Feedback loops allow for two-way communication (1-5)

- Recognition systems highlight both individual and collective contributions (1-5)

Engage Sustainability Assessment:

Motivation Systems:

- AI initiatives connect clearly to organisational purpose (1-5)

- Employees understand how AI improvements benefit their work (1-5)

- Recognition systems acknowledge both technical and emotional intelligence (1-5)

- Career development paths include AI-human collaboration skills (1-5)

Learning Infrastructure:

- Regular opportunities exist for cross-functional AI learning (1-5)

- Failure analysis leads to systematic improvements (1-5)

- Best practices are captured and shared effectively (1-5)

- Innovation comes from multiple organisational levels (1-5)

Scoring Guide:

- 64-80: Ready for advanced Radiate and Engage systems

- 48-63: Build foundational transparency and engagement practices first

- 32-47: Focus on basic communication and recognition systems

- Below 32: Establish psychological safety and basic feedback mechanisms

Phase 2: Design (Weeks 3-6)

Create Your Radiate Strategy:

Authentic Transparency Plan:

- Identify what successes and failures you'll share publicly
- Design formats that balance vulnerability with confidence
- Establish regular communication rhythms (monthly town halls, quarterly deep dives, annual comprehensive reviews)
- Create multiple channels for different stakeholder groups

Translation Framework:

- Develop templates for converting technical metrics into human impact stories
- Train leaders in storytelling that connects AI improvements to personal and organisational meaning
- Create visual dashboards that show both quantitative results and qualitative insights

Build Your Engage Architecture:

Recognition Evolution:

- Design AI-powered systems that identify collaboration and innovation examples
- Create peer-to-peer recognition mechanisms
- Establish leadership recognition of both technical achievements and emotional intelligence contributions
- Build celebration rituals that reinforce collaborative culture

Learning Systems:

- Establish cross-functional AI learning cohorts
- Create systematic failure analysis and improvement processes

- Design innovation challenges that encourage AI-human collaboration
- Build mentorship networks that span technical and cultural expertise

Phase 3: Implementation (Weeks 7-18)

Launch Your Radiate Systems:

Week 7-8: Transparency Infrastructure

- Launch regular leadership communication with authentic sharing
- Establish feedback mechanisms for stakeholder response
- Begin sharing both successes and learning from challenges

Week 9-12: Story Translation

- Train leaders in converting metrics to meaning
- Launch human impact storytelling alongside technical reporting
- Create diverse communication formats for different audiences

Week 13-18: Amplification and Evolution

- Scale successful communication approaches
- Integrate stakeholder feedback into ongoing radiate strategy
- Build sustained rhythms for transparent sharing

Activate Your Engage Practices:

Week 7-10: Recognition Launch

- Implement AI-powered recognition systems

- Train managers in acknowledging both technical and emotional contributions
- Launch peer recognition mechanisms

Week 11-14: Learning Infrastructure

- Start cross-functional AI learning cohorts
- Establish innovation sharing systems
- Create mentorship connections across technical and cultural expertise

Week 15-18: Culture Integration

- Connect recognition and learning to career development
- Integrate collaborative AI practices into performance evaluation
- Build leadership capabilities across multiple organisational levels

Phase 4: Sustained Evolution (Ongoing)

Continuous Radiate Improvement:

- Regularly assess communication effectiveness through stakeholder feedback
- Evolve transparency practices based on organisational maturity
- Adapt storytelling approaches to changing AI capabilities and business context
- Maintain authentic leadership voice while scaling communication systems

Ongoing Engage Enhancement:

- Use AI insights to identify emerging collaboration opportunities

- Evolve recognition systems based on changing work patterns and values

- Adapt learning systems to new AI technologies and organisational needs

- Build increasingly sophisticated cultural intelligence capabilities

The Leadership Transformation: From Manager to Cultural Architect

Implementing Radiate and Engage effectively requires a fundamental shift in leadership identity. You move from managing projects to architecting culture, from controlling information to orchestrating transparency, from motivating individuals to building sustained collaboration systems.

This transformation challenges leaders to:

- **Embrace Vulnerability as Strength:** Sharing failures and uncertainties becomes a source of credibility rather than weakness, building trust through authenticity rather than perfection.
- **Think in Systems, Not Events:** Sustained engagement requires building cultural practices that endure beyond individual initiatives or leadership changes.
- **Balance Individual and Collective Recognition:** Celebrate personal contributions while reinforcing interdependent success and shared achievement.
- **Integrate AI and Human Intelligence:** Use technological capabilities to enhance rather than replace human connection, emotional intelligence, and cultural wisdom.

- **Measure What Matters Most:** Track both performance metrics and engagement indicators, using AI insights while honouring human experience and wisdom.

The Competitive Advantage of Authentic Radiate and Engage

Organisations that master Radiate and Engage develop what I call "Transformation DNA" - the cultural capability to implement, adapt, and evolve AI initiatives more effectively than competitors. This creates sustained competitive advantage because:

- **Trust Accelerates Adoption:** When stakeholders trust leadership communication and feel genuinely engaged, they adopt new AI tools and processes faster and more effectively.
- **Innovation Comes From Everywhere:** Transparent sharing and sustained engagement unlock creative potential across all organisational levels, not just technical teams.
- **Resilience Through Relationship:** Strong cultural foundations help organisations navigate AI implementation challenges, technical failures, and market changes more successfully.
- **Attraction and Retention of Talent:** Authentic, engaging cultures attract people who want to contribute to meaningful AI-human collaboration rather than just technical implementation.
- **Stakeholder Confidence:** External stakeholders - customers, investors, partners - develop greater confidence in organisations that demonstrate authentic transparency and sustained employee engagement.

Completing the SHARE Cycle

Radiate and Engage complete the SHARE framework by ensuring that:

- **Synthesize** (connecting scattered intelligence) leads to insights that get shared transparently

- **Harness** (coordinating collective action) creates results worth celebrating and learning from

- **Align** (uniting stakeholders) builds the trust necessary for authentic transparency

- **Radiate** amplifies success while honoring failures and building credibility for future initiatives

- **Engage** sustains collaboration through recognition, learning, and cultural evolution

Together, these elements create what systems thinkers call a "reinforcing loop" - each practice strengthens the others, building organisational capability that becomes increasingly powerful over time.

Your Leadership Challenge

As you implement Radiate and Engage in your organisation, remember that the goal isn't perfect execution - it's authentic progress. Start with small experiments in transparency and engagement, learn from what works and what doesn't, and gradually build the cultural practices that will sustain AI-human collaboration over years and decades.

The most important question isn't whether you're ready to Radiate and Engage perfectly, but whether you're willing to begin authentically. Your stakeholders don't need you to have all the answers from you; they need you to be honest about the questions, transparent about the journey, and committed to building something meaningful together.

Your Chapter Challenge: Which stories about AI-human collaboration in your organisation deserve to be radiated more widely?

The future belongs to organisations that can combine technological capability with human wisdom, operational excellence with emotional intelligence, and individual achievement with collective success. By mastering Radiate and Engage, you're building the cultural foundation for sustained innovation and human flourishing in an AI-enhanced world.

In our final chapter, we'll explore how the complete CARE, DARE, SHARE framework transforms not just individual organisations, but entire ecosystems of human-AI collaboration. The journey from personal leadership development to cultural transformation to societal impact represents the ultimate expression of emotionally intelligent leadership in the age of artificial intelligence.

Chapter 13 Takeaways & Reflection

Sustainable transformation happens when leaders radiate authentically and engage systematically. Your don't need to be perfect – you need to be real.

◇ **Key Takeaways**

- **Authentic transparency accelerates trust and adoption:** Sharing failures & successes builds credibility. When people see leaders learning from mistakes, they engage with change, not resistance.
- **MOMENTUM sustains AI-human collaboration:** Motivate through meaning, Organise for ongoing learning, Measure human and technical success, Evolve recognition systems, Nurture cross-functional relationships, Trust through transparent communication, Unify around shared outcomes, Multiply leadership capabilities.
- **Radiate means strategic amplification, not corporate PR:** Effective radiating translates technical achievements into human impact stories, demonstrates what's possible for future change, and creates organisational intelligence through meaningful transparency.
- **Engagement systems build culture:** Sustainable collaboration requires recognition for both individual contributions and collective success, learning infrastructure that captures and shares innovation, and leadership development across multiple organisational levels.
- **Storytelling scales authentic connection:** AI can identify most compelling human stories behind successes, but human emotional intelligence translates into org meaning, cultural transformation.
- **Transformation DNA creates lasting competitive advantage:** Organisations that master Radiate and Engage develop the cultural capability to implement, adapt, and evolve faster and better than competitors. Trust accelerates everything.

◇ **Reflection Prompts**

- *What failure in your organisation deserves transparent sharing?*
- *Which stories of AI-human collaboration need wider amplification?*
- *How could authentic transparency about your challenges actually strengthen stakeholder confidence?*

Chapter 14: The Future You're Creating

Heart x Mind x AI = Exponential Leadership.

Right now, somewhere, a leader who has completed this journey is making a decision that will ripple through hundreds of lives. But unlike the leader I described in the Foreword, this leader knows something transformative: how to care deeply without losing analytical rigor, how to dare boldly while staying grounded in human wisdom, and how to share transparently while executing with precision. They've resolved the paradox that stops most leaders in their tracks. They understand that in our rush to embrace AI, we don't need to lose our humanity - we need to amplify it. They understand that empathy isn't weakness but strategic intelligence, that vulnerability builds rather than breaks trust, and that the most powerful transformations happen not to people, but with them. And they have escaped the great Rationality Mirage. And, in so doing, they have not just become better leaders - they have begun to build a better future.

Just as June 15, 2021, was etched in my memory as the day I realized everything I thought I knew about leadership was incomplete, today marks the day you have completed your journey of discovery into everything you need to know about leading with both heart and intelligence.

The Leader You've Become

Recently, I received a message that stopped me in my tracks. It came from one my former business leaders at Aegon:

"I wanted you to know - we implemented Care, Dare, Share in my current company, across all our teams, like we did at Aegon. Last quarter, we launched our most successful product ever. But that's not why I'm writing. Yesterday, my teammate J. told me she finally felt heard at work. She said our team meetings had become places where she could bring her whole self. I realized we aren't just changing our processes – we are changing who we are as leaders."

This was the last piece of validation on CARE, DARE, SHARE that I needed. It moved me and it inspired me to finalise this book. Not for the P&L metrics that improve or the efficiency that climbs, but for the moment when a leader discovers they can create the conditions where people flourish.

You began this journey in the Foreword with a simple but profound question: *Are you ready to lead with both heart and intelligence?*

Now, fourteen chapters later, you have your answer.

Try this: Take the CARE, DARE, SHARE Compass assessment again (Chapter 1), and compare it to where it was when you started. Reflect on what possibilities this expansion opens up for your organisation or your community?

What You've Built

Look back at where we started. In Chapter 1, I shared how stepping into the CEO role at Aegon NL taught me that the most powerful intelligence of all isn't artificial - it's human. We discovered that transformation fails when leaders forget the people behind the numbers.

Since then, you've built something remarkable: a complete operating system for human-centred leadership in the age of AI.

Through **CARE**, you learned to lead with empathic intelligence:

- In Chapter 2, you discovered how to **Connect** with emotional presence, moving from control to a genuine human relationship

- Chapter 3 taught you to **Analyse** insights at scale, turning AI into an amplifier of empathy rather than a replacement for human understanding

- Chapter 4 showed you how to **Respond** with tailored empathy, ensuring that every action carries both analytical precision and emotional resonance

- Chapter 5 revealed how to **Empower** others with distributed emotional intelligence, creating systems that scale human wisdom

Through **DARE**, you developed the courage to innovate with heart:

- Chapter 6 ignited your ability to **Dream** with strategic imagination, grounding bold visions in real human needs

- Chapter 7 equipped you to **Assess** opportunities through rigorous evaluation that honors both data and intuition

- Chapter 8 taught you to **Refine** solutions until they become emotionally resonant and culturally integrated

- Chapter 9 empowered you to **Execute** with confidence, treating AI implementation as a human transformation led by senior leaders and preparing for the scaling-up

Through **SHARE**, you mastered trust at scale:

- Chapter 10 showed you how to **Synthesize** collective knowledge, becoming the leader who helps the room become smarter together

- Chapter 11 taught you to **Harness** AI for collaboration, orchestrating intelligence rather than hoarding it

- Chapter 12 revealed how to **Align** stakeholders through emotional intelligence, creating unity through understanding rather than compliance

- Chapter 13 demonstrated how to **Radiate** and **Engage** beyond organisational boundaries, extending your impact into the wider ecosystem

You have completed your journey through the Leadership Expansion map, and you now understand how to set the **CARE, DARE, SHARE Leadership Flywheel** in motion. You have seen how each component connects: how deep CARE provides the foundation for courageous

DARE, and how successful DARE creates the momentum that is scaled through SHARE.

CARE, DARE, SHARE Leadership Flywheel

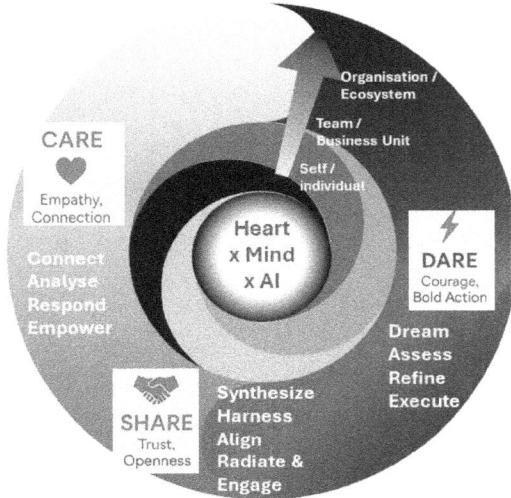

Fig. 6. The CARE, DARE, SHARE Leadership Flywheel: from self to organisation-wide iterations of the CARE, DARE, SHARE methodology create the foundation for successful long-lasting transformations.

This is no longer just a theoretical map; it is your operational blueprint. It represents the integration of heart and intelligence you now possess. Your legacy as a leader will be defined by your ability to keep this flywheel spinning: to continually listen with empathy, act with courage, and scale trust, creating an organisation where both humanity and technology thrive in a virtuous cycle.

What you have built is more than an operating system for leadership. It is a response to the defining challenge of our era. AI doesn't automate leadership; it demands we deploy humanity at scale. You have completed the operating manual for the Generative Leader - the one who uses empathy (Care), courage (Dare), and connection (Share) to make that future a reality. The choice to lead with heart and AI is not merely a competitive advantage, the way to avoid the 70-80% of transformations that fail, it is a profound act of leadership that will determine the very character of your future workplace and ensure the creation of a more human organisation.

The Paradox You've Resolved

Remember the central tension we identified in the Foreword? *If you lean only on AI, you risk losing the soul of your organisation. If you ignore AI, you risk being outpaced, fast.*

You've resolved this paradox not through compromise, but through integration.

You've learned that AI's greatest power isn't in replacing human judgment - it's in amplifying human empathy. Where others see technology versus humanity, you see technology *in service of* humanity.

When Sarah from Chapter 8 needed a response to her fears, you combined AI insights with human wisdom to create a solution that was both scalable and deeply personal. When the teams in Chapter 11 struggled with fragmented intelligence, you orchestrated collaboration that honoured both algorithmic efficiency and human connection.

This is your leadership signature now: the seamless integration of heart and intelligence, creating conditions where both humanity and technology thrive.

The Ripple Effect

The transformation you've undergone extends far beyond your immediate sphere. Consider the mathematics of influence:

If you implement CARE, DARE, SHARE with even ten direct reports, and they each influence ten others, your leadership philosophy touches 100 lives. If those 100 each impact ten more, you've influenced 1,000 people. The exponential effect of human-centred leadership amplified by intelligent systems creates change that ripples through entire industries.

But the real power isn't in the numbers - it's in the nature of the change itself.

Unlike transformations imposed from above, the changes you create are *embraced* from within. Because you've learned to care deeply, dare boldly, and share transparently, the people you lead don't just execute your vision - they co-create with you. They don't just implement your strategies - they improve them with their own insights and experiences.

This is the difference between change management and change leadership. You're not managing people through transformation - you're inspiring them and leading them into a future they help design.

The Integration Challenge

As you move forward, you'll face the temptation to revert to old patterns when pressure mounts.

There will be moments when purely analytical approaches seem faster, when vulnerability feels risky, when listening feels inefficient.

In those moments, remember this: CARE, DARE, SHARE isn't about being soft - it's about being both strong and wise. It's not about slowing down - it's about moving at the speed of trust rather than the speed of fear. And you will be surprised that the speed of trust is actually often ultimately faster than the speed of fear.

The leaders who sustain this approach understand that emotional intelligence and artificial intelligence aren't opposing forces - they're complementary capabilities that, when combined, create outcomes neither could achieve alone.

Your AI-Enhanced Humanity

Let me share what I believe is the most important insight from our journey together:

The future doesn't belong to leaders who choose between human wisdom and artificial intelligence. It belongs to leaders who understand that AI's highest purpose is to make us more human, not less.

When AI handles routine analysis, you're freed to focus on the uniquely human work of building trust, inspiring purpose, and navigating moral complexity. When AI provides patterns and predictions, you can invest your time in the irreplaceable work of understanding context, reading between the lines, and caring for the souls of your organisation.

You've learned that the most sophisticated AI insights mean nothing if they can't be translated into "potato language" - the kind of simple, warm communication that creates genuine shared understanding rather than impressive-sounding complexity that leaves people behind.

Your humanity isn't threatened by AI - it's enhanced by it. And your AI capabilities aren't constrained by human wisdom - they're guided by it toward outcomes that serve our highest aspirations.

As you stand at this crossroads, two distinct futures become visible. You must see them clearly.

- **One is the future you are now equipped to prevent.** It is a world where AI's cold logic has won. Workplaces hum with hyper-efficiency, but they are silent. Decisions are made by dispassionate algorithms, performance is tracked to the millisecond, and human interaction is a managed variable. In this future, employees are not collaborators; they are data points on a dashboard, and their fragmentation is the direct result of leading by spreadsheet. This is the future where we have dared with data but failed to care with wisdom, where AI serves the system, and humanity serves AI.
- **Now, picture the future you have learnt to build with CARE, DARE, SHARE.** It is a world where technology serves humanity's highest aspirations. Here, AI handles the mundane, freeing the human mind to do what it does best: to connect with emotional presence, to solve complex problems

with ingenuity, and to dare with strategic imagination. Leaders use AI not as a tool of surveillance, but as a partner for insight, allowing them to focus on mentoring, inspiring, and creating cultures where people feel safe to fail forward. This is the future your leadership makes possible, one where technology does not diminish our humanity, but amplifies it.

The Invitation Forward

These two futures are not an inevitable fate. They are a choice.

The leader I described in the Foreword - drowning in data but blind to what truly matters - is not some distant executive. They could be you. The boardroom where that decision is being made could be yours. Is that what you want?

The fulcrum on which the future of work will pivot is you. The case studies you have read about are not just stories of success; they are proof that a more human future is possible when leaders, like you, decide to create it. Your legacy will be measured not by the technology you implement, but by the humanity you unleash.

The tools are in your hands. The frameworks are in this book. The capacity for heart is within you. The questions that matter are now yours to answer: What is the most human thing I can do? How can AI amplify this choice? What future am I creating, right now?

The future is heart-led and AI-powered.

Go create it.

The Questions That Matter

As you close this book and begin applying these principles, three questions will guide your continued growth:

What is the most human thing I can do in this situation? This question cuts through complexity to reveal actions that honour dignity, build trust, and create connection.

How can AI amplify this human choice? This question transforms technology from a replacement for human judgment into an amplifier of human wisdom.

What future am I creating through this decision? This question ensures that your immediate choices serve your long-term vision for human flourishing, enhanced by intelligent technology.

These questions will serve you whether you're leading a team of five or an organisation of fifty thousand, whether you're navigating a crisis or capitalizing on opportunity, whether you're implementing new technology or strengthening human culture.

The Framework in Action: Case Studies in Transformation

Before you can build your own legacy, you must have conviction in the tools. The true test of any leadership framework is not its elegance in theory, but its power in practice - across different industries, cultures, and challenges. In this final chapter, we move from blueprint to proof, exploring how leaders have applied the principles of Care, Dare, and Share to drive profound transformations in some of the world's most demanding sectors. Here are five concrete examples of CARE, DARE, SHARE applied in real life.

Case Study: Schneider Electric - Manufacturing's Digital Renaissance

Schneider Electric, a global leader in energy management and automation, has been at the forefront of the "Fourth Industrial Revolution" by transforming its own factories into models of efficiency, sustainability, and human-centric innovation. A prime example is their factory in Le Vaudreuil, France, which has been recognized by the World Economic Forum as a "Sustainability Lighthouse," a beacon for the future of manufacturing. This case study will explore how Schneider Electric's approach at Le Vaudreuil exemplifies the "Care, Dare, Share" framework, demonstrating how a legacy factory can be reimagined to lead in the digital age.

The Challenge: A Brownfield Factory in a Competitive Landscape

The Le Vaudreuil factory, a "brownfield" site (meaning it's an existing facility, not a new build), faced the same challenges as many traditional manufacturers: aging infrastructure, siloed operations, and the need to increase efficiency and sustainability while remaining competitive. The leadership team recognized that incremental improvements would not be enough. They needed a fundamental transformation to prepare for a future defined by digitization and decarbonization.

The CARE, DARE, SHARE Journey

CARE: Empowering the Workforce

Schneider Electric's leadership understood that digital transformation is not just about technology; it's about people. They placed a strong emphasis on "Care" by investing in their employees and fostering a culture of collaboration and empowerment.

- **Upskilling and Reskilling:** Instead of replacing their existing workforce, Schneider Electric focused on upskilling and reskilling their employees. They provided extensive training to equip workers with the digital skills needed to thrive in a "smart factory" environment. This included training on how to work with new technologies like augmented reality, collaborative robots (cobots), and data analytics dashboards.

- **A People-Centric Approach:** The company adopted a "bottom-up" approach to innovation, actively seeking input from the factory floor. They implemented a digital platform, "EcoStruxure Industrial Advisor – Lean Management," which allows any employee to suggest improvements, flag issues, and contribute to the factory's continuous improvement. This tool has been rolled out to over 70,000 workers globally, resulting in a 4-5% average increase in site performance.

- **Creating a Safer, More Engaging Workplace:** The new technologies were not just about efficiency; they were also about improving the work environment. For example, augmented reality applications provide maintenance staff with real-time data and instructions, reducing the risk of errors and improving safety. This focus on employee well-being has been a key factor in the successful adoption of new technologies.

DARE: Boldly Embracing Innovation

Schneider Electric "dared" to invest in cutting-edge technologies and new ways of working, transforming the Le Vaudreuil factory into a showcase of Industry 4.0.

- **The EcoStruxure Platform:** The foundation of the transformation is Schneider Electric's own "EcoStruxure" platform, an open, interoperable, IoT-enabled architecture. This platform allows for the seamless integration of connected products, edge control, and analytics, providing a holistic view of the factory's operations.

- **Advanced Technologies in Action:**
  - **Industrial Internet of Things (IIoT):** Sensors connected to digital platforms provide real-time data on everything from energy consumption to machine performance. This has enabled the factory to optimize energy management, leading to a 25% reduction in power use and a 25% decrease in CO_2 emissions.

  - **Augmented Reality:** Maintenance technicians use the "EcoStruxure Augmented Operator Advisor" on tablets to overlay real-time data and virtual objects onto physical machinery. This has reduced maintenance costs by 30% and increased Overall Equipment Effectiveness (OEE) by 7%.

- **5G Connectivity:** In partnership with Orange, the factory was the first in France to trial an indoor industrial 5G private network. This high-speed, reliable connectivity supports advanced use-cases like augmented reality and telepresence robots for remote factory tours.

- **AI and Predictive Analytics:** The factory uses AI-powered analytics to predict maintenance needs, prevent downtime, and optimize production schedules. A zero-reject water recycling station, monitored by AI, has led to a 64% reduction in water use.

SHARE: Fostering a Culture of Transparency and Collaboration

The "Share" principle is evident in how Schneider Electric has democratized data and fostered a culture of open communication and collaboration.

- **Data Transparency:** Dashboards throughout the factory display real-time operational data, giving every employee insight into production performance, energy usage, and other key metrics. This transparency empowers workers to make informed decisions and take ownership of their work.

- **Sharing Best Practices:** The Le Vaudreuil factory is not an isolated success story. It is part of Schneider Electric's global "Smart Factory" initiative, which encompasses nearly 300 factories and distribution centers in over 40 countries. The lessons learned and best practices from Le Vaudreuil are shared across this network, accelerating the digital transformation of the entire company.

- **External Collaboration:** Schneider Electric actively collaborates with partners like Orange and PTC to push the boundaries of industrial innovation. They also share their expertise with other companies, hosting virtual and in-person tours of the Le Vaudreuil factory to demonstrate the benefits of digital transformation.

The Outcome: A Model for the Future of Manufacturing

The transformation of the Le Vaudreuil factory has yielded impressive results:

- **Sustainability:** 25% reduction in energy use, 25% reduction in CO_2 emissions, 17% reduction in material waste, and a 64% reduction in water use.

- **Efficiency:** 7% increase in Overall Equipment Effectiveness (OEE) and a 30% reduction in maintenance costs.

- **Business Growth:** The implementation of 4IR technologies has contributed to a 54% increase in business growth.

- **Employee Empowerment:** A more engaged, skilled, and empowered workforce.

Case Study: The European Bank - Leadership in Flow

Throughout this book, I've shared glimpses of the CARE, DARE, SHARE transformation at the European bank I have helped for many months - moments when Zaya, their conversational banking app powered by AI, triggered surprising insights, or when listening to frontline teams revealed more than any metric could. You've seen pieces of this story in our discussions in several chapters. But those were snapshots.

Now, let's zoom out and see the full picture: how Care, Dare, and Share came together to enable a radical shift, not just in technology, but in leadership, culture, and performance. This is the story of how the framework moves from theory to a living, breathing practice.

The Challenge: Achieving Growth While Having Limited Resources

As we have seen through the chapters, fundamentally, the challenge for this bank was to find ways to grow in its market, while the other larger banks had more presence in the form of branches and more financial and human resources to attract and keep customers.

The CARE, DARE, SHARE Journey

CARE: Listening Beyond the Metrics

The journey began, as it always must, with CARE.

When the CEO of the bank asked me to help out, on the back of what I had achieved at Aegon NL and in other situations, the business was full of smart people and solid strategies - but also silos, and sometimes fatigue, and uncertainty. AI initiatives were in motion, but felt, at times, disconnected. Teams were delivering on their KPIs, but sometimes not with the same sense of a shared goal.

Instead of jumping to restructure or rebrand, we slowed down to connect. We engaged in structured listening - through workshops, customer journey mapping, and unfiltered reviews of the immense data we already had.

We treated every piece of feedback not as a data point, but as a human story.

It revealed that, while a basic level of functionality is table stakes, consumers, generally, do not expect the highest level of technological sophistication, but they do value to be well understood, including emotionally. And with growing AI capabilities, that expectation is commensurately growing.

This was the heart of CARE in action: recognizing that sustainable transformation starts with emotional truth.

We took these insights seriously, making them the foundation for everything that followed. It wasn't always comfortable, but it built the trust we needed to move forward.

DARE: Acting with Insight and Courage

CARE gave us clarity, but it took DARE to move things forward. There was a choice. The conventional playbook said to compete with other banks, the bank needed a better banking app and more branches or a lot more marketing - a multi-year, multi-million-pound endeavour.

This is where the team dared to ask a different question. As I described in Chapter 6, "What if we're asking the wrong question?". "Who says you need to start with current accounts to build banking relationships?".

The CARE work had identified the strengths to build on: a leading position in credit cards, a great credit cards app, and a beloved, albeit simple, AI chatbot in the first version of Zaya.

So the playbook got flipped entirely....a daring act! The future would be built not on the weaknesses, but on the strengths, envisioning a revolutionary conversational banking service that started with credit cards and was powered by a much smarter Zaya.

DARE meant choosing strategic discomfort over surface-level fixes. AI was no longer an add-on, but a core member of the team and of the delivery. Instead of piloting tech in isolated pockets, entire customer journeys got redesigned holistically - involving customers, colleagues, and systems at every step.

Teams got empowered with a clear intent and a shared, audacious customer-centric goal.

SHARE: Connecting for Collective Momentum

But it was the SHARE phase that turned a bold vision into a self-sustaining reality. As in every organisation, moats or "knowledge islands" - where insights from Zaya, marketing, and operations existed in isolation – would emerge.

So they began running cross-functional synthesis sessions to consciously connect these islands. They moved from data handoffs to continuous learning loops. For example, when marketing analytics suggested certain customer segments had a natural affinity for the bank's brand, they didn't just guess why. They pulled data from every source at their disposal to co-create new campaigns grounded in a synthesized, 360-degree view of the customer. Very impactful marketing campaigns, which are still being referred to in that European country as great examples of customer connection, got launched as a result of this. They were slightly quirky, slightly bold, and very emotionally relevant to customers. They resonated with them.

The collaboration tools became spaces for meaning-making, not just task-tracking. And people started telling the story: not just of business wins, but of people stepping up, connecting across boundaries, and shaping the future together.

They did more than align strategies, they radiated belief. Soon, engagement scores began to rise, and colleagues started shifting from, "Well, it is hard to realise because...." To "Yes, we can. Let me come back on how to shape it....".

The Outcome: Transformation with Heart, Mind, and AI

The numbers spoke for themselves: income up by high single digits, profits up by more than 50%. Customer satisfaction up. Zaya got recognition in the country. But those weren't the most powerful indicators.

Zaya became more than a chatbot integrated with an app; it became an instrument of customer empathy, a source of truth that guided the bank's customer strategy.

The teams became stewards of shared intelligence, working in partnership to solve real problems for real people. And the leaders of this transformation, learned to orchestrate less from a position of having all the answers and more from a place of shared insight, emotional connection, and bold, collective intent.

That is the power of CARE, DARE, SHARE in practice. Not a checklist, but a rhythm. A mindset. A leadership signature that makes all the difference.

Case Study: Novartis - "Patient-Centric Revolution" A New Model for Patient Outcomes

In the high-stakes world of pharmaceuticals, the greatest challenge isn't just discovering a new molecule; it's navigating the decade-long, billion-dollar journey to get that medicine to the patients who need it.

For decades, the clinical trial process has been notoriously slow, costly, and profoundly difficult for patients. This case study explores how Novartis, a global healthcare leader, applied the principles of Care, Dare, and Share to fundamentally reimagine this process, using AI to place patient well-being at the very heart of drug development.

The Challenge: The Human Cost of an Inefficient System

The journey of a clinical trial patient is one of hope mixed with an immense burden. Imagine a leadership meeting at Novartis reviewing trial data. The charts show an 85% patient dropout rate - a staggering statistic treated as a cost of doing business. But a leader practicing CARE asks a different question: "What is the human story behind that number?"

The story is one of exhaustion. A patient driving four hours for a 15-minute check-up. The anxiety of navigating complex protocols while feeling sick. The feeling of being a "subject" in an experiment, not a partner in a cure.

It was this empathic insight that sparked Novartis's transformation. The leadership Dared to ask: "What if we designed the system around the patient's life, not just the data we need?". This question led to their AI-powered "Nerve Live" platform, not as a tool for better data collection, but as an engine for a more humane process. They realized the fastest path to a cure was not a more efficient lab, but a more compassionate trial.

The CARE, DARE, SHARE Journey

CARE: From Data Points to Patient Partners

Novartis's transformation began with a deep commitment to understanding the patient journey in granular, emotional detail. Instead of relying solely on clinical data, the company began to CARE by listening with new tools and a new mindset.

- Empathic Insights at Scale: Novartis leveraged AI and Natural Language Processing to analyse millions of anonymized data points from patient forums, social media, and medical literature. This helped them identify the biggest friction points in clinical trials: the burden of travel, the anxiety of uncertainty, and the feeling of being disconnected from the research team.
- Designing for People: These insights directly informed the design of more patient-friendly trials. The company began prioritizing decentralized trials that allowed patients to participate from home, using wearable devices and telemedicine to reduce the need for hospital visits. They created patient-facing apps that provided clear, simple information, turning confusion into confidence. By caring about the emotional and logistical burdens, Novartis shifted the model from one that extracted data from patients to one that supported patients through the process.

DARE: Building the 'Nerve Centre' of Clinical Trials

Armed with a deep understanding of patient needs, Novartis Dared to build a solution that would have been unimaginable a decade ago. They invested in a bold, AI-powered platform to serve as the "digital control tower" for their global clinical trials.

- Predictive Power: This platform, known as Nerve Live, uses predictive analytics to forecast trial enrolment rates, identify the best clinical sites, and anticipate potential delays before they happen. By analysing over a decade of historical trial data, the AI can pinpoint which locations and which doctors will be most successful at recruiting and retaining patients for a specific disease, reducing trial start-up times significantly.

- Real-Time Orchestration: Nerve Live provides a single source of truth for trial operations worldwide, allowing teams to monitor progress in real-time. This has enabled Novartis to manage its portfolio of hundreds of ongoing trials with unprecedented agility, making data-driven decisions that accelerate timelines while ensuring patient safety remains the top priority. This was a dare to move from reactive problem-solving to proactive, intelligent orchestration.

SHARE: Creating a Collaborative Intelligence Ecosystem

The true transformation came when Novartis began to Share the intelligence from Nerve Live across its entire ecosystem, breaking down traditional silos between departments and even with external partners.

- Internal Knowledge Flow: Insights generated by Nerve Live weren't siloed within the clinical operations team. They were shared with drug discovery teams to inform future research, with medical affairs teams to better support doctors, and with commercial teams to prepare for a successful product launch. This created a continuous learning loop where every trial made the entire organisation smarter.
- External Collaboration: Novartis fostered a culture of open innovation, partnering with tech leaders like Microsoft to enhance its AI capabilities and with academic institutions to advance the science of drug development. By sharing its anonymized insights and best practices, Novartis helped elevate the standard for the entire industry, reinforcing the idea that a rising tide of shared intelligence lifts all boats.

The Outcome: Faster Medicines, Better Lives

The results of Novartis's patient-centric transformation have been profound, creating a new benchmark for the industry:

- Accelerated Drug Development Timelines: By using AI-powered platforms like Nerve Live to optimize trial design and execution, Novartis has been able to significantly shorten the drug development lifecycle. The company has successfully shaved one to two years off the typical 10-year timeline for bringing a new drug to market

- Improved Patient Experience and Retention: The shift to more decentralized, patient-friendly trials directly addresses one of the industry's biggest challenges. While the industry average sees up to 85% of trials failing to retain enough patients, Novartis's empathic approach has led to higher patient retention rates, ensuring studies can be completed successfully and on schedule.
- Enhanced R&D Efficiency: Shortening the development timeline by one to two years represents a 10-20% acceleration in R&D, a massive efficiency gain in an industry where time to market is critical. This allows for a more effective allocation of capital and resources, enabling investment in a broader pipeline of innovative therapies.
- Greater Predictability and Success: The Nerve Live platform allows Novartis to manage its portfolio of approximately 500 ongoing clinical trials in real time. Its predictive analytics for site selection and enrolment forecasting increase the probability of trial success by identifying and mitigating potential issues before they arise.

By putting CARE at the heart of their strategy, Novartis unlocked a powerful truth: the fastest path to scientific innovation is through human empathy.

Case Study: The Logistics Company

The Challenge: Navigating a Complex, High-Stakes World

This logistics group, I have been helping, one of the top 40 globally, operates in a sector defined by immense pressure: tight delivery windows, complex global supply chains, a massive carbon footprint, and a constant need to ensure the safety and efficiency of tens of thousands of employees worldwide. The pandemic had further exposed vulnerabilities in visibility, planning, and agility. Recognizing that incremental change wouldn't suffice, they decided to launch an ambitious transformation around digitization and automation of tasks. But to be successful, it needed the buy-in of its employees in the digitization of many of its processes.

In discussions with their board and leadership, they decided to apply the CARE, DARE, SHARE approach.

The CARE, DARE, SHARE Journey

CARE: Investing in People and the Planet

The transformation began by focusing on its two most critical stakeholders: its people and the global community.

- **Caring for Employees**: The company understood that a digital transformation could create anxiety about job security. Instead of just automating tasks, they launched a massive upskilling initiative to empower their workforce. They created a program to train employees in the complexities of modern customs and trade, and they invested heavily in digital skills training to help their team work alongside new technologies like robotics and AI. By focusing on making employees' jobs safer, easier, and more valuable, they turned potential resistance into engaged participation.

- **Caring for the Planet**: Acknowledging its environmental impact, the company committed to drastic carbon footprint reduction targets. This wasn't just a corporate slogan; it became a powerful rallying cry, showing customers and employees that the company was committed to a sustainable future. This was very coherent with and supportive of the messages given in the Caring for Employees programs, and it also created a strong justification for the automation of many tasks. The initiative involved analysing every aspect of their operations to find opportunities for decarbonization, from electrifying their vehicle fleet to designing sustainable warehouses. But the beauty was that in doing such in-depth

319

analysis, opportunities were also found around streamlining processes, further automating, and simplifying things. So, in identifying ways to care for the planet, they were also identifying ways to care for employees and to improve their operational excellence.

This dual focus on employee empowerment and environmental stewardship created the foundation of trust and purpose needed for the company to make its next bold moves.

DARE: Bold Investments in Next-Generation Logistics

Grounded in its commitment to its people and the planet, the company dared to invest heavily in a suite of technologies designed to create a smarter, faster, and greener logistics network.

This was not about isolated pilots but a systematic overhaul of their operations, focusing on concrete, high-impact areas:

- Robotics and Automation: The company deployed hundreds of collaborative robots in its warehouses across the globe. These robots don't replace workers but assist them, traveling up to 10 miles per shift to bring items to human pickers. This dramatically reduced walking time and physical strain, allowing employees to be more productive and focused on higher-value tasks.
- AI and Data Analytics: The company started using AI to optimize everything from delivery routes to shipment processing. AI algorithms analyse traffic patterns, weather, and delivery density in real-time to create the most efficient routes for its couriers, saving fuel and time. In its hubs, AI-powered cameras and scanners can process parcel data in milliseconds, improving sorting accuracy and speed.
- Electrification of the Fleet: The company also started investing to electrify its delivery fleet. They aimed to progressively ensure that at least half of their fleet would be electrified over a 10-year time span.

This disciplined execution of a bold vision demonstrates how daring to invest in the right technologies can create a powerful competitive advantage.

SHARE: Radiating Success and Engaging the Ecosystem

The company recognized that the challenges of global logistics and sustainability were too large for any company. So the final phase of their transformation has been to share their knowledge, capabilities, and vision with customers, partners, and the wider industry.

They started by actively helping customers decarbonize their own supply chains, by sharing access to sustainable warehouses.

It then started engaging in partnerships with tech companies on robotics, and with energy providers on EV charging infrastructure.

The Outcome:

- Productivity in warehouses using collaborative robots has increased by 25-30%
- The deployment of AI and data analytics has contributed to consistent improvements in operational efficiency and delivery times.
- They are on target for their significant CO_2 reductions, and the company is on track to meet its ambitious target of having at least 50% of its fleet electrified over a 10-year time span.

Case Study: The Multi-Regional Accounting Services Firm

This case study details how a major professional services firm, I was involved with, applied the principles of Care, Dare, and Share to integrate generative AI into its core operations, aiming to redefine efficiency, empower its workforce, and create a new paradigm for client value.

The Challenge: The Productivity Paradox in a Knowledge-Based Industry

In the world of professional services - audit, tax, and consulting - the primary asset is human expertise. However, even the most brilliant minds at a firm like this large accounting firm are often buried in mountains of low-value, repetitive work: sifting through thousands of documents, summarizing complex regulations, drafting standard reports, and preparing presentations. This "productivity paradox" creates a dual challenge: it leads to burnout and disengagement among highly skilled professionals and limits the time they can spend on the strategic, creative, and deeply analytical work that clients value most. The challenge for this firm was the need to augment its human capital to meet the escalating demands for speed, insight, and innovation in a digital-first world. The pool of talent was finite in the region, and therefore, they needed to find a way to enable their best talent to "find more hours" in the day.

The CARE, DARE, SHARE Journey

CARE: Listening to the Overburdened Professional and the Demanding Client

- **Caring for the Expert Workforce:** together with the firm's leadership, we began by caring about the daily reality of its 2,000+ employees in one of their key regions. We listened to the frustrations of auditors spending weeks on compliance checks that could be automated, and consultants bogged down by research instead of strategy. We recognized that the path to a more fulfilling career and better work-life balance lay in freeing people from digital drudgery. This deep care for the employee experience - the desire to make work more meaningful - became the human-centric driver for the AI strategy.

- **Caring for the Client's Evolving Needs:** We also listened intently to clients. In an age of instant information, clients were no longer satisfied with backward-looking reports. They demanded faster insights, predictive analysis, and proactive advice. The firm cared about moving from a reactive service provider to a proactive strategic partner. They understood that to deliver this next level of value, their teams needed tools that could process information at machine speed, freeing them up for the critical thinking and relationship-building that machines cannot replicate.

This dual CARE - for the professional growth of their people and the strategic success of their clients - created the powerful "why" behind the decision to make a massive and daring bet on generative AI.

DARE: A Hundred Million Bet on an AI-Augmented Future

Having established the human and client-centric need for change, the firm dared to fundamentally reinvent its operating model. As part of an investment worth several hundred million dollars, it committed to deploying generative AI across its entire organisation in one of its large key regions. Their dare was not simply to adopt a new technology, but to build a secure, proprietary AI platform and, most importantly, to upskill every single employee to become an AI-proficient professional. This was a bet that the future of professional services would be defined not by humans versus machines, but by humans augmented by machines.

What we did:

- **Build a Secure, Proprietary Tool (MyPal):** Recognizing the immense data security and client confidentiality risks of public AI models, the firm dared to invest in its own proprietary generative AI tool, which we will call for confidentiality reasons "MyPal", for the purpose of this book. Built in collaboration with some of the software giants in AI, this platform provided the power of a large language model within a secure, private environment. This was a dare to prioritize trust and responsibility over the convenience of off-the-shelf solutions.

- **Upskill Everyone:** the firm dared to make AI literacy a core competency for every employee, from junior associates to senior partners. We launched a massive internal training program to ensure that every professional understood how to

323

use generative AI effectively, ethically, and securely. This was not just about teaching people how to write prompts; it was a fundamental dare to change the skill profile of the entire firm.

- **Lead with "Responsible AI" Principles:** From the outset, the firm dared to put ethics at the forefront of its AI rollout. We established a clear framework to govern the use of the tools, focusing on accuracy, fairness, transparency, and data privacy. This was a dare to build a culture of digital stewardship, ensuring that efficiency gains would never come at the expense of professional integrity.

SHARE: Creating a Collaborative Intelligence Platform

The firm's leadership understood that the true power of AI would be unlocked not in isolated use-cases, but when it became a shared platform for collective intelligence. The final phase of the strategy has been to share the AI tools across all their multi-region set-up and, more importantly, the learnings, to create a collaborative ecosystem both within the firm and with their clients.

They started by sharing MyPal with every employee: The rollout of MyPal to all 2,000+ employees was a powerful act of sharing. It democratized access to cutting-edge technology and created a unified platform where insights and efficiencies could be shared across service lines. An auditor could use it to summarize new regulatory standards, while a financial planning consultant used it to, for example, challenge business plans for their clients' new market entry strategies. This shared tool began to break down knowledge silos and create a common language of innovation.

The use of MyPal itself became a shared learning experience. By analysing how teams were using the tool, the firm could identify best practices and innovative applications. These insights were then shared back with the entire firm through ongoing training and workshops. This created a powerful network effect: the more people used the platform, the smarter the entire organisation became about how to leverage AI.

Finally, the firm's most significant act of sharing has been to turn its internal transformation into a client service. Having gone through the journey of AI adoption, governance, and upskilling themselves, the firm realised it could start sharing that firsthand expertise to help its clients navigate their own AI transformations. This created a whole new stream of activity for them, sharing the hard-won wisdom from their own experience, building deeper, more strategic partnerships in the process.

The Outcome:

- **Massive Upskilling:** The firm is on track to train its entire workforce on AI tools and principles, creating one of the country's most AI-proficient professional teams.

- **New Service Offerings:** the firm is leveraging its internal AI experience to build a rapidly growing advisory practice, helping clients with AI strategy, governance, and implementation.

- **Thought Leadership in Responsible AI:** The firm has established itself as a leading voice on the ethical and responsible deployment of AI, sharing its frameworks and learnings with the broader business community.

The Common Thread - Humanity Transforms

What do a French factory, a European bank, a Swiss pharmaceutical company, a multi-regional accounting services firm and a global logistics company have in common?

In each case, leaders succeeded not by focusing on technology alone, but by **channelling** technology through profoundly human insights. Schneider Electric cared for its workforce by upskilling rather than replacing people, creating bottom-up innovation platforms that gave every employee a voice. Virgin Money dared to flip the conventional banking playbook, building on emotional truths revealed through deep customer listening rather than chasing competitors' strategies. Novartis shared intelligence across its entire ecosystem, transforming clinical trials from data extraction exercises into patient partnership journeys.

Each organisation discovered that its greatest competitive advantage wasn't its AI or IoT platforms, but its ability to weave human empathy into the fabric of technological transformation. They didn't just implement digital tools - they reimagined entire systems around human needs, fears, and aspirations.

This powerfully reinforces the central truth: **Data informs. Humanity transforms.**

Your Integrated CARE, DARE, SHARE plan

As you have read through the chapters, you are now convinced that CARE, DARE, SHARE is the right approach to embrace. But you might wonder how it all comes together in one integrated plan?

This is an example of a high-level roadmap over an 18-24 months time span. Of course, it needs to be tailored to your specific circumstances.

Summary Timeline

- **Months 1-6:** Foundation (CARE) - Build emotional intelligence and trust

- **Months 7-12:** Innovation (DARE) - Deploy AI with human wisdom

- **Months 13-18:** Collaboration (SHARE) - Create collective intelligence

- **Months 19-24:** Mastery - Integrate and scale transformation

Total Timeline: 18-24 months for complete implementation

The Care, Dare, Share Masterplan

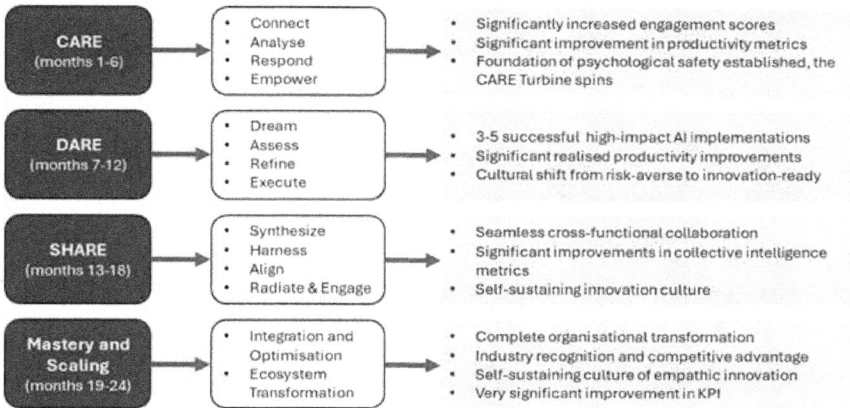

CARE (months 1-6)	• Connect • Analyse • Respond • Empower	• Significantly increased engagement scores • Significant improvement in productivity metrics • Foundation of psychological safety established, the CARE Turbine spins
DARE (months 7-12)	• Dream • Assess • Refine • Execute	• 3-5 successful high-impact AI implementations • Significant realised productivity improvements • Cultural shift from risk-averse to innovation-ready
SHARE (months 13-18)	• Synthesize • Harness • Align • Radiate & Engage	• Seamless cross-functional collaboration • Significant improvements in collective intelligence metrics • Self-sustaining innovation culture
Mastery and Scaling (months 19-24)	• Integration and Optimisation • Ecosystem Transformation	• Complete organisational transformation • Industry recognition and competitive advantage • Self-sustaining culture of empathic innovation • Very significant improvement in KPI

Fig. 7. The CARE, DARE, SHARE Masterplan.

At Aegon NL, it took us 18-24 months to achieve the transformational improvements we were targeting. The most successful leaders from the case studies in this book achieved significant results within 6-12 months but required 18-24 months for complete cultural transformation and sustainable competitive advantage.

The key success factors to be successful are:

1. **Leadership commitment:** Must be genuine, not performative

2. **Resource allocation:** Requires dedicated team members, not just additional duties

3. **Change readiness:** Organisation must be prepared for cultural transformation, i.e. there needs to be the realisation that something must change

4. **Measurement discipline:** Regular assessment and course correction are essential

5. **Patience with process:** Sustainable change takes time; rushing creates superficial adoption

While not rushing is essential, there could be some **accelerating factors:**

- **Strong existing culture:** Can reduce timeline by 3-6 months

- **CEO/senior leadership commitment:** Essential for staying on track

- **Prior change management experience:** Reduces resistance and speeds adoption

- **Available resources:** Dedicated teams can move 50% faster

Or, conversely, potential **obstacles** that would slow things down:

- **Cultural resistance:** Can add 6-12 months to the timeline

- **Complex legacy systems:** May slow DARE implementation by 3-6 months

- **Limited resources:** Part-time implementation can double the timeline

- **External crises:** Market disruptions can pause progress for months

Here is the detailed breakdown of possible timing:

Phase 1: Foundation Building (Months 1-6)

CARE Framework Implementation

Month 1: Connect

- Week 1-2: Leadership assessment using The CARE, DARE, SHARE Compass tool (24 questions detailed in Chapter 1)

- Week 3-4: Begin systematic listening tours (e.g. 2 clients per week, 3-5 internal conversations per stakeholder group, adapting it in function of where your focus is)

- Set up 45-minute conversation rhythms: weekly one-on-ones, monthly skip-levels, quarterly stakeholder rounds (detailed in Chapter 2)

Months 2-3: Analyse

- Deploy AI-powered sentiment analysis and engagement surveys

- Establish "Actionable-Truth-Zone" with monthly "Brutal Truth" sessions (detailed in Chapter 3)

- Begin predictive empathy applications (burnout prediction, customer churn analysis)

- Implement emotional data ethics framework

Months 4-5: Respond

- Apply ACTED (Acknowledge, Co-Design, Tailor, Enable, Demonstrate) (detailed in Chapter 4)

- Launch 30-day implementation plan for tailored empathic responses

- Begin measuring the effectiveness of your demonstrating care

Month 6: Empower

- Implement the Six Pillars of Empowerment Model (detailed in Chapter 5)

- Establish emotional literacy training programs

- Create listening systems and feedback loops

- Begin embedding emotional logic into decision-making processes

Expected Outcomes by Month 6:

- Significantly increased engagement scores

- Significant improvement in productivity metrics
- Foundation of psychological safety established, the CARE Turbine spins

Phase 2: Strategic Innovation (Months 7-12)

DARE Framework Implementation

Months 7-8: Dream

- Vision workshops using the five AI strategies (Operational Streamlining, Outcome Optimization, Empowered Workforce, Knowledge at Scale, Growth Acceleration) (detailed in Chapter 6)
- Future-back thinking exercises
- Cross-industry inspiration mapping
- Constraint-free ideation sessions with AI scenario modelling

Months 9-10: Assess

- Apply 8-Question Filter to all AI use-cases (detailed in Chapter 7)
- Deep assessment using AI-powered analysis across impact, complexity, team readiness, and data quality
- Select top 3-5 initiatives scoring 8+ points
- Develop detailed implementation blueprints

Month 11: Refine

- Launch intelligent pilots using SCALE (Signals, Context, Adaptation, Learning, Evolution) (detailed in Chapter 8)
- Apply emotional calibration and cultural integration
- Design for scalability with reuse and documentation
- Begin impact amplification through network effects

Month 12: Execute

- Implement IMPACT (Intentional Communication, Measured Implementation, People-First Adaptation, Agile Monitoring, Continuous Calibration, Transparent Results) (detailed in Chapter 9)

- Three-dimensional measurement: Performance, Learning, Strategic indicators

- Calculate Intelligent ROI including compound value creation

Expected Outcomes by Month 12:

- 3-5 successful high-impact AI implementations

- Significant realised productivity improvements

- Cultural shift from risk-averse to innovation-ready

Phase 3: Collective Intelligence (Months 13-18)

SHARE Framework Implementation

Months 13-14: Synthesize (detailed in Chapter 10)

- Map knowledge ecosystem across formal/informal sources

- Design Synthesize architecture with AI-powered insight aggregation

- Establish Synthesize rituals (monthly cross-functional sessions, quarterly strategic reviews)

- Build organisation-wide Synthesize skills

Month 15: Harness

- Implement FLOW (Find, Listen, Orchestrate, Weave) (detailed in Chapter 11)

- Deploy collaborative intelligence tools and systems

- Create "Intelligence Bridges" across teams and boundaries

- Establish dynamic learning clusters

Months 16-17: Align

- Apply UNITY (Understand, Navigate, Integrate, Trust, Yield) (detailed in Chapter 12)
- Conduct comprehensive stakeholder alignment assessment
- Run structured alignment workshops
- Implement 26-week alignment plan

Month 18: Radiate and Engage

- Launch MOMENTUM across eight dimensions (detailed in Chapter 13)
- Implement transparency systems and recognition practices
- Create sustained collaboration systems
- Establish continuous evolution processes

Expected Outcomes by Month 18:

- Seamless cross-functional collaboration
- Significant (e.g. 40%+) improvements in collective intelligence metrics
- Self-sustaining innovation culture

Phase 4: Mastery and Scaling (Months 19-24)

Months 19-21: Integration and Optimization

- Connect all three frameworks into a seamless operating system (detailed in Chapter 14)
- Advanced AI deployment with emotional intelligence integration
- Cultural transformation measurement and refinement

- Leadership depth development at all levels

Months 22-24: Ecosystem Transformation

- Extend impact beyond organisational boundaries

- Industry leadership and best practice sharing

- Sustainable competitive advantage establishment

- Next-generation leader development

Expected Outcomes by Month 24:

- Complete organisational transformation

- Industry recognition and competitive advantage

- Self-sustaining culture of empathic innovation

- Very significant (e.g. 50-100%) improvement in key performance indicators

Your Leadership Legacy Starts Now

Every meaningful transformation starts with leaders who model the change they seek. You are now equipped to be such a leader.

You can treat empathy as strength, courage as clarity, and vulnerability as the foundation of trust. You can implement change that doesn't just happen *to* people but *with* them. You can create organisations where technology serves humanity's highest aspirations.

The path forward requires exactly what you've developed: the ability to lead with both heart and intelligence, to care deeply while daring boldly, to share transparently while executing excellently.

The most powerful act in our frenetic digital age remains what it always was: slowing down and actually listening. This is what separates successful transformations from the 70% that fail - not poor execution, but poor listening. You now know how to listen with both empathy and intelligence. Use that listening to create understanding.

Use that understanding to build trust. Use that trust to inspire transformation that endures.

I am confident that the date you finish reading this book will be etched in your memory as the moment you committed to creating a future where technology amplifies the best of human nature.

Return to your CARE, DARE, SHARE Compass one more time (Chapter 1). The triangle that maps your leadership footprint has expanded beyond where you started. This expanded footprint is your legacy in the making.

Your leadership journey has the potential to demonstrate that in our quest to build smarter organisations, we never need to lose sight of what makes us fundamentally human.

This is collaborative leadership - where AI amplifies human capability rather than replacing it. Where empathy isn't a "soft skill" but a strategic imperative. Where vulnerability becomes the foundation of unshakeable trust.

The future is heart-led and AI-powered.

Are you ready to create it?

Onwards and upwards with CARE, DARE, SHARE.

About the Author

Allegra Patrizi is a seasoned CEO, board member and founder, who has led transformative change across the financial services and technology sectors for over 25 years.

As CEO of Aegon The Netherlands, she led the doubling of the company's value and the scaling of its subsidiary KNAB into one of the country's leading digital banks. At Virgin Money, she was the Managing Director of all business and commercial areas. During her tenure, the bank saw profits grow over 60%, and received awards for its AI applications. Her C-level experience has also encompassed roles as Chief Risk Officer, Chief Commercial Officer, and Chief Technology Officer. Her board experience, spans large corporations like Leaseplan (now part of Ayvens) and D'Ieteren Group, as well as innovative fast growing fintechs.

Today, Allegra's work focuses on advising companies of all sizes, on transformations at the intersection of technology, strategy, and empathy. She is the founder of Silver-Stripes Ventures Ltd, which builds agentic AI solutions, and the creator of Claridora.AI, a leading AI insights platform for boards and executives.

Her leadership philosophy - **Care, Dare, Share** - has guided her work across continents and industries. A former McKinsey partner, airplane pilot, international equestrian, and cookbook author, Allegra brings a unique blend of clarity, courage, and emotional intelligence to everything she does. True citizen of the world, she lives with her family between Italy, Belgium, the UK, and Switzerland.

TO BOOK ALLEGRA PATRIZI,
WWW.ALLEGRAPATRIZI.COM **OR**
BOOKING@ALLEGRAPATRIZI.COM

Compendium

For readers ready to go beyond reflection into real-time application, I've created a companion resource: *The Leader's Compendium: From Insight to Action*. This is not a summary - it's your practical toolkit. Whether you're preparing for a strategy meeting, coaching a team member, or navigating a complex transformation, the Compendium offers "just-in-time" tools, checklists, and frameworks drawn directly from the CARE, DARE, and SHARE pillars. You'll find diagnostic tools, actionable playbooks, and leadership journal prompts to help you turn principles into daily practice. Consider it your field guide for leading with clarity, courage, and connection.

It is available on www.AllegraPatrizi.com and www.Care-Dare-Share.com .

It includes the following sections:
The Leader's Compendium: From Insight to Action

Section 1: Your Leadership Compass

Section 2: "In the Moment" Playbooks

Section 3: Framework Reference Guide

Section 4: Your Leadership Journal

Section 5: Sentences for Emotionally Intelligent Leaders

Section 6: Timelines

Section 7: Diagnostic tool for your plan (assess any plan of yours against the Care, Dare, Share approach)

Section 8: Frequently Asked Questions

www.ingramcontent.com/pod-product-compliance
Lightning Source LLC
Chambersburg PA
CBHW071323210326
41597CB00015B/1330